The Poems of Herman Melville

The Poems of
Herman Melville

Edited by Douglas Robillard

The Kent State University Press

Kent, Ohio, & London

© 2000 by The Kent State University Press, Kent, Ohio 44242

Library of Congress Catalog Card Number 99-052872

ISBN 0-87338-660-4

Manufactured in the United States of America

Revised edition

First edition of *Poems of Herman Melville* (without *Clarel*) published by
College and University Press Services, Inc., © 1976.

07 06 05 04 03 02 01 00   5 4 3 2 1

Library of Congress Cataloging-in-Publication Data
Melville, Herman, 1819–1891.
[Poems]
The poems of Herman Melville / edited by Douglas Robillard.—
Rev. ed.
p.   cm.
Includes bibliographical references.
ISBN 0-87338-660-4 (pbk. : alk. paper) ∞
I. Robillard, Douglas, 1928– II. Title.
PS2382.R63   2000
811'.3—dc21   99-052872

British Library Catalog-in-Publication data are available.

To Grace —

Contents

Acknowledgments   *xiii*
Introduction   *1*

Battle-Pieces
   The Portent   *53*
   Misgivings   *53*
   The Conflict of Convictions   *54*
   Apathy and Enthusiasm   *56*
   The March into Virginia   *58*
   Lyon   *59*
   Ball's Bluff   *61*
   Dupont's Round Fight   *62*
   The Stone Fleet   *62*
   Donelson   *63*
   The Cumberland   *76*
   In the Turrett   *77*
   The Temeraire   *78*
   A Utilitarian View of the Monitor's Fight   *80*
   Shiloh   *81*
   The Battle for the Mississippi   *82*
   Malvern Hill   *83*
   The Victor of Antietam   *85*
   Battle of Stone River, Tennessee   *87*
   Running the Batteries   *88*
   Stonewall Jackson   *90*
   Stonewall Jackson (ascribed to a Virginian)   *91*
   Gettysburg   *93*
   The House-Top   *94*
   Look-out Mountain   *95*

Chattanooga   95

The Armies of the Wilderness   97

On the Photograph of a Corps Commander   104

The Swamp Angel   105

The Battle for the Bay   106

Sheridan at Cedar Creek   110

In the Prison Pen   111

The College Colonel   112

The Eagle of the Blue   113

A Dirge for McPherson   113

At the Cannon's Mouth   114

The March to the Sea   115

The Frenzy in the Wake   118

The Fall of Richmond   119

The Surrender at Appomattox   120

A Canticle   120

The Martyr   122

"The Coming Storm"   123

Rebel Color-Bearers at Shiloh   124

The Muster   125

Aurora-Borealis   126

The Released Rebel Prisoner   127

A Grave Near Petersburg, Virginia   128

"Formerly a Slave"   129

The Apparition   129

Magnanimity Baffled   130

On the Slain Collegians   130

America   132

On the Home Guards   134

Inscription   134

The Fortitude of the North   134

On the Men of Maine   135

An Epitaph   135

Inscription   135

The Mound by the Lake   136

On the Slain at Chickamauga   136

An Uninscribed Monument   136

On Sherman's Men   137

On the Grave of a Young Cavalry Officer   137

A Requiem   *138*
On a Natural Monument   *138*
Commemorative of a Naval Victory   *139*
Presentation to the Authorities   *140*
The Returned Volunteer to His Rifle   *140*
The Scout Toward Aldie   *141*
Lee in the Capitol   *164*
A Meditation   *169*
Notes to *Battle-Pieces*   *171*
Notes Supplement   *179*
Editor's Notes to *Battle-Pieces*   *187*

Excerpts from *Clarel*
Part One. Jerusalem, Cantos 29–33   *193*
Part Two. The Wilderness, Cantos 29–35   *209*
Part Four. Bethlehem, Cantos 10–16   *228*
Editor's Notes to *Clarel* excerpts   *255*

John Marr and Other Sailors
John Marr   *263*
Bridegroom Dick   *269*
Tom Deadlight   *281*
Jack Roy   *282*
The Haglets   *283*
The Aeolian Harp   *290*
To the Master of the "Meteor"   *291*
Far Off-Shore   *292*
The Man-of-War Hawk   *292*
The Figure-Head   *292*
The Good Craft "Snow-Bird"   *293*
Old Counsel   *294*
The Tuft of Kelp   *294*
The Maldive Shark   *294*
To Ned   *295*
Crossing the Tropics   *296*
The Berg   *296*
The Enviable Isles   *298*
Pebbles   *298*
Editor's Notes to *John Marr and Other Sailors*   *299*

Timoleon   *305*
After the Pleasure Party   *310*
The Night-March   *314*
The Ravaged Villa   *315*
The Margrave's Birthnight   *315*
Magian Wine   *316*
The Garden of Metrodorus   *317*
The New Zealot to the Sun   *317*
The Weaver   *318*
Lamia's Song   *319*
In a Garret   *319*
Monody   *319*
Lone Founts   *320*
The Bench of Boors   *320*
The Enthusiast   *321*
Art   *322*
Buddha   *322*
C——'s Lament   *322*
Shelley's Vision   *323*
Fragments of a Lost Gnostic Poem of the 12th Century   *323*
The Marchioness of Brinvilliers   *324*
The Age of the Antonines   *324*
Herba Santa   *325*
Venice   *327*
In a Bye-Canal   *327*
Pisa's Leaning Tower   *328*
In a Church of Padua   *329*
Milan Cathedral   *329*
Pausilippo   *330*
The Attic Landscape   *332*
The Same   *332*
The Parthenon   *333*
Greek Masonry   *334*
Greek Architecture   *334*
Off Cape Colonna   *334*
The Archipelago   *334*
Syra   *335*
Disinterment of the Hermes   *337*

The Apparition   *338*
In the Desert   *338*
The Great Pyramid   *339*
L'Envoi   *340*
Editor's Notes to *Timoleon, Etc.*   *340*

Bibliography   *345*

Acknowledgments

I wish to thank Northwestern University Press for permission to use quotations from the Northwestern/Newberry editions of Melville's *Pierre, Clarel, Correspondence,* and *Journals.* I am very grateful for all the help given me during the book's production by Erin Holman, Joanna Hildebrand Craig, Will Underwood, Christine Brooks, and others at The Kent State University Press.

Introduction

Melville's Poems

Herman Melville is one of America's greatest poets, his best poems worthy to take their place beside the poetry of Walt Whitman and Emily Dickinson. The Melville who is the author of *Moby-Dick, Billy Budd,* "Benito Cereno," "Bartleby, the Scrivener," and other fascinating fictions is already generously given his due by readers and scholars. However, Melville the poet is not, and he is therefore the most neglected major poet in America. His fiction apparently possesses an appeal that his poetry, by and large, seems to lack. Still, as we study his work, it is worth remembering that Melville devoted many more years to the composition of poetry than he gave to prose writing and that, even if he had not written his fiction, the quality, variety, and imposing energy of his poems should entitle him to a prominent place in American literature.

This volume of Melville's poems—unlikely, perhaps, to help raise his reputation as a poet—is intended to be different from the volumes of selected poems edited by Robert Penn Warren and Hennig Cohen. Both make excellent selections, but, inevitably, both leave out some of Melville's most interesting poems. It is probable that Melville makes his very best effect when the volumes of his shorter poems are read straight through. He always seems to have a principle of construction in mind for each book, and this effect is lost in a selection of the "best" or most characteristic of his poems. With this in mind, I have printed the complete texts of *Battle-Pieces and Aspects of the War, John Marr and Other Sailors,* and *Timoleon.* The ideal of completeness breaks down when confronted with the length and bulk of *Clarel,* but I have selected some blocks of complete cantos, which, I hope, will give some idea of the poem's narrative movement as well as its excellence, range, and multiple interests.

There has been no collected edition of the poems since H. P. Vincent's *The Collected Poems of Herman Melville* (1947).The Northwestern-Newberry volume in the new collected works has been promised for years and may be out soon. We have been fortunate to have some fine studies of Melville as a poet. Cohen's notes to his selection and to his edition of *Battle-Pieces* offer much valuable information about the poems and their sources. Warren's introduction and notes to his selection are the work of a sensitive poet and acute critic, and so his statements must be weighed carefully. Walter Bezanson's introduction and extensive notes to *Clarel* are a permanent addition to our stock of knowledge of that difficult poem, and the additions in the Northwestern-Newberry edition must also be considered. *The Mystery of Iniquity* (1972), the book-length study of the poetry by William H. Shurr, is still the most balanced and complete scholarly investigation of all of Melville's poems.

The Poetry of Melville's Late Years by William Bysshe Stein (1970) does not deal with *Battle-Pieces* or *Clarel,* and its readings of the late poems are often quirky and in need of challenge or supplementary information and interpretation; but it is an alert, attractive book that often shakes our comfortable ideas about the poems and forces us to further engagement with the difficulties that Melville the poet can offer. *The Civil War World of Herman Melville* by Stanton Garner (1993) is extremely important for its treatment of the poems in *Battle-Pieces.* It offers backgrounds for every poem and interpretations of the poems within the context of their time of composition. Several chapters of *After the Whale* by Clark Davis (1995) carefully discuss the poetry and are distinguished by their perceptive accounts of the works, which suffer from what Davis calls "a willful dissociation, a frequent refusal to envision this long period of generic uncertainty as a whole."

It is to be hoped that the second volume of Hershel Parker's magisterial biography and the greatly enlarged new edition of *The Melville Log* will further aid students of this important period of the poet's life. William Dillingham's *Melville and his Circle:The Last Years* (1996) undertakes some parts of the task of unraveling certain aspects of Melville's reading and discusses some of the poetry with accuracy and discernment. But there is a great deal more to the last fifteen years of Melville's life and creative expression than Dillingham attempts to encompass.

Over the years, essays on various topics have provided us with more information and enlightenment. Pieces by Richard Harter Fogle, Lawrence H. Martin Jr., Jane Donahue, Darrel Abel, and Laurence Barrett set forth some important distinctions and helped mark the way for students. More recent essays by Bryan Short, John Bryant, Robert Sandberg, Robert Milder, Edgar A. Dryden, and Juana Djelal have given us some captivating accounts of individual poems and poem groups. In *Critical Essays on Melville's Billy Budd, Sailor*, edited by Robert Milder (1989), there are pieces by Milder and Milton Stern that offer important insights into the poetry while discussing other matters. These all help to establish Melville as the remarkable poet he undoubtedly is.

Some aspects of Melville's poetry seem to present almost insuperable barriers to their interpretation and appreciation. In some instances he burdens poems with epigraphic captions that appear to offer discordant or contrary elements to otherwise clear-looking poetic texts. In others, changes of mind, reflected in manuscript revisions, mix with earlier concepts to produce poems that remain unclear, whatever the effort to unravel their meanings. He is often a difficult poet, his lines reduced to the barest statement of what he means. Because he is a patient poet, reworking his lines as often as he deems it necessary, the lines are sometimes loaded, "every rift," with difficult words. What can one make, for example, from the line "Sibylline inklings blending rave" in the poem "Magian Wine," or "Of God the effluence of the essence, / Shekinah intolerably bright" from the poem "In the Desert"? And what is one to make of titles? From a view of revisions, it seems that "C——s Lament" may be intended to be about Coleridge. But what does Coleridge have to do with the poem that Melville presents? Even knottier is the brief "Fragments of a Lost Gnostic Poem of the 12th Century," which consists of only two quatrains (a third eliminated during revisions). The title raises questions: Are these fragments from a short poem or a long one? Do they fit together, or are they separated by many verses, or even by pages of the "original" poem? What makes the poem gnostic? Why specify that it is of the twelfth century and not some other epoch? And is the poet, or Melville, adapting the pose that he is simply a transcriber of someone else's poem rather than its author?

That these questions, among many others, must be asked

indicates that Melville is a difficult poet at least partly because he is a learned poet. His description of Pierre Glendenning might serve as an announcement of his own mode of learning:

> A varied scope of reading, little suspected by his friends, and randomly acquired by a random but lynx-eyed mind, in the course of multifarious incidental, bibliographic encounterings of almost any civilised young inquirer after Truth, this poured one considerable contributory stream into that bottomless spring of original thought which the occasion and time had caused to burst out in himself. (*Pierre* 283)

Though the man described is a young hero and the book was written by a man still young, the phrases delineate well Melville's own intense search for Truth in his varied reading. Markings and marginal comments written in the books he read testify to the depth of his response to the act of reading and show him always as professional, seeking what he can find usable in the literature of the past. It has been noted that Melville's reading did often seem random and superficial, but that can hardly be true. Rather, say that though he seemed to skim the books he encountered, his "lynx-eyed mind" absorbed fully what he read, organized it to serve him in his work, and, remembered precisely for years, served his curious and capacious talents to allow him to produce profound prose and poetic creations.

I

After his intensive engagement with prose fiction and nonfiction, from about 1845 to 1857, Melville undertook what for him was a relatively new venture, the composition of poetry. His attitude toward this change seems ambivalent, at least in his public references to it. Writing to his brother, Tom, on May 25, 1862, he playfully talked about his poetry. He had passed his manuscripts on to a trunk maker, he said, who would use them for linings. If Tom should buy a new trunk, he might "just peep at the lining & perhaps you may be rewarded by some glorious stanza stareing [*sic*] you in the face & claiming admiration" (*Correspondence* 377).

The "whole stock" of manuscripts—"my own doggerel," he called them—that he had so ingloriously disposed of probably included those for a volume of poetry he had assembled in 1860 and attempted, unsuccessfully, to have published. In his copy of Thomas Hoods's poems, acquired just before this letter, he had marked the epigram entitled "The Poet's Fate":

> WHAT is a modern Poet's fate?
> To write his thoughts upon a slate;—
> The Critic spits on what is done,—
> Gives it a wipe,—and all is gone.

On a more serious note, he had marked in a volume of William Cullen Bryant's poems some lines from "The Past":

> Full many a mighty name
> Lurks in thy depths, unuttered, unrevered;
> With thee are silent fame,
> Forgotten arts, and wisdom disappeared.

However, he knew, as he had known from the construction of his fictions, what an effort went into artistic creation. In his poem "Art," he made a list of

> What unlike things must meet and mate:
> A flame to melt—a wind to freeze;
> Sad patience—joyous energies;
> Humility—yet pride and scorn;
> Instinct and study; love and hate;
> Audacity—reverence.

The seriousness of this dedication to his art, whether prose or poetry, undercuts the public utterances and the stance he chose to take over the long and difficult years of work in New York Customs and toil on the poems. Earlier writers took the view that the poetry was a great falling off from the powerful and engaging novels and tales. Melville would have been astonished by such a characterization of his writings. His creative explorations would continue to be far ranging, intense, passionate, and deeply philosophical, right up to the time of his death.

There had been a long preparation for these ventures into poetic composition. From his earliest years as a reader, Melville had made poetry an integral part of his study. As a schoolboy he had encountered in his text, Murray's *English Reader,* the poems of Cowper, Young, and Pope. A school prize awarded him in 1831 was *The London Carcanet*, which contained passages "from the most distinguished writers"—Thomas Moore, Lord Byron, and Walter Scott—as well as selections of prose. When Melville made his first, juvenile attempt at writing, in 1839, his "Fragments from a Writing Desk" showed that he had been reading Byron, Moore, Milton, and Thomas Campbell, among others. Passages with an autobiographical tinge in *Omoo* and *Redburn* indicate familiarity with these writers and others.

But it was after returning from his sea journeys in 1845 that he began reading as a serious professional author, buying books, marking as he read, and often writing marginal comments on their pages. In 1848 he acquired Dante in the Cary translation and James MacPherson's *Fingal*. In *Mardi*, written in the same year, there is evidence of his reading of Dante. When he acquired a set of Shakespeare in seven volumes and a two-volume set of Milton's poems in 1849, he marked the works of both writers copiously as he read. In "Lycidas," for instance, he took note of the passages that had to do with authorship, carefully underlining the passage that requires the poet to "strictly meditate" the thankless Muse. Reading Book 6 of *Paradise Lost*, where the armies of the Lord are arrayed against those of Satan, with "a dreadful interval" between them (l. 105), Melville annotated the passage with the quotation "The deadly space between," reminded at this point of Thomas Campbell's "Ode on a Naval Victory." The fact that he was able to use the phrase years later in *Billy Budd* to describe the difficult necessity of probing the character of Claggart makes clear how he grasped and stored what was valuable.

Melville's Ishmael and Pierre Glendenning prove themselves as well read as their creator. This wide reading must have meant much to him as he began to write poetry with the intention of publication. By 1860 he had prepared a volume of poems and attempted, unsuccessfully, to have it published. Hershel Parker has offered a full account of this venture in his essay "The Lost Poems (1860)," indicating what Melville was reading at the time and speculating on what may have been the contents of the lost volume. It seems possible that the manuscripts of this abortive collection of poems went to line the productions of the ominous trunk maker. In later years, an ironic echo in the poem *Clarel* has the young Clarel finding a manuscript lining his own trunk.

During the years of the Civil War, Melville gained, through his experiences and through reading, what he would need for the composition of *Battle-Pieces*. But his reading in poetry was wider and of more consequence. Bezanson says that "he wanted to cast his net to bring in the primary resources of poetic tradition—epic, ballad, and song" (*Clarel* 526) and lists the poems of Collins, Churchill, Moore, Heine, Arnold, and Mangan, among others. Mangan's *Poems* (1859) contained not only poetry by that partially gifted writer but also his unreliable translations ("versions" might be a better word) of poems by Goethe, Schiller, Tieck, Freiligrath, Rueckert, and others, giving Melville at least some conspectus of European continental poetry.

Most of the Civil War poems, according to Melville's own account, were written after the fall of Richmond, which took place April 3, 1865. Between that time and publication of *Battle-Pieces and Aspects of the War* in August 1866, Melville worked at shaping the volume. It is his most public performance; that is to say, in it he feels obliged to add a prose "Supplement" in which he can address the nation and make his ideas and feelings known, even if it destroys what he calls "the symmetry of this book." While the supplement certainly does interfere with the book's symmetry, it does allow Melville the opportunity of voicing his deepest feelings about the war and its aftermath. In the closing paragraph he says, "Let us pray that the terrible historic tragedy of our time may not have been enacted without instructing our whole beloved country through terror and pity; and may fulfillment verify in the end those expectations which kindle the bards of Progress and Humanity." This noble sentiment fully justifies the carefully framed title. The book does not consist only of battle pieces; it is deeply concerned with aspects of the war, the most important of which is clearly the Aristotelian catharsis the poet expects and hopes for.

Individual poems in the volume have been praised, studied, and excerpted as anthology pieces. "The Portent," which opens the tragic story, has probably drawn the most commentary, and, indeed, it is one of Melville's most polished performances as a poet. Its fourteen lines, divided into two stanzas, might remind one of a sonnet; but, if so, it is a sonnet with its lines curtly clipped, its shape wrenched, its pictorial rendering of the execution of John Brown vivid and terrible, and its prophetic, seerlike tone at the conclusion deep with the tinge of tragedy. The scene is vivid and heart-wrenching:

> Hanging from the beam,
> Slowly swaying (such the law),
> Gaunt the shadow on your green,
> Shenandoah!
> The cut is on the crown
> (Lo, John Brown)
> And the stabs shall heal no more.

The poet paints a picture not displayed in any of the periodicals of the time. They showed Brown on the scaffold before the execution but did not show the hanging corpse. The Shenandoah River flows into the Potomac at Harpers Ferry, the scene of Brown's disastrous attack, and the word "Shenandoah" becomes synecdoche for Virginia and for the Southern states. Brown's "streaming beard" is like the tail of a meteor, and the meteor prefigures a vision of the war, brought on by the death of the "weird," prophetic Brown.

For an author as committed as Melville was to the portrayal of life at sea, the naval poems among the *Battle-Pieces* have a special resonance. "The Stone Fleet," a lament for the scuttled whaleships designed to blockade the harbor at Charleston, is given to an "old sailor" who mourns the loss of something noble from the past and meditates upon the irony that the deed has only made the harbor clearer for passage. "Nature," the old man declares, "is nobody's ally." The battle of the *Monitor* and the *Merrimac* suggests "to an Englishman of the old order" the dismantling of the *Temeraire*, one of the greatest of the old wooden ships and thus the end of the era of sailing ships in naval warfare. Likewise, the armed and armored warship of the present is the theme for "A Utilitarian View of the *Monitor's* Fight," where "the gaud of glory" is replaced by "plain mechanic power." War loses its "Orient pomp" and now moves among "trades and artisans." Everything

now goes "by crank, / Pivot, and screw, / And calculations of
caloric."

Some of the *Battle-Pieces* concerned with the struggles on
land have the grave quality of elegy and memorial. In "Shiloh"
the battle is already over, and the speaker in the poem pronounces
celebratory words for the dead:

> But now they lie low,
> While over them the swallows skim,
> And all is hushed at Shiloh.

The tiny singing birds, wheeling and skimming over the grave
sites, bring some relief to the scene of the fierce battle in which
more than twenty thousand troops had lost their lives. "Malvern
Hill," the scene of another bitter struggle, celebrates a battle taking place only three months after Shiloh, but it is again recollect-
ed in tranquility, in the following spring, by the elm trees spared
in the battle:

> We elms of Malvern Hill
> Remember every thing;
> But sap the twig will fill;
> Wag the world how it will,
> Leaves must be green in Spring.

The overwhelming power of the natural world is beyond the
reach of humanity and its insistent and destructive quarrels with
itself.

Not all the *Battle-Pieces* have this quiet sense of belatedness
and commemoration. "Running the Batteries" describes the battle above Vicksburg "as observed from the anchorage," and the
city is well within the circle of destruction: "A flame leaps out;
they are seen; / Another and another gun roars." In "The Battle
for the Mississippi" ships struggle and limp from the fray: "The
oaken flag-ship, half ablaze, / Passed on, and thundered yet." "At
the Cannon's Mouth" bears the epigraph "Destruction of the
Ram Albemarle by the Torpedo-Launch" and begins, "Palely intent,
he urged his keel / Full on the guns."

It is impossible to guess why Melville chose some subjects among the many available to him and why he rejected others. He writes of Shiloh, Malvern Hill, Gettysburg, and Sherman's march to the sea, but he neglects the exploits of Colonel Grierson, who led his troops from Tennessee to Louisiana, killing and capturing Confederate soldiery and destroying much of the South's war supplies. In turn, John Morgan's raid through Ohio destroyed Federal property until Morgan was captured. The attack of black soldiers at Port Hudson, Louisiana, might have called up some of Melville's poetry, but he left the topic alone. One must assume that he carefully selected the battles to enunciate the themes that he wanted to display in the volume.

Melville moved his family from Pittsfield to New York City in 1863, just missing the draft riots of July. His poem "The House-Top," to which he carefully gives a particular tone by the subtitle, "A Night Piece," is an imaginative reconstruction of the awful scene with his judgment of the results. As in the case with a number of the other poems in the volume, Melville is not content to let it stand on its own, but he offers a note for the line "man rebounds whole aeons back in nature." This "rebound" underlines the poet's view that mankind, for all its modernity, is still near the viciousness of its own past. The note reinforces the poetic and philosophical position that, says Froissart, one "dare not write the horrible and inconceivable atrocities committed," alluding to the remarkable sedition in France during his time. The like may be hinted of some proceedings of the draft rioters.

The allusion to Froissart (1333–1400), and the quotation, tie the atrocities of 1863 to a violent and bloody past that hangs heavily over the present time. The blank verse allows Melville a deliberative pace for his description:

No sleep. The sultriness pervades the air
And binds the brain—a dense oppression, such
As tawny tigers feel in matted shades,
Vexing their blood and making apt for ravage.
Beneath the stars the roofy desert spreads
Vacant as Libya. All is hushed nearby.

The heat and oppressive feeling, the animal images, and the emptiness of the scene contribute to the impression: things may as well be occurring in Africa as in New York, and the time might be at any time in the past. The riots have proved the error of the "faith implied, / Which holds that Man is naturally good," a theme that echoes through many of the poems in the volume.

Slavery is one aspect of the war that gets very little treatment in the book. Only one poem, "Formerly a Slave," exhibits—from the distance Melville often puts between his poetry and its subjects—some fairly conventional feelings. It is possible that he would not have spoken at all about this important matter had he not attended a showing of artworks. The poem's epigraph makes clear the occasion: "An idealized portrait, by E. Vedder, in the Spring exhibition of the National Academy, 1865." Vedder (1836–1923) spent much of his life in Italy but lived in New York during the war years and submitted several paintings to the Academy. Melville, always sensitive to pictures, attempts to describe the portrait and use it as a basis for his reflections. The muted tone and generalized language indicate little feeling about "the peculiar institution" and its bitter results. The poet sees some prophetic quality in the aspect of the woman who was formerly a slave, but he assumes that her people will not come into their own for a very long time.

In his introduction to his selection of Melville's poems, Robert Penn Warren speaks of these in *Battle-Pieces* as being a log of Melville's attempt to make sense of his feelings about the war. As a log charts a ship's speed and progress as well as weather and navigational events of importance, this volume charts Melville's bewildered progress through the years of the war and the events after the surrender, both in what it records and what it leaves out. He might have begun the book with poems on the raid on Harpers Ferry or on the trial of John Brown, but, instead, chooses a moment after these events. Brown has just been executed, his body "swaying," his face hidden by the cap with its "anguish none can draw," but the anguish that the poet means is not merely personal but large—national—in scale. There is an "afterward" quality about other poems in the collection, indicating, at least partly, that Melville wrote after learning of the events he was portraying, sometimes years later. But it also indicates the poetic stance that he wished to assume, of brooding on the events some time past and the lessons they bear. It is only the last poems in the volume that must have been written just as their events were taking place that help to round out the story that Melville wants to tell.

The poet has a dream-vision of the war in its fantastic aspects. In "The Apparition," a poem he calls "A Retrospect," he sees the struggle as a volcanic eruption bursting through the apparently calm and pastoral surface of the world. Such a destructive event, caused by "the unreserve of Ill," is only a matter of "the scared sense" being deceived. But that hopeful thought gives way to a pessimistic conclusion:

> So, then, Solidity's a crust—
>   The core of fire below;
> All may go well for many a year,
> But who can think without a fear
>   Of horrors that happen so?

The retrospect is followed by memorial poems dedicated to those lost in the war: the slain collegians; the home guards; those who fell at Pea Ridge, Second Manassas, Fredericksburg, Chickamauga, Kenesaw Mountain; and the soldiers and the sailors lost in naval engagements.

Narrative poems, bringing the action to the fore, demonstrate, sometimes erratically, Melville's proven skills as a storyteller. On the one hand, "Donelson" does not work well, though the poet uses a number of technical effects: a letter, newspaper headlines, conversations, timed reports. On the other hand, "The Scout toward Aldie," a lengthy narrative about the attempt by Union forces to seek out and fight Colonel John Mosby and his raiders, is a successful versified tale. The Confederate officer achieves mythic status: "As glides in sea the shark, / Rides Mosby through the green dark." In April 1864 Melville was able to visit some of the battle scenes in Virginia and some of the scenes of Mosby's exploits, even joining a scouting party on a patrol. The poem is enriched by the observation and use of pertinent detail, but the poem moves well beyond the details open to Melville's observation. The story is skillfully handled, transitions are sharply marked to keep the narrative moving, and the poetic language is precise and fresh.

The book is uneven, as any volume of poems is likely to be. It contains weak poems, poems that plainly contradict Melville's statement that they "were composed without reference to collective arrangement" and that the poet functioned only "to have but placed a harp in a window, and noted the contrasted airs which wayward winds have played upon the strings." If there is anything to be learned from a reading of the volume straight through as it appears, it is that the arrangement is carefully attended to. That is why some of the weaker poems have the air of having been composed to fill in an idea, a theme, a sense of direction, a particular "aspect of the war." Melville's sense of structure is, as always, admirable. The volume, far from being a random collection, functions as a comprehensive book. Reviews appearing at the time of publication showed, for the most part, a lack of understanding. The poetry was called "epileptic"; "its rhymes are fearful," said a reviewer. *Harper's New Monthly Magazine,* having published some of the poems before book publication, praised Melville's work. Another comment pointed out that "no one but Mr. Melville could have written it, and few besides himself would have cared to write it."

II

Just before the end of 1866, Melville became a civil servant, working for the Custom House in New York. The family was happy about the regular employment, his mother noting that his being compelled to go to business had improved his health. What Melville thought of his changed condition is not recorded. His employment lasted through several administrations in Washington. Finally, in 1885, at the age of sixty-five, he retired.

During his retirement he busied himself with a heavy course of reading and with the composition of his poetry. *Clarel: A Poem and a Pilgrimage* was published in 1876. Melville's dedication makes clear how it was possible for him to have the poem published: "By a spontaneous act, not very long ago, my kinsman, the late Peter Gansevoort, of Albany, N.Y., in a personal interview provided for the publication of this poem, known to him by report, as existing in manuscript. Justly and affectionately the printed book is inscribed with his name." Publisher G. P. Putnam would surely not have published it otherwise. After all, it was a narrative poem in four books and a total of more than 18,000 lines. Melville was to refer to it as "a metrical affair, a pilgrimage or what not." In a brief note to be encountered by a prospective reader before he even begins reading the work itself, Melville voices an ironically stated view: "If during the period in which this work has remained unpublished, though not undivulged, any of its properties have by a natural process exhaled; it yet retains, I trust, enough of original life to redeem it at least from vapidity. Be that as it may, I here dismiss the book—content beforehand with whatever future awaits it." The author would not have been surprised to learn that the poem has had a difficult future. Less than five hundred copies were sold, most of the few reviews were dismissive, and later commentary has often been hostile.

Most long poems are far from satisfying, and *Clarel* is hardly an exception. But in its details it is frequently a marvelous piece of work. Melville was led to the concept of a long narrative poem by the examples that he studied: Spenser's *The Faerie Queene*, Milton's *Paradise Lost*, Wordsworth's *The Prelude, or the Growth of a Poet's Mind*, and Byron's *Childe Harold's Pilgrimage*. Byron may have given him the idea of a pilgrimage. Wordsworth's account of the growth of a mind may also have furnished an idea, for the young Clarel does grow (at least a little) during the brief time span of the poem.

Clarel is a vast edifice. Melville does, however, provide a sort of guide through its varied rooms and vistas by concocting a fairly simple plot. Clarel, a young American studying for the ministry, comes to Palestine, as other tourists have done, to see for himself what there is to see. His attitude is probably that which Melville took to his own pilgrimage: "In pursuance of my object, the saturation of my mind with the atmosphere of Jerusalem, offering myself up a passive subject, and no unwilling one, to its weird impressions, I always rose at dawn & walked without the walls" (*Journals* 86). This passivity is strongly marked in the poet's construction of Clarel's character; as a result, the young man, unlike such vivid personages of Melville's creation as Tommo,

Redburn, and Ishmael, is a weaker and less interesting figure than he might have been.

A love plot involving Clarel and the beautiful Ruth takes up fairly little of the poem and is interrupted by the death of her father. Kept from her, Clarel leaves Jerusalem with a party of tourists and proceeds east to the Dead Sea and then north to the monastery at Mar Saba. From there the party returns to Bethlehem and then to Jerusalem, where Clarel learns that Ruth and her mother have died. He is overcome with grief. His friends must leave him, and he mourns alone during the holy season between Palm Sunday and Easter.

This plot does not move the poem's narrative very far. Instead, during Clarel's touring pilgrimage a complex argument emerges about the problem of religious faith, especially when faced by the tides of unbelief and science in the nineteenth century. The disillusioning aspect of landscape adds to the weight of the discussion. "No country will more quickly dissipate romantic expectations than Palestine," Melville notes, "particularly Jerusalem. To some the disappointment is heart sickening" (*Journals* 91). The reading that Melville did after his pilgrimage and while he was planning and writing the poem reflected and supplemented his own impressions and ideas. Like others who took this tour, he found himself gripped by history, by the long centuries of pilgrimage and writing. Bezanson credits him with reading Thomas Wright's edition of *Early Travels in Palestine* (London: Bohn, 1848) for some of his material; Wright's book is a fascinating anthology that reprints the writings of travelers in the Holy Land from about the eighth through the seventeenth centuries. Some are reverential and some look skeptically at the legends and at the realities of life and belief in this narrow world. The impression Clarel has of Jerusalem matches what Melville experienced when he saw the city. The young student finds blankness and blindness

> in walls of wane,
> Sealed windows, portals masoned fast,
> And terraces where nothing passed
> By parapets all dumb (1.1.163–66)

He and a friend "rove the storied ground— / Tread many a site

that rues the ban / Where serial wrecks on wrecks confound"
(I.x.1–3).

As *Battle-Pieces* is about aspects of the war, this poem is about
aspects of landscape, religious feeling, and cultural and historical
labyrinths. Looking down at Jerusalem from a tower is like viewing the City of Dis or, rather, "some print, / Old blurred, bewrin-
kled mezzotint" (1.36.30–31). Again, as in *Battle-Pieces*, in *Clarel*
there is a feeling of remove from the physicality of the scene.
Clarel rambles through the city becoming acquainted with all
there is to see, and he begins to meet and be drawn to other
people. There is Celio, a young Italian man, his body distorted by
a humped back that has caused him to be bitter and skeptical
about his religious faith. At the site of the Ecce Homo Arch, he
meditates and says of God, "Smite or suspend, perplex, deter— /
Tortured, shalt prove a torturer" (1.13.98–99). Clarel visits the
Wailing Wall,

> an Ararat
> Founded on beveled blocks how wide,
> Reputed each a stone August
> of Solomon's fane (I.xvi.89–92)

As he views it, he first sees Ruth and immediately falls in love.
When Clarel visits the "rifled *Sepulcher of Kings*," Melville has an
opportunity for disputation and takes it, in splendid verse:

> Hewn from the rock a sunken space
> Conducts to garlands—fit for vase—
> In sculptured frieze above a tomb:
> Palm leaves, pine apples, grapes. These bloom,
> Involved in dearth—to puzzle us—
> As 'twere thy line, Theocritus,
> Dark Joel's text of terror threading:
> Yes, strange that Pocahontas-wedding
> Of contraries in old belief—
> Hellenic cheer, Hebraic grief.
> The homicide Herods, men aver,
> Inurned behind that wreathage were. (I. 28.25–36)

In this brief span of poetry, we see much that has entered the

Melvillean battery of thought: the love of art, the notion of dearth (a term crucial to his work), the knowing allusions to Greek poetry and his deep Biblical knowledge, the contrariety between styles of thought in "Hellenic cheer" and "Hebraic grief." Contrariety, by its very nature, fascinates Melville, and he delights in observing it in almost all states of being.

After the tragedy in Ruth's family, Clarel joins the pilgrims who leave Jerusalem on a guided tour that will take them to the Dead Sea and then north as far as Mar Saba. Since the group is a varied one, there is room for letting each character develop a consistent, individual view. Derwent, an Anglican pastor "of facile wit" who usually assumes the "last adopted style" of thinking (2.1.35, 55), is a bit contemptible in that company of deeply committed men, but he often scores points in his own debating way. Vine and Rolfe are men whom Clarel met before deciding to go on his tour, and each is important to Melville's plan. The first is an artist whose "charm of subtle virtue shed / A personal influence." He is not a "sackclothed man; / Howbeit, in sort Carthusian / Though born a Sybarite" (1.29.22–24, 38–40). A complex person, then, with powerful qualities of character and, as Clarel will learn, dismal weaknesses, Vine is often taken to be a partial portrait of Melville's great friend Nathaniel Hawthorne, who combined most of those contrarieties in his troubled self. On the other hand, Rolfe is clearly an idealized heroic figure—Melville's portrait of himself as he would like to be. The description breathes Clarel's (and Melville's) admiration:

He rose, removed his hat to greet,
Disclosing so in shapely sphere
A marble brow over face embrowned:
So Sunium by her fane is crowned.
One read his superscription clear—
A genial heart, a brain austere—
And further, deemed that such a man
Though given to study, as might seem,
Was no scholastic partisan
But supplemented Plato's theme
With daedal life in boats and tents,
A messmate of the elements;
And yet, more bronzed in face than mind,

Sensitive still and frankly kind—
Too frank, too unreserved, may be,
And indiscreet in honesty. (I.31.9–25)

The passage is worth quoting at length and studying closely, for it reveals much about its author, his sense of what is valuable in human beings and his love of knowledge unhampered by narrow scholarly or selfish pursuits. The details cover a wide range of ideas. The fane at Sunium was, in Melville's time, taken to be a temple to Athena, goddess of wisdom. The uncommon but handsome word "daedal," revealing in its insistence, makes Rolfe one of the company of Daedalus, "the cunning worker" who is the patron of artists' and craftsmen's guilds, an excellent counter to his studious nature. "Daedal" may also mean "of the earth." Melville may have encountered this word in his careful reading of *The Faerie Queene*, where Spenser opens the third book with praise for Queen Elizabeth and offers an interesting statement about art:

> But living art may not least part expresse,
> Nor life-resembling pencill it can paynt,
> All were it Zeuxis or Praxiteles:
> His daedale hand would faile, and greatly faynt,
> And her perfections with his error taynt (III.ii.10–14).

Another Spenserian use of the word emphasizes its earthly connection: "Then doth the daedale earth throw forth to thee / Out of her fruitfull lap aboundant flowres" (IV.x.45) reminds us that Rolfe's face is "embrowned" and that he is "more bronzed in face than mind." The remainder of the stanza compares the work of poet and painter, and the poet worries that the poet may suffer from "want of words" to achieve his object. Rolfe has words and is perfectly able to hold his audience in thrall with his discourses on subjects ranging from history to art to religious feeling. Launched into a description of the marvelous city of Petra and the building called El Deir, he defines art precisely and curtly:

> Mid such a scene
> Of Nature's terror, how serene
> That ordered form. Nor less 'tis cut

> Out of that terror—does abut
> Thereon: there's Art. (2.30.41–45)

Rolfe is the steadying influence, the final arbiter and balanced thinker in the group of rather unbalanced pilgrims.

By creating personages such as these, and a number of lesser but still important characters—Nehemiah, Mortmain, Margoth, Ungar, and Agath among them—and by speaking often in his own voice, Melville provides himself with articulate, voluble men who can range widely over history, thought, and personal observations to inform the discourse of the poem. The discussions that take up most of the poem's bulk become a virtual pandect of the century's thought, laying out the contrarieties of belief, agnosticism, skepticism, and atheism, as well as the pain that doubts can cause.

What do these pilgrims talk about? Some examples may help. A Syrian monk tells his story: "'Twas sin, he said, that drove him out / Into the desert—sin of doubt." After much searching, he is given a whisper of truth that says

> Content thee; in conclusion caught
> Thou'lt find how thought's extremes agree—
> The forethought clinched by afterthought,
> The firstling by finality. (2.18.141–44)

In many ways, this idea obtains throughout the poem. Rolfe, "in burst," makes a remarkable answer:

> Barque, Easter barque, with happier freight
> Than Leon's spoil of Inca plate;
> Which vernal glidest from the strand
> Of statues poised like angels fair;
> On March morn sailest—starting, fanned
> Auspicious by Sardinian air;
> And carriest boughs through Calpe's gate
> To Norman ports and Belgian land,
> That the Green Sunday, even there,
> No substituted leaf may wear,
> Holly or willow's lither wand,
> But sprays of Christ's canonic tree,

Rome's Palma-Christi by decree,
The Date Palm; ah, in bounty launch,
Thou blessed Easter barque, to me
Hither one consecrated branch. (2.19.1–16)

Rolfe's words manage to give the religious flavor to the pilgrimage and the poem, and his wisdom, among the pilgrims, is easily
established.

But, immediately, as part of Melville's plan, Margoth—a stranger, a geologist, willing to dispute all biblical topics, a representative of the materialistic atheism of the nineteenth century—
jokes away the theological musings of the other pilgrims with
"punning mock and manner." "Jura limestone, every spur," he
says of the mountain range:

Yes, and though signs the rocks imprint
Which of Plutonic action hint,
No track is found, I plump aver,
Of Pluto's footings—Lucifer (2.19.67–71).

By such abrasive oppositions, such intensely held and strongly
articulated views, Melville advances the argument. All of the carefully chosen pilgrims and hangers-on are given the chance to air
their thoughts in an often subtle chiaroscuro of persuasion. Derwent, the Anglican optimist, is made ridiculous for his ideas. Vine,
the most disappointing figure in the poem, is intelligent and
sensitive enough to hold a central place in Melville's large canvas.
But the portrayal of his weakness becomes clear to Clarel, who
sees about this figure he would gladly admire the "trembling over
of small throes" and is forced to call it "an evil sign: / No more
need dream of winning Vine / Or coming at his mystery" (3.7.37–39).

Clarel's great difficulty during the course of the poem is that
he has a powerful desire to be inspired by religious faith although
he has little feeling for it. This ill-based and abusive necessity
causes the young divinity student to stumble about among clashing views, always seeking one clear line of belief that can suit him.
The pilgrimage he makes through this confusing and chaotic set
of philosophies, and the humbling experiences of his journey
through past and present, as well as the terrible crisis of losing
Ruth, the lover he means to help him regain some stability, all

bring him to some sort of conclusion at the very end of the
poem:

> Unmoved by all the claims our times avow,
> The ancient Sphinx still keeps the porch of shade;
> And comes Despair, whom not her calm may cow,
> And coldly on that adamantine brow
> Scrawls undeterred his bitter pasquinade.
> But Faith (who from the scrawl indignant turns)
> With blood warm oozing from her wounded trust,
> Inscribes even on her shards of broken urns
> The sign o' the cross—*the spirit above the dust!* (4.35.3–11)

As though to indicate that the dance of tetrameter lines, with its
quick, often jabbing, explanations and theories, is over and that
there is some resolution, Melville here turns to the slower, more
weighty pentameter line. The narrator of the whole long poem
can then advise his young protagonist to "keep thy heart, though
yet but ill-resigned— / Clarel, thy heart, the issues there but
mind" (27–28). His is finally able to offer some balm of comfort:
"Emerge thou mayst from the last whelming sea, / And prove
that death but routs life into victory" (33–34). But we notice that
even the comfort is provisional. Clarel just "may" be able to emerge
from the veritable sea of conflict, contrariety, and grief that has
been overwhelming him and find some kind of questionable
triumph.

The work we know as *Clarel: A Poem and Pilgrimage in the Holy
Land* is too lengthy, detailed, and difficult to be apprehended in a
few explanatory words. A full explication would have to be a
longer book than the poem itself. After all, as he wrote, the author
had dwelt upon these matters for years—not only because they
made an interesting topic for a poetic narrative, but because they
engaged his own deepest doubts and concerns. When he visited
Hawthorne at Liverpool in 1856, just before setting out on his
pilgrimage, the older writer noted astutely and affectionately in
his journal that Melville "persists—and has persisted ever since I
knew him, and probably long before—in wandering to and fro
over these deserts, as dismal and monotonous as the sand hills
amid which we were sitting. He can neither believe, nor be comfortable in his unbelief; and he is too honest and courageous not

to try to do one or the other." Hawthorne did not live to read
Clarel. But if he had, he would have readily recognized what he
saw in the Melville of 1856, a glowering and stubborn determi-
nation to discover what ached within his spirit and to (somehow)
settle it.

III

In the years that followed publication of *Clarel*, Melville continued to write poems of varying length, mining his experiences of
the sea and travel, his observation of the arts and his deep love for
them, and the results of his reading in history, religion, and philosophy, as well as the odd recurrent stories that seemed most
significant to him. During this time he worked for New York
Customs until he was able to retire at the end of 1885. During the
next few years he began bringing some of that work to completion, arranging first for the publication of a volume of poems,
John Marr and Other Sailors with Some Sea-Pieces in 1888. The firm
of Theodore L. De Vinne & Company brought out the book in
twenty-five copies, perhaps all that Melville felt he could afford to
have done.

His motives for using this method of publication for both *John
Marr* in 1888 and *Timoleon* in 1891 were complex, but sensible.
One reason must have been that he was carefully preparing final
texts of his poems and ordering them in his books and then
having them printed to preserve a public record of his writings,
to appear as he wanted them to do and establish the effects that
he envisioned. This venture was entirely successful; any printings
of the two volumes must depend upon these two small but precisely worked out editions. Another reason is that by becoming
his own publisher and reducing the function of publishers to
mere printers, he established final authority for what went into
the volumes. There would be no interfering editors to make or
even suggest changes, no revisions, exclusions, or additions to
satisfy any external agency. Melville assumed entire responsibility
for his books. One judges that if he had lived longer, he would
have done something similar for the volume he called *Weeds and
Wildings* and another volume, or perhaps more than one more,
which would have been revised and printed in editions that would

be small but of great consequence. The case of *Billy Budd* may have turned out differently. The story might well have been accepted by a magazine or by a commercial publishing house for book publication. But this is speculative, since Melville never had the opportunity to carry out his wishes, whatever they might have been.

The elaborate and careful arrangement of *John Marr and Other Sailors* is artful. A prose introduction introduces John Marr, a sailor who has cut himself off from the sea. The physical details, handled briefly, form a kind of scenario for what might well have been a successful novel. After a youthful stint at sea, Marr has worked on land as a sailmaker and then a carpenter. He has had a wife and a child, both of whom die in the prairie village where he has settled and are buried near a native burial mound left by "a race only conjecturable." Marr is described: "swarthy and black-browed, with eyes that could soften or flash, but never harden, yet disclosing at times a melancholy depth." Like Rolfe in *Clarel*, he is another avatar of Melville, this time an aging man wounded by the blows of life and fate. The inland people who surround him do not understand him or his sea tales; the rolling prairie about him is like the "bed of a dried-up sea," and he himself seems "an absentee from existence." But, as it turns out, it is the rigor of this condition that drives him into memories of his past and turns him into a poet.

Melville is careful to establish that the present-day (1880s) appearance of the prairie is much different than it was in the time of Marr, some fifty years before. Now there are "places overpopulous with towns over-opulent," farms with a "superabundant wheat-harvest," a scene "now everywhere intersected with wire and rail." In John Marr's time it had been a place without "so much as a traceable road," where one "steered by the sun" and in a ride from one encampment to another, "travel was much like navigation." The vivid contrast of past with present is a constant theme in Melville's poetic output, emphasized in *Battle-Pieces* by the differences in sea battles between the great wooden ships— "hearts of oak"—of the past and the armored ironclads and submarines of the Civil War. The poems of *John Marr* cover a long time span, from the eighteenth century to the 1870s, just before the publication date of the volume.

Proceeding from this account of John Marr's sense of loneliness, hurt, and exile, the poems present sailors, ships, and the sea in varied situations. He and his shipmates have a firm belief: "*Life is storm—let storm.*" They have, for the most part, taken things "as fated merely." The old sailor called Bridegroom Dick muses, in 1876, on scenes from his past; since he is past sixty-five, he must be older than Melville, and his memories of the sea go further back. Even older is Tom Deadlight, who is dying, at the age of ninety-eight, in 1810. His memories cover a long period of eighteenth-century British naval action and lore. Jack Roy is not given a date to situate him in history, but he reflects the careless cheer of the young sailor. These are the "visionary ones" invoked by Marr from the treasure hoard of his persistent retrospection. As the poet says in "The Aeolian Harp," the visions are a "rendering of the Real. / What that Real is, let hint / A picture stamped in memory's mint." This mint of memory offers a way out of the arid, soul-killing daily commonplaces of life.

Of these opening poems in the sequence, "Bridegroom Dick" has attracted the most attention. It is the longest of the poems and contains substantial information that can be linked to Melville's life. Dick is not Melville, and, unlike John Marr, he has not suffered the loss of his wife. Instead, in a companionable way, he can share his recollections and feelings with her. But he is also an aged sailor, examining his past and finding much in it that is memorable. For him, the land is not a place of exile where a former seaman is landlocked; in October, a balmy time with the year "in decay," he speaks of "mellowing" as he reflects upon the many sailors he has known or heard of: "they are all gone, I think, / Leaving Bridegroom Dick here with lids that wink."

The poem once more rehearses a familiar Melvillean theme, the changes wrought by time, technological advances, differing social attitudes and actions, and the ever-pressing younger generations pushing into the scene and pushing aside the elderly and infirm. He regards this state of affairs with little bitterness and with considerable humor, for he continues to be part of the world he is observing. He is a kind of aging Ishmael, or perhaps an aging White-Jacket, looking back on a long career in the difficult and often tragic world of seafaring, and he views it with a mix of nostalgia and a certain amount of sadness:

Wife, where be all these chaps, I wonder?

Trumpets in the tempest, terrors in the fray,
Boomed their commands along the decks like thunder;
But silent is the sod, and thunder dies away.

Unlike other poems in the collection, which are often brief to the point of being gnomic, "Bridegroom Dick" has a breadth of expressive vision. Like the "John Marr" prose passage, it too reads like a scenario for a planned but never written novel. And what a novel it might have made with its scenes of battle and its varied characters given satiric or otherwise memorable names—Tom Tight, Captain Turret, Lieutenant Long Lumbago, and Commander All-A-Tanto. They are mixed in with real names from Dick's sailing past—Decatur, Perry, Porter, Scott, and Guert Gan (who is Guert Gansevoort, a relative of the Melville family). The poem illustrates generously the theme that John Marr had articulated: "Life is storm—let storm."

Having established at once a view that the ailing John Marr should follow in his quest for the past, the book proceeds to other characters who are deep in his memory. Tom Deadlight, "a grizzled petty-officer," his mind wandering, fastens incoherently upon a long and colorful past and sings of it in the measures of "a famous old sea-ditty." Unlike Dick, the dying old man in his last moments of life rambles as the cadences of the old song "attune the last fluttering of distempered thought." In a long life, Tom has not been able to organize his actions and feelings into a coherent pattern as the younger Bridegroom Dick has, and, as a result, the poem lacks the geniality of the earlier piece. Instead, it is informed by a cold and cutting blast of the sea's terrors; "distempered" is an excellent description of Tom's view of things, informed by a dour and sardonic humor: "Dead reckoning is good for to sail for the Deadman; / And Tom Deadlight he thinks it may reckon near right."

Third in this ill-matched group of "other sailors" recalled by John Marr is Jack Roy, his name, perhaps, a Melvillean pun on the French *roi*. He is a "manly king o' the old *Splendid's* crew." Marr characterizes him as a Mercutio aboard the ship and puns him again as a playing card, a Jack who is never "relishing the knave" and who is not "overmuch the king." His effervescent spirit is caught in a vivid simile: "Like the dolphin off Africa in rainbow a-sweeping— / Arch iridescent shot from seas languid sleeping."

Individuals all, these three men are also representative men of the seagoing life that the poet/sailor has lived, and their particular views govern much of what will occur later in the volume.

A highly interesting aspect of these first poems in *John Marr* is the ways in which they incorporate prose with poetry. The prosy Melville, whose prose has much of poetry in it, tries again and again to weld the arts of prose and poetry together in his work. This activity came early, in the lyrics interspersed through much of *Mardi*. It continues in *Moby-Dick* in the reworking of a familiar hymn for Chapter 9, "The Sermon," and in the dramatic and lyric scene played out in Chapter 40, "Midnight, Forecastle." In *Battle-Pieces* Melville works prose into the poetry of poems like "Donelson" and uses headnotes and epigraphs to have prose intrude upon the poetry. He then adds a set of notes, in prose, to the poems, presumably to give them a dimension that he feels will not sit well in the limited structure of some of the poems. His prose conclusion to the volume takes a longer step in its attempt to wrench the two—his prose and his poetry—together in a creative pattern that is held together by will and expediency. The prose in *John Marr* serves the poet's needs by adding fact to fancy, again in the prose scenario that opens the volume and in the epigraphs that provide some factual and prosy additions to certain poems. In *Timoleon*, as we shall see, the poet often adds prosy title or epigraph to enhance the poem and make more clear his intent. It is generally assumed that *Billy Budd* grew from the headnote to a poem, "Billy in the Darbies," a case of the prose countering and then overriding the poetry.

We find a similar pattern being followed in the poems that Melville left unpublished at his death. The volume entitled *Weeds and Wildings.* A prose dedication, "To Winnefred," opens the proposed volume. In the third part, the poem "Rip Van Winkle's Lilac" is preceded by a lengthy prose piece, a scenario rather than a story, dealing in part with Rip's earlier life and offering a digression upon the art of painting. Two poems of some length, "At the Hostelry" and "Naples in the Time of Bomba," mix prose and poetry in various engaging ways. It appears that Melville had not been able to work out all the details of joining prose and poetry in these unpublished works. Presumably, given the time and good health, he would have done further work on this fascinating experimental part of his poetic work.

After these introductory poems, two sections of the book, entitled "Sea Pieces" and "Minor Sea Pieces," move from the human to the inhuman element, the sea in all its power and cruelty. There are powerful images of the unchecked and often brutal and unmatchable strength of this alien world that mankind cannot hope to engage on anything like even terms. "The Aeolian Harp" displays a wreck "adrift, / Long time a thing forsaken; / Overwashed by every wave / Like the slumbering kraken." In "Far Off-Shore," where there is no shipwreck, the tragic drama of loss and death has advanced to its hopeless conclusion upon a raft that had held out hope for survivors: "None upon the lashed spars lying, / Quick or dead." Scenes like these inform a poem like "Old Counsel," in which the seasoned shipman can caution younger sailors: "brother, be not over-elate— / *All hands save ship!* Has startled dreamers."

Even the cautionary advice is not enough, for other dangers are part of the oceanic experience. "The Maldive Shark" portrays the beast in fearful terms like "his saw-pit of mouth," "his ghastly flank," "his Gorgonian head," and show him finally as the "pale ravener of horrible meat." "The Berg" likewise insists upon the iceberg's fearfulness, showing its "mortal damps," its "dankish breath"; it is a "lumbering lubbard" and cause for warning and dread:

Impingers rue thee and go down,
Sounding thy precipice below,
Nor stir the slimy slug that sprawls
Along thy dead indifference of walls.

These are the terrors of the sea, to be guarded against continually but that still overcome the humans who venture out upon it. Melville appears to have been dissatisfied with the last line of "The Berg." In a copy of the published volume, an alternative revision is offered: "Along thy dense stolidity of walls." He must have recognized the enormous problem involved in trying to articulate a combination of words like "dense stolidity" but did not want to let the poem go without trying it out. And, indeed, the revision improves upon the rather generalized "dead indifference."

"The Haglets" is one of the most striking poems in the book and certainly one of Melville's best. It has a history of rethinking and revision not available for other poems in the volume. In his journal of the pilgrimage to Palestine, Melville, aboard ship, noted on December 7, 1856, that during the evening, "captain told a story about the heap of arms affecting the compass" (*Journals* 56). In *Clarel* he uses Agath, the timoneer, to tell a version of this exemplum, this brief narrative told to illustrate a moral point. The aged sailor, "with dullish eye / Of some old reminiscence," is prevailed upon to tell of sailing from Egypt, bound for Venice on a ship called *The Peace of God*, an ironic name since the cargo consists of cannons to be melted down to make new artillery. A passenger, a Moor, has taken aboard a chest containing swords, and his cabin is directly beneath the compass. The metal affects the compass during a gale and the "mutinous bad crew" drinks and carouses as the ship hits rocks and is wrecked (*Clarel* 3.12.25–130).

Among Melville's manuscripts is a poem entitled "The Admiral of the White," which tells a different story. It describes a naval vessel led astray to its destruction upon the rocks, its compass affected by the French swords it has taken. Apparently, the scene has shifted from merchant shipping to the mishaps of the British navy in its struggles with France. A suitable date might be the time of the Seven Years War, during the 1750s and 1760s, though the poem gives no readily recognizable details to set the historical framework. This fleet has won its battle: "We've beaten the foe, their ship blown below, / Their flags in St. Paul's Church we'll rear." Part of the prize, the French captains' swords, cause the compass to veer from a true reading and the ship is wrecked. There is no indication of where this tragedy takes place, though we are told that the British ship is bound home, that it is the end of the year, and that the ship strikes "high-beetling" rocks. The meter and sound of the poem are reminiscent of the sea poems of Thomas Campbell. Its anapests mingled with the iambs give the poem a headlong motion to match the headlong movement of the ship to disaster.

The short, balladlike version of "The Admiral of the White" seems to have been composed after publication of *Clarel*, possibly between 1876 and 1885, and represents an intermediate stage in Melville's conception of his tale. In 1885 Melville published in the *New York Tribune* a poem with the same title, a longer work of thirty stanzas. It tells the story of the British ship after its successful struggle with "the arm'd Plate Fleet." Its spoils include "Toledoes great, grand draperies too, / Spain's steel and silk, and splendors from Peru," indicating that Melville has changed the historical time and situation. It again uses tetrameter lines but with a pentameter line at the end of each stanza, and the pace is slower and more deliberate because Melville has given up the nervous pace of the anapestic meter. In this form it is already an effective work of poetic art, a poem quite close to the great final version. The haglets have assumed their place in this version as birds of fate; the men are at their quarters in the storm that blows up, wondering how they have been betrayed into a destructive course. All fail to "heed the blades that clash in place / Under lamps dashed down that lit the magnet's case." But the poet had not finished his work on the poem. He found that he had much more to say and that the content and form of this version would not do. Seeing the poem in print was likely the impetus for further handling of the theme.

A manuscript of the new poem, the final version, is worthy of study. Melville leaves instructions for the printer, indicating that "The greater part of this piece (The Haglets) is marked off (in blue pencil) into stanzas of eighteen lines each. I think the seventh and thirteenth lines should be *indented*." The new version begins with title and the first three stanzas from the newspaper version, with Melville changing the title and removing the note that indicated that it was "by the author of OMOO" and other works and giving the copyright date. He wants more space between the second and third stanzas. Then he begins the additions with the line "The eddying waters whirl astern," adding twelve lines to make up his first eighteen-line stanza. And here we can see how his enlarged vision of the poem has come to change it with metaphorical and mythic additions. The ship's prow, "a seedsman, sows the spray"; its hull "leaves a Milky Way." In an essay in *ELH* that is reproduced in a shortened version in his book on the poetry, William Bysshe Stein has written an illuminating comment on the mythical adornments to the poem. The essay raises "The Haglets" to a place it deserves, as one of the

finest of Melville's poems, a tribute to his skills that should elim-
inate at once all complaints about his less-than-professional
approach to his art. One judges a poet by his best work, not by the
pieces that are interesting but less than impressive.

The poem combines two of Melville's most deeply felt themes:
the power and indifference of the natural world and the workings
of fate, the enigmatic force that controls so much of what humans do. Fate is represented by the haglets, the sea birds that
move purposively about the doomed ship, weaving a web of
destruction. The poet sees them as shuttles working on the loom
of fated actions, a subject he had treated in the forty-seventh
chapter of *Moby-Dick*, "The Mat-Maker." There Ishmael pondered on "chance, free will, and necessity—no wise incompati-
ble—all interweavingly working together." The novel even hints
of this device in the title of its first chapter, "Loomings."

In the poem, the birds

> weave and inweave,
> Then lock the web with clinching cry
> Over the seas on seas that clasp
> The weltering wreck.

The date of the poem's incident must be of the eighteenth century, during the wars that England fought with Spain. In its final
form, the poem is a remarkable demonstration of Melville's dramatic and poetic skills. The longer stanzas slow the movement
even more than the 1885 version had slowed the earlier "Admiral
of the White." The shift of title to emphasize the sea birds rather
than the Admiral points to what Melville wants the reader to see
in the poem—the workings of fate, the catching of the human
within the web of events that it cannot control. The final images,
as he had foreseen even before the substantial revisions and additions, have an elegiac and conciliatory sound. The violence of the
destruction is over, and the Admiral and his men have sunk into
their unfathomable sleep, the "wizard sea enchanting them / Where
never haglets beat." This is the language of "Billy in the Darbies,"
the poem given to the doomed Billy Budd, meditating upon his
death when "they'll lash me in a hammock, drop me deep /
Fathoms down, fathoms down, how I'll dream fast asleep." But
"The Haglets" moves beyond this thanatopsis to thaumaturgy:

On nights when meteors play
And light the breakers dance,
The Oreads from the caves
With silvery elves advance;
And up from ocean stream,
And down from heaven far.
The rays that blend in dream
The abysm and the star.

Elves, a wizard sea, and the Oreads, the mountain nymphs, all commingle in Melville's pictorial imagination in a dream that mutes the terrors of Fate and its stringent dictates.

However, while the "Sea Pieces" and some of the "Minor Sea Pieces" portray the sea in its grandeur and unyielding power and indifference to the human, at least one poem, "The Tuft of Kelp," shows something different, its curative and purifying powers. The little epigrammatic poem exhibits this paradoxical view well:

All dripping in tangles green,
Cast up by a lonely sea
If purer for that, O Weed,
Bitterer, too, are ye?

The ocean is a bitter element and likely to embitter all who must endure it. But, almost as a throwaway line, is its power to purify, to provide a catharsis for weed or human. John Marr seeks the catharsis of sea memories but, at this point in the book, has not won free from their embittering purification. The poem is strategically placed within the pattern of the book to indicate the manner in which the sailor/poet may achieve respite and balm from his encounters with the sea, the burden of history, and the aching thoughts of his past life.

In the final section of the poems, "Pebbles," the poet sings once more of the implacable sea, never appeased, even by the wrecks it causes. "Man, suffering inflictor, sails on sufferance there," and is as often as not the victim of its "elemental mad ramping of ravening waters." But, perhaps just as often, it can be seen in the light of "Christ on the Mount, and the dove in her nest!" Therefore, we are prepared as John Marr resumes his personal and terrifying engagement with the sea, which has meant so much to his younger life and now persists, in his memory, to act upon his wounded spirit in a miraculous way:

Healed of my hurt, I laud the inhuman Sea—
Yea, bless the Angels Four that there convene;
For healed I am even by their pitiless breath
Distilled in wholesome dew named rosmarine.

The diction is heavy with the sense of shock:"hurt,""inhuman," "pitiless." But, paradoxically, other words contradict and reveal the meaning of the journey the sailor has taken through his strange realm: "healed," "bless," "wholesome." "Healed" is used twice within the four lines to emphasize the change that has been wrought in the poem's protagonist. The last word in the poem, and in the book, is itself magical: *ros marinus* is "dew from the sea" and, in English, turns to "rosemary," the attractive flower of re-membrance. As Marr had said in his first poem, "myriads mem-ory traces, / To enfold me in a dream," and it is this dream of memory that allows him to recover from his hurt and be healed and whole again.

It is tempting to see the volume of poems biographically, as Melville's own effort to heal himself by a return to his long-lost sea experiences. But that seems a reductive and somewhat unsat-isfactory way to study it. John Marr is not Melville. His experi-ences are different, and they have on him a different effect than those of Melville's life had on him. Every writer uses bits and pieces of himself and his being in creating his art, but he is at liberty to meld them into his fictive plan and mold the whole into a result that is more shapely and suggestive than the often confus-ing welter of contradictory events in one's daily life. Near the end of *Billy Budd*, written during the same period as "The Haglets," Melville steps forth to speak movingly of the dictates of art:"The symmetry of form attainable in pure fiction cannot so readily be achieved in a narration essentially having less to do with fable than with fact. Truth uncompromisingly told will always have its ragged edges; hence the conclusion of such a narration is apt to be less finished than an architectural finial" (chap. 29). Symmetry and the rounded sense of completeness are artificial and artistic products. The writer is the shaper of his fiction, fact, and fable; they are the unlike things that meet and mate to provide something more subtle and more complete than they ever could be when not fused into a new form.

IV

It had taken Melville the twelve years since the publication of *Clarel* to compose and put together the poems of *John Marr* into a pattern that satisfied him. He was left only three years of life, but in that brief time he managed to accomplish much. In 1891, just a few months before his death, he, at his own expense, brought out *Timoleon, Etc.*, a volume in the paperback format and in an issue of only twenty-five copies, just as he had done for *John Marr.*

This small-scale activity has been interpreted as Melville turning his back on readers and printing the volumes only as gifts for friends and family. But, on the contrary, it seems to be the poet's effort to bring his work before the public and to make sure that as much of it as possible would be in final form rather than left incomplete and in manuscript. By putting the poems into print in a form that would always be available, he was avoiding the difficulty that scholars have with Emily Dickinson's poetry, most of which was left in manuscript with revisions and alternate readings that will always plague readers who can never quite decide what would have been the poet's final thoughts in her finest works. Then, too, there was the additional advantage of having full control of what went into the books without interference from editors. The publisher became nothing more than a printer, and the author had great freedom. Writing to Hawthorne in June 1851, Melville had complained that he would "at last be worn out and perish, like an old nutmeg grater, grated to pieces by the constant attrition of the wood, that is, the nutmeg." He went on: "What I feel most moved to write that is banned,—it will not pay. Yet, altogether, write the *other* way I cannot." By acting as his own editor and publisher, he could write "the other way" without fear of being banned.

This situation certainly applies to some of Melville's work as well. *Billy Budd* was written during these last years and was left incomplete at Melville's death. Posthumous publication—almost thirty years later—gives rise to much speculation about the text and its meanings. Even the genetic text, prepared by Harrison

Hayford and Merton Sealts, which shows, to great advantage, Melville's alternative ideas about words, phrases and larger units, does not present us with a text that can be considered final. The same can be said for *Weeds and Wildings*, a volume of poetry that Melville was trying to get into final shape during the last months of his life, as well as a considerable number of poems left in manuscript.

Despite Melville's best efforts, the poems in this new volume do not, at first glance, seem to jell into a coherent whole that would be greater than the sum of its parts. His recognition of this disadvantage is reflected in his titles. A manuscript version of the title is *Timoleon and Other Ventures in Minor Verse;* the final, printed version of the title is *Timoleon, Etc.* Both versions of the title have a rueful tinge, the author apparently giving up his opportunity to make his title one that would encompass and fuse together the book's separate members. The use of the dismissive "et cetera" seems a particularly ironic comment upon the work he was doing.

However, it is possible to see several strands that link up the varied poems. Melville used an important device in a number of the poems, an epigraph which gives additional information that, for some reason, he does not want to include within the lines of the poems. That for "Timoleon," the narrative that opens the book, is "(394 B.C.)." The last poem in the volume, "L'Envoi," bears the epigraph "The Return of the Sire de Nesle A.D. 16—." With dates at beginning and end, the volume certainly depends on history for at least some of its effects, and other poems reinforce the view. The very short poem, with a very long title, "Fragments of a Lost Gnostic Poem of the 12th Century," is another announcement of the burden of the past. The nineteenth century makes its appearance in "C——'s Lament," which seems to be about Coleridge, and "Shelley's Vision"; both have to do with the artistic and social concerns of poets still alive during Melville's early life. "The Marchioness of Brinvilliers" casts a modulated light on a sensational case of multiple murders in seventeenth-century France. "The Bench of Boors" is a meditation upon a painting by David Teniers (1610–1690), and "The Age of the Antonines," undated in the poem, returns us to the Roman Empire of the second century after Christ. Although they take the form of the jottings of a perceptive tourist, other poems require the historic sense: "The Great Pyramid," "The Parthenon," "Milan's

Cathedral," and "Pisa's Leaning Tower" all juxtapose the Egyptian and European past against a thoughtful consideration of nineteenth-century America.

There is no central figure, like John Marr, to hold the poems together, but the measured voice of an artist, a poet, considers his own art and the great efforts of painters, architects, and poets. Likewise, the volume, as a whole, rather resembles the work of two of Melville's favorite poets who traveled to find scenes and subjects for their poems. Wordsworth's "Memorials of a Tour in Italy, 1837," has poems about Raphael, Michelangelo, and the Pillar of Trajan, as well as translations from Michelangelo. Heinrich Heine's *Reisebilder*, his pictures of travel in Europe, also appealed to Melville, and in his volume of Heine in translation he annotated this section with the marginal note "the poetical part of the Reisebilder." In the journal kept of his 1856–57 pilgrimage to the Holy Land and then to the art centers of Europe, he pondered creating what might have been a volume of poetry with the title "Frescoes of Travel by Three Brothers" with a note of some subjects that might be covered: "Rosseau [*sic*], Cicero, Byron, Haydon, Venice, Olympus, Parthenon, Leonardo." And, of course, to go with these poetic travelogues were some in prose: Goethe's notes on his travels in Italy, Washington Irving's *The Sketch Book*, James Fenimore's *Gleanings from Europe*, Charles Dickens's *American Notes* and *Pictures from Italy*, and Hawthorne's posthumously published journals of his stay in England and Italy. *Timoleon* fits comfortably within the orbits of these books as a touristic stroll through an earlier world compounded of art and architecture, religious discords, the enigmatic violence of human behavior, the ambiguous but largely indifferent movement of a natural world that does no one any special favors, and, perhaps the virtual impossibility of love.

However, studying the volume as a whole to find if there is a coherent pattern to its selection and placement of poems, one sees, perhaps, an emergent theme. After all, Melville could have chosen other poems that he had written for this volume, but instead he settled on these, and so he must have had an idea in mind for the book's structure. A clue can be found in "L'Envoi," the last poem in the volume. An "envoi" was usually envisaged as a final stanza in a poem that was meant to act as a summation of the poem. Melville's "envoi" is a whole poem, a summation of the meaning of the whole book. His Sire de Nesle has spent virtually a lifetime searching for a sensible pattern in the life he leads and in the world about him. He discovers, finally, that his "thirst is slaked" by all he has learned of the "terrible" earth. Most of all, he has learned that "knowledge poured by pilgrimage / Overflows the banks of man." He is like an aging version of Clarel, the pilgrim who ceaselessly attempts to gain such knowledge of his world.

The poems in the volume, most of them, anyhow, outline what this personage has learned. "Timoleon" deals with the immense problem of putting love of the institution, the state, above familial affections and the shock of being rejected by members of that institution. "After the Pleasure Party," in a manner somewhat similar to "Timoleon," records the revenge of love on the pure search for knowledge. Several poems, like "The Night March" and "The Margrave's Birthnight," question the existence of a divine being, and "Buddha" and "Fragments of a Lost Gnostic Poem" have something to say about the condition of religion in our time. A number of poems rehearse the difficulties of the artistic life, the pressures of artistic creation, and the often inevitable waste and destruction of the products of the arts in an ever more commercial and superficial world. "The Age of the Antonines" and several of the Greek poems contrast ages of coherent thinking and, hence, immortal art with the rather hateful present of the nineteenth century. Three poems at the end of the volume bring back the theological argument; but now, with the added formulation of religious feeling, that enters the arena of the sublime. A sight of "The Apparition," the Parthenon, causes the poet to revise somewhat his opinion of mankind, allowing that revision to be credited to Diogenes. The power of the sun in the poem "In the Desert" calls forth a genuinely religious feeling: "Of God the effluence of the essence, / Shekinah intolerably bright!" "The Great Pyramid" seems an expression of man's unconquerable nobility of purpose in its almost inhuman tangibility. Human it undoubtedly is, as the poet acknowledges: "Craftsmen, in dateless quarries dim, / Stones formless into form did trim." It is this welter of contradictory experiences that causes the pilgrim to turn homeward and inward.

A major poem in the collection, "After the Pleasure Party" has drawn a good deal of discussion. Its epigraph, "Lines Traced Under an Image of Amor Threatening," introduces the lines that set out, substantially, the premise of the poem. Amor, a demigod of erotic love, threatens those who possess "pride from love exempt." The tale is of Urania, the girl whose name comes from that of the Muse of astronomy. She has been exempt from love in her scientific pursuits, but now, stirred by Amor, she has become "Vesta struck with Sappho's smart." A title once intended for the poem was "A Boy's Revenge, or After the Pleasure Party," and another possibility that Melville tried was "Urania, or After the Pleasure Party." These two possibilities encompass each side of the argument, the "boy" of the first being Amor. The subject is an ancient one; Hippolytus, for instance, follows the dictates of the goddess Artemis, thus rejecting sex and enraging Aphrodite, who raises passionate love for him in his mother-in-law, Phedra, and then causes his destruction. Urania is horrified to learn how "soon or late, if faded e'en, / One's sex asserts itself." She cries out in protest against Nature:

> Why has thou made us but in halves—
> Co-relatives? This makes us slaves.
> If these co-relatives never meet
> Self-hood itself seems incomplete.
> And such the dicing of blind fate
> Few matching halves here meet and mate.
> What Cosmic jest or Anarch blunder
> The human integral clove asunder
> And shied the fractions through life's gate?

"Meet and mate" reminds us of the unlike things that must meet and mate in "Art" to produce a work of art. Life, unlike art, requires a perfect mating, and the act of correlation is left to blind fate, a disaster for the woman. The poet does not attempt to solve this harsh riddle. "One knows not," he repeats and offers what seems a story that may be beside the point. Urania considers the possibility of the nun's life in a convent and then contrasts it, passionately, with the appeal to Athene, the helmeted goddess whose statue she has seen at the Villa Albani in Rome. But the appeal—to be raised "far from strife / Of that which makes the sexual feud / And clogs the aspirant life"—is not to be answered.

The vengeful work of Amor is stronger than the asexual, independent being of Athene.

In his journal for February 28, 1857, Melville records a visit to the Villa Albani, where he had seen such a statue of the helmeted Athene. Though he did not mention the statue in his brief note, it fed his imaginative reconstruction of the feminist dilemma and struggle, providing him with an alternative to what he usually saw of the submissive woman of his time. The cautionary "one knows not" allows tentative conclusions, a familiar device from Melville's fiction. Having told the reader of "Bartleby the Scrivener" that he cannot provide further information, the lawyer narrates "one little item of rumor" that may throw some light on the story. The narrator of "Billy Budd" refrains from saying what passes between Captain Vere and the doomed Billy, preferring to conclude that "what took place at this interview was never known," but he still feels free to offer some conjectures. The ambiguity that results enriches the texture of story and poem with possibilities.

The gnomic little poem called "Fragments of a Lost Gnostic Poem of the 12th Century" is a tantalizing piece of Melvillean indirection. The poet assumes the guise of one who has done nothing more than preserve all that is left of what is possibly a very long work—two presumably detached quatrains that may belong to different parts of the "lost" poem—and presents them complete with the asterisks to prove that they should be read separately and may have little enough to do with one another. For instance, the "here" in the first line of the second quatrain cannot refer to the first quatrain but must have something to do with a lost portion of the poem. The fragmentary state of the poem gives Melville the opportunity to engage in the "ontological heroics" that he prizes without the benefit or burden of lengthy diatribes, philosophical discourse, or explications; he is not required to tell why he is dealing with a poem of the twelfth century rather than one of a much earlier period when gnosticism could be thought of as being much more active. Unlike scholars who carefully study all the background of a manuscript, he is free to avoid saying where the fragments have turned up or speculate on how long the poem might have been, or how much poetry intervenes between the recovered quatrains.

William B. Dillingham links the "indolence" of the second fragment with James Thomson's "Indolence: A Moral Essay."

During the 1880s, a young British reader, Charles James Billson, wrote to Melville and subsequently sent him some of the books written by Thomson (1834–1882). Melville was pleased with the gifts and read a number of Thomson's poems, especially "The City of Dreadful Night," a piece that may have fitted his mood at the time. Writing to James Billson, he noted of the poem that "one can hardly overestimate it, massive and mighty as it is,—its gloom is its sublimity" (*Correspondence* 514). Thomson's poem discussed ideas that had moved Melville for years. The poem begins:

> Lo, thus as prostrate, "In the dust I write
> My heart's deep language and my soul's sad tears."
> Yet why invoke the specters of black night
> To blot the sunshine of exultant years?
> Why disinter dead faith from moldering hidden?
> Why break the seals of mute despair unbidden,
> And wail life's discords into careless ears?

Melville was preparing to resign his position at New York Customs and planned to work on his volumes of poetry. It must have been disquieting to have someone—just dead—wondering if it were not better to remain mute and not reengage in the almost desparate act of publication. How much of "life's discords" would Melville want to attempt to pour into "careless ears"?

The manuscripts show that Melville composed a third "fragment" that he no doubt considered for inclusion in the poem but finally cancelled·

> Flowers are illlusion and they die
> Take away the corps of the rose
> For fragrance it doth putrify
> The test of a thing is its close.

Quite as aphoristic as the two preceding "fragments," this one may have been rejected before Melville could work on it very much. In the second line, he may have intended the word "corps" to be "corpse," and in the third line "fragrance" is far from clear in its odd spelling. No punctuation, such as the poet was fond of using as embellishment to his words, appears here.

The rest of the poem shows the effects of a considerable amount of reconsideration and revision. The poem seems to have cost Melville a great deal of effort. The title may have been "Lost Poem" at some stage, and a notation "from the Greek," may have been intended as part of the title. In place of the word "matter" in the third line of the first quatrain, Melville originally wrote "Apollyon," a curious first choice for the line. Apollyon appears in the Bible (*Revelation* 9.11) as "the angel of the bottomless pit, whose name in the Hebrew tongue is Abaddon, but in the Greek tongue hath his name Apollyon." The name is indeed from the Greek, from "apollynal," meaning "to utterly destroy." The use of the name "Apollyon" seems to fit what the poet had in mind when his suggested title included "from the Greek." And in the fourth line of the quatrain, "His ancient brutal claim" had earlier read "His old abysmal claim." Another interesting change in the poem appears in the line "Indolence is heaven's ally here," where the word "indolence" replaces "the do nothing." The change introduces a more poetic, more freighted word into the text, and a word like "indolence" works richly with the vision of heaven in its struggle with hellish "energy."

All of this may seem too much discussion of what after all is only one poem in a collection of more than forty separate pieces, but it does give us a look into the mind of the poet in action, as it were, while it turns over one idea and then another. We can see at least something of the dynamics of creating a poem. The poems about the arts have a major place in the collection and make an important aesthetic and ethical statement about Melville's work. The poem "Art" does not make an appearance until fifteen other poems, some about the arts, have made their way before the reader. It is an artistic credo, pointing out the great difficulty there is to achieve form and, at the same time, "pulsed life create." Creation is indeed a massive effort that requires bringing "unlike things" together so that they mate and fuse, a powerful chemical reaction. The mystic heart of Jacob is invoked for his great agonistic act with the angel, in this case "the angel—Art." All of the discordances of human existence are thus drawn into a single complete event. In some similar way, the brief poem "In a Garret" takes the conventional theme of the artist who trades the notion of wealth for creation "to grapple from Art's deep / One dripping trophy." Melville supplies an alternative but rejected title,

"Schiller's Ambition," and notes, perhaps as another rejected title, "The Spirit of Schiller." Following soon after these statements of purpose is a pair of important poems about literary artists. "Shelley's Vision" records the eventual triumph of the poet's art over the power of contemporary disdain: "Hate the censor." The poet sees himself as martyr, a Saint Stephen to the mob. "C———'s Lament" seems to have offered Melville some difficulties. The available manuscripts show him considering a variety of titles: "Coleridge's Lament," "Threnody," "Anacreon's Threnody," "Simonides' Threnody." Melville's insistence upon the two poetical terms, "lament" and "threnody," is part of a careful scheme. The threnody is a song of lamentation, a dirge, a funeral song, and, usually, an encomium for the dead. A nearly contemporary poem that Melville likely knew was Emerson's "Threnody on His Young Son." A lament is similar in that it is also a poem of grieving, often for a person but sometimes for a position. The Anglo-Saxon "Deor's Lament" is an example, as is Sackville's "Lament" for Henry, Duke of Buckingham, whose words are introduced by the last line of Sackville's induction: "On cruel Fortune, weeping, thus he plain'd."

The burden of C———'s lament is the loss of youth with all its glories. It is "more than wine," for within it "man and nature seemed divine." The poem could thus be a lament for the loss suffered by any of the possible persons whom Melville considered as protagonist and speaker. The poem, however, has a further significance, to be seen in its final stanza:

> But will youth never come again!
> Even to his grave-bed has he gone,
> And left me lone, to wake by night
> With heavy heart that erst was light?
> O, lay it at his head—a stone!

This poem should recall "Monody," a poem that appears a bit before it in the collection. A monody, like a threnody or a dirge, is a lyric sung by one with a sense of loss, either for a loved one or again, perhaps, for a place in life. Milton's epigraph to "Lycidas" indicates that the poem is a monody. Melville's annotation to the poem in his copy of Milton reads "Written at age of 29," indicating his keen sense that the loss being lamented is the loss of youth, with all its promise. Matthew Arnold's "Thyrsis" is described by Arnold as a monody, and, again, the loss of youth, in his lamentation for Clough, is the theme of the lamentation.

Of the poems in *Timoleon*, "Monody" has drawn much comment, where it is usually taken for a poem about Hawthorne. The association is persuasive when the poet sings "To have known him, to have loved him, / After loneness long." That Melville seems to have intended it as a monody—that is, a dirge intended for public performance, to be followed, after a short interval, by a threnody—says much about how he considered the themes of the collection. "Monody" does have a personal sound about it, and it could be about Hawthorne. This would make it another poem about art. But it could also be about the loss of youth, or the loss of one particular youth, Melville's son, Malcolm, who killed himself in 1867 at the age of nineteen. "Loneness" and "lone" are repeated motifs in the two poems that seem thus linked. Both feature a heaviness of heart that must be relieved, and both feature a grave in which is buried something of inexpressible value. Again, a poem appearing between the two dirges is "Buddha," which prays—to whatever extent the poet can pray—for Nirvana, asking it to "absorb us in your skies, / Annul us into thee." There can, perhaps, be some easing of pain in the promise of nirvana.

A number of the art poems concern themselves with the visual arts. Melville gives the title "Fruit of Travel Long Ago" to a group of poems that deal, at least in part, with the architectural visions of Europe, Egypt, and the Middle East that he encountered during his travels in 1856–57. It has been assumed, based upon that title, that some of the poems may have been written as far back as the 1850s. But the title could be more ambiguous than we think; although the travel had occurred long ago, the "fruit," the poems, may be very late and not written till the 1880s. There are several striking poems in this group. "Milan Cathedral" is portrayed as a miracle of art—its pinnacles "like to ice-peaks snowed," its statues of saints ascending as "multitudinous forks of fire." In "Pisa's Leaning Tower" the poet sees the structure leaning over as though it contemplates suicide. "Venice" portrays that city, rising from the sea, as "reefs of palaces" rising from the sea and compares its manmade beauty with that of coral, a natural artwork "freaked with many a fringe / Of marble garlandry." The

Parthenon is viewed from a distance and then much nearer, until
the last tile is shown and it can be called "art's meridian." Melville
sees this wealth of beauty merged with Nature and sums up his
view in the poem "Greek Architecture":

> Not magnitude, not lavishness,
> But Form—the Site,
> Not innovating wilfulness,
> But reverence for the Archetype.

The architectural becomes a symbol for all of art, visual and
poetic, which makes its appeal by its insistence upon form. Melville
had stated that view in *Clarel* in the passage in which Rolfe
describes the shape of the buildings of Petra. "One starts," he says,
"In Esau's waste are blent / Ionian form, Venetian tint." In "The
Weaver" the artist labors "at a lonely loom," his work taking all his
time, so that his "face is pinched, the form is bent, / No pastime
knows he nor the wine." He has to live, as the poet says, reclusive
and abstinent in order to work at the shrine of art.

Having traveled a good part of the world, Melville was conscious of the terrible effects of time and change and of the harsh
work of men who destroy the accomplishments of the arts. A
brief poem, "The Ravaged Villa," is a picture of destruction of
vase and fountain; worst of all, "flung to kiln, Apollo's bust /
Makes lime for Mammon's tower." Apollo is the greatest of mu-
sicians, having defeated the satyr Marsyas in a musical contest. He
controlled the arts and sciences, poetry, philosophy, astronomy,
mathematics, medicine, and the other sciences and is thus the god
to be most revered by any artist. Mammon, who stands for wealth,
is a false god inspiring avarice. In the New Testament, both Matthew and Luke caution that one "cannot serve God and mammon." In contrast to the gracious artistry of the villa, the tower is
unembellished and dedicated only to getting and spending.

A skimpier poem, "Disinterment of the Hermes," is harmed
by its weighty moralistic tone. The statue itself is well described
as one of the "forms divine in adamant fair," since the term "adamant" is a stone harder than stone, not to be broken down.
When the poet expresses the view that an archeological dig that
brings up such treasures is better than digging for gold, he is
melding together two unlike historical events, the California gold

rush and the archeological discoveries mentioned in his cancelled epigraph, "Suggested by the Disinterment of the Hermes by the German Commission." (The statue of Hermes, a great piece of sculpture immediately identified as by Praxiteles, was discovered in 1877.) In the poem Melville implies, as he does in a number of other poems, the unlikely conjunction of a past filled with art, aesthetic feeling, and spirituality with a late-nineteenth-century economic spirit of avarice and barrenness.

Other poems simply record the poet's enchantment of vision, and, often enough, their deific remove from the lower human element. "Off Cape Colonna" celebrates the ruined Greek temple which, from its prospect at a height, can be effectively viewed from the sea. The phrase "sublimed to fancy's view" again fuses two unlike things. "Fancy," with its origins in "fantasy," is, in Coleridgean terms, a distinct faculty of the human psyche. Jean-Paul Richter, one of Melville's favorite writers, considered the *Phantasie* "the power of making all parts into a whole," and a *Phantast* is a dreamer, a visionary. The idea of fancy is an unstable one, unclear in all that it can encompass. In his poem "Good-bye my Fancy," Walt Whitman sees it as a "dear mate, dear love," and speculates that if it does not die with him, it will, possibly, engage in the after life by "ushering me to the true songs."

The use of "sublimed" offers some problems as well. Melville assuredly knew Burke's *A Philosophical Inquiry into the Origin of Our Ideas of the Sublime and Beautiful*. The book was part of his library, and, furthermore, he was acquainted with the artistic and aesthetic theories of earlier times. Since the term "sublime" means, in its simpler forms, "at a height," or "elevated," he finds the columns of the temple at a physical height as well as at an ennobling prospect—hence, his bringing the two words "aloof" and "aloft" together. The aloofness of loftier art is reflected in the second stanza by the serenity of these godlike ruins that have seen the wreckage of ships. Melville especially calls attention to the destruction exhibited in William Falconer's *The Shipwreck*, a long poem he knew well. In the "Extracts" in *Moby-Dick*, Melville quotes from the poem and in other works seems to exhibit a knowledge of Falconer's other poetry as well.

One of the most striking of his poems comes near the end of the volume. "In the Desert" records his reaction to the Egyptian desert. The poem has a personal element in its use of "me"; a

canceled version had the impersonal "Egypt's." Likewise, the poet
changed the title from "Horace in Egypt," and the third line of
the first stanza at one point read "May so the weak-eyed Horace
affright." If, as seems likely, he is referring to the Roman poet
Horace (Quintus Horatius Flaccus, 65–8 B.C.), he may have had
in mind to bring forward another artist with testimony about the
harsh part of the world he is experiencing. A brief note in his
journal for January 3, 1857, records that the desert in Egypt is
"more fearful to look at than ocean." Melville, always the seagoing writer, often sees landscape as seascape. In the prose introduction to *John Marr*, his sailor-poet, an avatar of Melville himself,
sees the mid-American prairie as "the bed of a dried-up sea" and
the rolling prairie land with its "fixed undulations" as "smooth as
those of ocean becalmed."

The substitution of "Theban flamens" adds its weight of history and theology. Thebes was the ancient capital of Egypt; when
Aaron turns his rod into a serpent, the Pharaoh calls for his flamens,
or priests: "the wise men and the sorcerers: now the magicians of
Egypt, they also did in like manner with their enchantments"
(*Exodus* 7:11). The "Hebrew wizards," or the "dubious" wizards
before revision, croon of the Pharaoh's night in *Exodus* 10:21–23.
The "oriflamme," an inspiring symbol, is the "fiery standard" of
the Hebrew God against the priests and sorcerors of the Egyptian
faith. A canceled passage meant to follow this fiery outburst reads:
"The lucid ether with such glow / Engirds the universe roundabout, / The world floats as *in vacuo.*" This portion of the poem
was probably cut, since the second stanza already emphasizes the
ethereal. In the final stanza, the holy light, "intolerably bright," is
the effluence, or emanation of the essence, the ethereal, which is
the fifth essence. The desert seems a battleground of religious
orthodoxies.

The most powerful of the architectural poems is "The Great
Pyramid." Upon seeing the pyramids in 1857, Melville recorded
a rush of unordered impressions in his journal, but the predom-
inant feeling was one of awe at the size and bulk of these human
structures. "Pyramids still loom before me," he writes, "something vast, indefinite, incomprehensible, and awful." "Might have
been created with the creation," he adds a bit later (*Journals* 76).
These feelings go into the poem, the poet questioning, "is it
man's? / More like some Cosmic artisan's." He had noted that no

natural growth of ivy or lichen found its way upon the pyramids and repeats his vision of its being "sterile all and granite-knit." Like all other art, it possesses what humanity does not, a timeless quality:"Time's future infinite you dare." A cancelled epigraph— "And Moses was learned in all the wisdom of the Egyptians," from *Acts* 7:22—casts some light on Melville's thinking about the poem. The chapter summarizes the story of Moses, and the poet alludes to this tale in *Exodus* in his last stanza:

> Craftsmen, in dateless quarries dim,
> Stones formless into form did trim,
> Usurped on Nature's self with Art,
> And bade this dumb I AM to start,
> Imposing him.

Melville's tinkering with this stanza throws a fascinating light upon his poetic procedures. In the second line, he had written "shapeless" and "shape" but revised it to "formless" and "form," words resonant with meaning. In the poem "Greek Architecture," a few pages earlier, he had written "Not magnitude, not lavishness, / But Form—the Site." The act of capitalizing the term raises it, for him, to the highest significance. In the third line, "usurped" takes the place of the canceled "impose," an important change. To impose is to establish by authority; but to usurp is to seize without legal authority. The further reference to Moses in the fourth line has to do with the appearance of the Lord in the burning bush. When Moses inquires what name he shall give to his people in advising them to flee, the Lord's answer is "I AM THAT I AM" (*Exodus* 3:14). The final word of the poem is "him," but in a canceled version, "Him." The law of the Lord is by imposition, not usurpation.

A canceled final stanza is of much interest:

> From Fear the dream, from Power the thought
> A form analogous was wrought—
> Viewless in ages overcast,
> That Form and Thou shall last and last
> Though both be naught.

This stanza has undergone substantial revision:

From quarries of insubstantial thought
Another great I AM was wrought—
Tremendous in the overcast.
These two I-Am's shall last and last
    Though both be naught.

And even beyond these workings are changes. "A Form analogous" also appeared as "a God symbolical," and "These two I-Am's" may have been intended to be simply "These Twain." The poet is clearly testing his materials for their strength and rejecting those that will not hold, in the briefest space, the poetic thesis that he is presenting.

    Why is some knowledge of these labors necessary when we do possess final versions of the poem? It gives some impression of the work that Melville was willing to impose upon himself to get his poems right. In the poet's workshop, everything is tried—the words, like pieces of metal or adamant, put into place, tested, and then kept or rejected in favor of better words. Concision is sought, and anything that seems less than a final line is canceled. A stubborn integrity informs all of this writing down, this rethinking, this canceling and reviewing, this craftsmanship. To imagine for a moment that Melville had given up writing for a larger audience, whatever that was, and wrote only for a select company of family and friends, is to mistake his conception of the writer's responsibilities, perils, and rewards.

V

By the time Melville had paid for the publication of *Timoleon* and seen the volume through the press in the summer of 1891, he was probably very ill. He died on September 28 of that year, and so he was unable to carry out the projects that his active mind and spirit ceaselessly brought to the surface. There was the novella *Billy Budd*, more or less completed in draft but obviously in need of considerable revision to remove some inconsistencies in the narrative and probably in need of additional paragraphs, pages, and chapters. At his death, the manuscript was packed away, not to be brought back to light and published for more than twenty years.

Melville had also been working on a volume of poems to be entitled *Weeds and Wildings.* There were several tables of contents, setting out the probable order of the poems in a projected publication. Many of the poems bore the marks of thought and work, the alternative readings of lines and words still not clear. Beyond this proposed volume, many more poems lay in manuscript, with thoughtful alterations written down, considered but not yet decided upon. All of these works are of highest interest and should be studied carefully, both for their contributions to a knowledge of the poet and for their intrinsic poetic merit.

It is easy to see that, even in their incomplete state, a number of the poems take their place with the best that the poet Melville had to offer. "At the Hostelry" offers, among other things, a discussion of the picturesque in art. Painters of many periods are resurrected to give their views on the subject, and often Melville is concerned to characterize them as they drink, eat, and speak. Here, Melville is clearly drawing on his surprisingly complete knowledge of painters and paintings. Among the antagonists who speak of their concerns are Tintoretto, Michelangelo, Leonardo da Vinci, Paul Veronese, Rembrandt, Salvator Rosa, Franz Hals, Jan Steen, Jose Ribeira (known as Spagnoletto), Claude Lorrain, Adrian Brouwer, Gerard Douw, and Peter Paul Rubens. The discussion is clever and racy, the painters opinionated and passionate about their art and art theories. This symposium—covering centuries of art and ranging widely among nations—is a highly sophisticated discussion of some artistic matters that Melville wanted to put into print.

One of the very best of the manuscript poems is "Pontoosuce," but there is much to be debated in any discussion of the poem. The title, for instance, might well have been "The Lake," an alternative that Melville considered and that is used in the printing of the poem in the Constable edition of the poetry. Or the title might be "Pontoosuc." That, after all, is the name of the lake in western Massachusetts, not too far from the Melville home, Arrowhead. Did Melville add an "e" to the name to give it a more elegant and "poetic" sound, or are we the dubious inheritors of another case of his famous misspellings or his difficult orthography? If there are questions about the title, how many more questions can there be about a text that is not, by any means, the poet's final word? Similarly, in the two unpublished poems printed under the title "Camoens," there are possibilities for variant readings. Compare the printed versions in the Constable edition and the Vincent edition. There is some conflict about what is actually the beginning of "Camoens (Before)." The Constable edition (414) reads:"And ever must I fan this fire? / Thus ever in flame on flame inspire?" In Vincent (380) the beginning of the poem reads:"Restless, restless, craving rest, / Forever must I fan this fire, / Forever in flame on flame aspire?" Such variant readings make the possibility of a final text impossible.

It seems sensible, therefore, to stop with the poems that we know reached final draft, that the poet has allowed to stand in print. The scholarly examination of these texts has not yet reached publication, together with the necessary sifting of variant readings. When this work has been done, we will know even more about Melville as poet and be able to conjecture more about his reading and thinking during the later years of his life. What this mass of unpublished and, to some extent, unfinished material does show, however, is that Melville the poet continued his questing, his thinking, and his persistent urge to put forth the results of his art right to the end of his life. It was said of Franz Joseph Haydn and his unfinished string quartet (Opus 103) that he still possessed the passion and that only the physical vitality had been lost. (During the last few years of his life, he had been unable to compose.) But with Melville, all the signs indicate that he did retain his vitality right to the end of his life. Had he been given more time, no doubt *Billy Budd*, *Weeds and Wildings*, and the other manuscripts would have been worked over and completed and readied for publication. He had worked steadily as a writer from his twenty-fifth year. At the end of his life, he was still doing the job of the writer, putting before us his often grandiose plans of an orderly world of art and life.

Battle-Pieces ⟶

[With few exceptions, the Pieces in this volume originated in an impulse imparted by the fall of Richmond. They were composed without reference to collective arrangement, but, being brought together in review, naturally fall into the order assumed.

The events and incidents of the conflict—making up a whole, in varied amplitude, corresponding with the geographical area covered by the war—from these but a few themes have been taken, such as for any cause chanced to imprint themselves upon the mind.

The aspects which the strife as a memory assumes are as manifold as are the moods of involuntary meditation—moods variable, and at times widely at variance. Yielding instinctively, one after another, to feelings not inspired from any one source exclusively, and unmindful, without purporting to be, of consistency, I seem, in most of these verses, to have but placed a harp in a window, and noted the contrasted airs which wayward winds have played upon the strings.]

(1859)

Hanging from the beam,
  Slowly swaying (such the law),
Gaunt the shadow on your green,
  Shenandoah!
The cut is on the crown
(Lo, John Brown),
And the stabs shall heal no more.

Hidden in the cap
  Is the anguish none can draw;
So your future veils its face,
  Shenandoah!
But the streaming beard is shown
(Weird John Brown),
The meteor of the war.

MISGIVINGS
(1860)

When ocean-clouds over inland hills
  Sweep storming in late autumn brown,
And horror the sodden valley fills,
  And the spire falls crashing in the town,
I muse upon my country's ills—
The tempest bursting from the waste of Time
On the world's fairest hope linked with man's foulest crime.

Nature's dark side is heeded now—
  (Ah! optimist-cheer disheartened flown)—
A child may read the moody brow
  Of yon black mountain lone.
With shouts the torrents down the gorges go,
And storms are formed behind the storm we feel:
The hemlock shakes in the rafter, the oak in the driving keel.

THE CONFLICT OF CONVICTIONS[a]
(1860–61)

On starry heights
    A bugle wails the long recall;
Derision stirs the deep abyss,
    Heaven's ominous silence over all.
Return, return, O eager Hope,
    And face man's latter fall.
Events, they make the dreamers quail;
Satan's old age is strong and hale,
A disciplined captain, gray in skill,
And Raphael a white enthusiast still;
Dashed aims, at which Christ's martyrs pale,
Shall Mammon's slaves fulfill?

    (Dismantle the fort,
    Cut down the fleet—
    Battle no more shall be!
    While the fields for fight in æons to come
    Congeal beneath the sea.)

The terrors of truth and dart of death
    To faith alike are vain;
Though comets, gone a thousand years,
    Return again,
Patient she stands—she can no more—
And waits, nor heeds she waxes hoar.

    (At a stony gate,
    A statue of stone,
    Weed overgrown—
    Long 'twill wait!)

But God his former mind retains,
    Confirms his old decree;
The generations are inured to pains,
    And strong Necessity
Surges, and heaps Time's strand with wrecks.
    The People spread like a weedy grass,
    The thing they will bring to pass,

And prosper to the apoplex.
The rout it herds around the heart,
    The ghost is yielded in the gloom;
Kings wag their heads—Now save thyself
    Who wouldst rebuild the world in bloom.

     (Tide-mark
     And top of the ages' strife,
     Verge where they called the world to come,
     The last advance of life—
     Ha ha, the rust on the Iron Dome!)

Nay, but revere the hid event;
    In the cloud a sword is girded on,
I mark a twinkling in the tent
    Of Michael the warrior one.
Senior wisdom suits not now,
The light is on the youthful brow.

     (Ay, in caves the miner see:
     His forehead bears a blinking light;
     Darkness so he feebly braves—
     A meagre wight!)

But He who rules is old—is old;
Ah! faith is warm, but heaven with age is cold.

     (Ho ho, ho ho,
     The cloistered doubt
     Of olden times
     Is blurted out!)

The Ancient of Days forever is young,
    Forever the scheme of Nature thrives;
I know a wind in purpose strong—
    It spins *against* the way it drives.
What if the gulfs their slimed foundations bare?
So deep must the stones be hurled
Whereon the throes of ages rear
The final empire and the happier world.

(The poor old Past,
The Future's slave,
She drudged through pain and crime
To bring about the blissful Prime,
Then—perished. There's *a grave!)*

Power unanointed may come—
Dominion (unsought by the free)
   And the Iron Dome,
Stronger for stress and strain,
Fling her huge shadow athwart the main;
But the Founders' dream shall flee.
Age after age shall be
As age after age has been,
(From man's changeless heart their way they win);
And death be busy with all who strive—
Death, with silent negative.

     YEA AND NAY—
     EACH HATH HIS SAY;
     BUT GOD HE KEEPS THE MIDDLE WAY.
     NONE WAS BY
     WHEN HE SPREAD THE SKY;
     WISDOM IS VAIN, AND PROPHESY.

APATHY AND ENTHUSIASM
(1860–61)

I

O the clammy cold November,
   And the winter white and dead,
And the terror dumb with stupor,
   And the sky a sheet of lead;
And events that came resounding
   With the cry that *All was lost,*
Like the thunder-cracks of massy ice
   In intensity of frost—
Bursting one upon another

Through the horror of the calm.
   The paralysis of arm
In the anguish of the heart;
And the hollowness and dearth.
   The appealings of the mother
   To brother and to brother
Not in hatred so to part—
And the fissure in the hearth
   Growing momently more wide.
Then the glances 'tween the Fates,
   And the doubt on every side,
And the patience under gloom
In the stoniness that waits
The finality of doom.

   II
So the winter died despairing,
   And the weary weeks of Lent;
And the ice-bound rivers melted,
   And the tomb of Faith was rent.
O, the rising of the People
   Came with springing of the grass,
They rebounded from dejection
   After Easter came to pass.
And the young were all elation
   Hearing Sumter's cannon roar.
And they thought how tame the Nation
   In the age that went before.
And Michael seemed gigantical,
   The Arch-fiend but a dwarf;
And at the towers of Erebus
   Our striplings flung the scoff.
But the elders with foreboding
   Mourned the days forever o'er,
And recalled the forest proverb,
   The Iroquois' old saw:
Grief to every graybeard
   When young Indians lead the war.

THE MARCH INTO VIRGINIA

ending in the First Manassas
(JULY, 1861)

Did all the lets and bars appear
    To every just or larger end,
Whence should come the trust and cheer?
    Youth must its ignorant impulse lend—
Age finds place in the rear.
    All wars are boyish, and are fought by boys,
The champions and enthusiasts of the state:
    Turbid ardors and vain joys
        Not barrenly abate—
Stimulants to the power mature,
    Preparatives of fate.

Who here forecasteth the event?
What heart but spurns at precedent
And warnings of the wise,
Contemned foreclosures of surprise?
The banners play, the bugles call,
The air is blue and prodigal.
    No berrying party, pleasure-wooed,
No picnic party in the May,
Ever went less loth than they
    Into that leafy neighborhood.
In Bacchic glee they file toward Fate,
Moloch's uninitiate;
Expectancy, and glad surmise
Of battle's unknown mysteries.
All they feel is this: 'tis glory,
A rapture sharp, though transitory,
Yet lasting in belaureled story.
So they gayly go to fight.
Chatting left and laughing right.

But some who this blithe mood present,
    As on in lightsome files they fare,
Shall die experienced ere three days are spent—
    Perish, enlightened by the vollied glare;

Or shame survive, and, like to adamant,
The throe of Second Manassas share.

Lyon
Battle of Springfield, Missouri
(AUGUST, 1861)

Some hearts there are of deeper sort,
Prophetic, sad,
Which yet for cause are trebly clad;
Known death they fly on:
This wizard-heart and heart-of-oak had Lyon.

"They are more than twenty thousand strong,
We less than five,
Too few with such a host to strive."
"Such counsel, fie on!
'Tis battle, or 'tis shame;" and firm stood Lyon.

"For help at need in vain we wait—
Retreat or fight:
Retreat the foe would take for flight,
And each proud scion
Feel more elate; the end must come," said Lyon.

By candlelight he wrote the will,
And left his all
To Her for whom 'twas not enough to fall;
Loud neighed Orion
Without the tent; drums beat; we marched with Lyon.

The night-tramp done, we spied the Vale
With guard-fires lit;
Day broke, but trooping clouds made gloom of it:
"A field to die on,"
Presaged in his unfaltering heart, brave Lyon.

We fought on the grass, we bled in the corn—
Fate seemed malign;

His horse the Leader led along the line—
    Star-browed Orion;
Bitterly fearless, he rallied us there, brave Lyon.

There came a sound like the slitting of air
    By a swift sharp sword—
A rush of the sound; and the sleek chest broad
    Of black Orion
Heaved, and was fixed; the dead mane waved toward Lyon.

"General, you're hurt—this sleet of balls!"
    He seemed half spent;
With moody and bloody brow, he lowly bent:
    "The field to die on;
But not—not yet; the day is long," breathed Lyon.

For a time becharmed there fell a lull
    In the heart of the fight;
The tree-tops nod, the slain steep light;
    Warm noon-winds sigh on,
And thoughts which he never spake had Lyon.

Texans and Indians trim for a charge:
    "Stand ready, men!
Let them come close, right up, and then
    After the lead, the iron;
Fire, and charge back!" So strength returned to Lyon.

The Iowa men who held the van,
    Half drilled, were new
To battle: "Some one lead us, then we'll do,"
    Said Corporal Tryon:
"Men! *I* will lead," and a light glared in Lyon.

On they came: they yelped, and fired;
    His spirit sped;
We levelled right in, and the half-breeds fled,
    Nor stayed the iron,
Nor captured the crimson corse of Lyon.

This seer foresaw his soldier-doom,
    Yet willed the fight.
He never turned; his only flight
    Was up to Zion,
Where prophets now and armies greet brave Lyon.

BALL'S BLUFF

a reverie

(OCTOBER, 1861)

One noonday, at my window in the town,
    I saw a sight—saddest that eyes can see—
    Young soldiers marching lustily
        Unto the wars,
With fifes, and flags in mottoed pageantry;
        While all the porches, walks, and doors
Were rich with ladies cheering royally.

They moved like Juny morning on the wave,
    Their hearts were fresh as clover in its prime
    (It was the breezy summer time)
        Life throbbed so strong,
How should they dream that Death in a rosy clime
        Would come to thin their shining throng?
Youth feels immortal, like the gods sublime.

Weeks passed; and at my window, leaving bed,
    By night I mused, of easeful sleep bereft,
    On those brave boys (Ah War! thy theft);
        Some marching feet
Found pause at last by cliffs Potomac cleft;
        Wakeful I mused, while in the street
Far footfalls died away till none were left.

DUPONT'S ROUND FIGHT
(NOVEMBER, 1861)

In time and measure perfect moves
    All Art whose aim is sure;
Evolving rhyme and stars divine
    Have rules, and they endure.

Nor less the Fleet that warred for Right,
    And, warring so, prevailed,
In geometric beauty curved,
    And in an orbit sailed.

The rebel at Port Royal felt
    The Unity overawe,
And rued the spell. A type was here,
    And victory of Law.

THE STONE FLEET[b]
an old sailor's lament
(DECEMBER, 1861)

I have a feeling for those ships,
    Each worn and ancient one,
With great bluff bows, and broad in the beam:
    Ay, it was unkindly done.
            But so they serve the Obsolete—
            Even so, Stone Fleet!

You'll say I'm doting; do but think
    I scudded round the Horn in one—
The Tenedos, a glorious
    Good old craft as ever run—
            Sunk (how all unmeet!)
            With the Old Stone Fleet.

An India ship of fame was she,
    Spices and shawls and fans she bore;

A whaler when her wrinkles came—
 Turned off! till, spent and poor,
     Her bones were sold (escheat)!
     Ah! Stone Fleet.

Four were erst patrician keels
 (Names attest what families be),
The Kensington, and Richmond too,
 Leonidas, and Lee:
     But now they have their seat
     With the Old Stone Fleet.

To scuttle them—a pirate deed—
 Sack them, and dismast;
They sunk so slow, they died so hard,
 But gurgling dropped at last.
     Their ghosts in gales repeat
     Woe's us, Stone Fleet!

And all for naught. The waters pass—
 Currents will have their way;
Nature is nobody's ally; 'tis well;
 The harbor is bettered—will stay.
     A failure, and complete
     Was your Old Stone Fleet.

DONELSON
(FEBRUARY, 1862)

The bitter cup
 Of that hard countermand
Which gave the Envoys up,
Still was wormwood in the mouth,
 And clouds involved the land,
When, pelted by sleet in the icy street,
 About the bulletin-board a band
Of eager, anxious people met,
And every wakeful heart was set

On latest news from West or South.
"No seeing here," cries one—"don't crowd"-
"You tall man, pray you, read aloud."

IMPORTANT.

We learn that General Grant,
    Marching from Henry overland,
And joined by a force up the Cumberland sent
    (Some thirty thousand the command),
On Wednesday a good position won—
Began the siege of Donelson.

This stronghold crowns a river-bluff,
    A good broad mile of leveled top;
Inland the ground rolls off
    Deep-gorged, and rocky, and broken up—
A wilderness of trees and brush.
    The spaded summit shows the roods
Of fixed entrenchments in their hush;
    Breast-works and rifle-pits in woods
Perplex the base.—
                  The welcome weather
    Is clear and mild; 'tis much like May.
The ancient boughs that lace together
Along the stream, and hang far forth,
    Strange with green mistletoe, betray
A dreamy contrast to the North.

Our troops are full of spirits—say
    The siege won't prove a creeping one.
They purpose not the lingering stay
Of old beleaguerers; not that way;
    But, full of vim from Western prairies won,
    They'll make, ere long, a dash at Donelson.

Washed by the storm till the paper grew
Every shade of a streaky blue,
That bulletin stood. The next day brought
A second.

Grant's investment is complete—
    A semicircular one.
Both wings the Cumberland's margin meet,
Then, backward curving, clasp the rebel seat.
    On Wednesday this good work was done;
    But of the doers some lie prone.
Each wood, each hill, each glen was fought for;
The bold enclosing line we wrought for
Flamed with sharpshooters. Each cliff cost
A limb or life. But back we forced
Reserves and all; made good our hold;
And so we rest.
                    Events unfold.
On Thursday added ground was won,
    A long bold steep: we near the Den.
Later the foe came shouting down
    In sortie, which was quelled; and then
We stormed them on their left.
A chilly change in the afternoon;
The sky, late clear, is now bereft
Of sun. Last night the ground froze hard—
Rings to the enemy as they run
Within their works. A ramrod bites
The lip it meets. The cold incites
To swinging of arms with brisk rebound.
Smart blows 'gainst lusty chests resound.

Along the outer line we ward
    A crackle of skirmishing goes on.
Our lads creep round on hand and knee,
They fight from behind each trunk and stone;
    And sometimes, flying for refuge, one
Finds 'tis an enemy shares the tree.
Some scores are maimed by boughs shot off
    In the glades by the Fort's big gun.
    We mourn the loss of Colonel Morrison,
    Killed while cheering his regiment on.
Their far sharpshooters try our stuff;

And ours return them puff for puff.
'Tis diamond-cutting-diamond work.
        Woe on the rebel cannoneer
Who shows his head. Our fellows lurk
        Like Indians that waylay the deer
By the wild salt-spring.—The sky is dun,
Foredooming the fall of Donelson.
Stern weather is all unwonted here.
        The people of the country own
We brought it. Yea, the earnest North
Has elementally issued forth
        To storm this Donelson.

FURTHER.

        A yelling rout
Of ragamuffins broke profuse
        To-day from out the Fort.
        Sole uniform they wore, a sort
Of patch, or white badge (as you choose)
        Upon the arm. But leading these,
Or mingling, were men of face
And bearing of patrician race,
Splendid in courage and gold lace—
        The officers. Before the breeze
Made by their charge, down went our line;
But, rallying, charged back in force,
And broke the sally; yet with loss.
This on the left; upon the right
Meanwhile there was an answering fight;
        Assailants and assailed reversed.
The charge too upward, and not down—
Up a steep ridge-side, toward its crown,
        A strong redoubt. But they who first
Gained the fort's base, and marked the trees
Felled, heaped in horned perplexities,
        And shagged with brush; and swarming there
Fierce wasps whose sting was present death—
They faltered, drawing bated breath,
        And felt it was in vain to dare;

Yet still, perforce, returned the ball,
Firing into the tangled wall
Till ordered to come down. They came;
But left some comrades in their fame,
Red on the ridge in icy wreath
And hanging gardens of cold Death.
  But not quite unavenged these fell;
Our ranks once out of range, a blast
  Of shrapnel and quick shell
Burst on the rebel horde, still massed,
  Scattering them pell-mell.
    (This fighting—judging what we read—
    Both charge and countercharge,
    Would seem but Thursday's told at large,
    Before in brief reported.—Ed.)
Night closed in about the Den
  Murky and lowering. Ere long, chill rains.
A night not soon to be forgot,
  Reviving old rheumatic pains
And longings for a cot.
  No blankets, overcoats, or tents.
Coats thrown aside on the warm march here—
We looked not then for changeful cheer;
Tents, coats, and blankets too much care.
  No fires; a fire a mark presents;
  Near by, the trees show bullet-dents.
Rations were eaten cold and raw.
  The men well soaked, came snow; and more—
A midnight sally. Small sleeping done—
    But such is war;
No matter, we'll have Fort Donelson.

                "Ugh! ugh!
'Twill drag along—drag along,"
Growled a cross patriot in the throng,
His battered umbrella like an ambulance-cover
Riddled with bullet-holes, spattered all over.
"Hurrah for Grant!" cried a stripling shrill;
Three urchins joined him with a will,
And some of taller stature cheered.

Meantime a Copperhead passed; he sneered.
　　　"Win or lose," he pausing said,
"Caps fly the same; all boys, mere boys;
　Any thing to make a noise.
　　　Like to see the list of the dead;
These '*craven Southerners*' hold out;
Ay, ay, they'll give you many a bout."
　　　"We'll beat in the end, sir,"
Firmly said one in staid rebuke,
A solid merchant, square and stout.
"And do you think it? that way tend, sir?'
Asked the lean Copperhead, with a look
Of splenetic pity. "Yes, I do."
His yellow death's head the croaker shook:
"The country's ruined, that I know."
A shower of broken ice and snow,
　　　In lieu of words, confuted him;
They saw him hustled round the corner go,
　　　And each by-stander said—Well suited him.

Next day another crowd was seen
In the dark weather's sleety spleen.
Bald-headed to the storm came out
A man, who, 'mid a joyous shout,
Silently posted this brief sheet:

　　　GLORIOUS VICTORY OF THE FLEET!

　　　FRIDAY'S GREAT EVENT!

　　　THE ENEMY'S WATER–BATTERIES BEAT!

　　　WE SILENCED EVERY GUN!

　　　THE OLD COMMODORE'S COMPLAINTS SENT

　　　PLUMP INTO DONELSON!

"Well, well, go on!" exclaimed the crowd
To him who thus much read aloud.
"That's all," he said. "What! nothing more?

"Enough for a cheer, though—hip, hurrah!
"But here's old Baldy come again—
"More news!"—And now a different strain.

nn69

Battle-Pieces

*(Our own reporter a dispatch compiles,
As best he may, from varied sources.)*

*Large re-enforcements have arrived—
    Munitions, men, and horses—
For Grant, and all debarked, with stores.*

*The enemy's field-works extend six miles—
The gate still hid; so well contrived.*

*Yesterday stung us; frozen shores
    Snow-clad, and through the drear defiles
And over the desolate ridges blew
A Lapland wind.
                    The main affair
    Was a good two hours' steady fight
Between our gun-boats and the Fort.
        The Louisville's wheel was smashed outright.
A hundred-and-twenty-eight-pound ball
Came planet-like through a starboard port,
Killing three men, and wounding all
The rest of that gun's crew,
(The captain of the gun was cut in two);
Then splintering and ripping went—
Nothing could be its continent.
    In the narrow stream the Louisville,
Unhelmed, grew lawless, swung around,
    And would have thumped and drifted, till
All the fleet was driven aground,
But for the timely order to retire.*

*Some damage from our fire, 'tis thought,
Was done the water-batteries of the Fort.*

*Little else took place that day,
    Except the field artillery in line
Would now and then—for love, they say—*

Exchange a valentine.
The old sharpshooting going on.
Some plan afoot as yet unknown;
So Friday closed round Donelson.

LATER.

Great suffering through the night—
A stinging one. Our heedless boys
Were nipped like blossoms. Some dozen
Hapless wounded men were frozen.
During day being stuck down out of sight,
And help-cries drowned in roaring noise,
They were left just where the skirmish shifted—
Left in dense underbrush snow-drifted.
Some, seeking to crawl in crippled plight,
So stiffened—perished
                                        Yet in spite
Of pangs for these, no heart is lost.
Hungry, and clothing stiff with frost,
Our men declare a nearing sun
Shall see the fall of Donelson.
    And this they say, yet not disown
The dark redoubts round Donelson,
        And ice-glazed corpses, each a stone—
            A sacrifice to Donelson;
They swear it, and swerve not, gazing on
A flag, deemed black, flying from Donelson.

Some of the wounded in the wood
    Were cared for by the foe last night,
Though he could do them little needed good,
    Himself being all in shivering plight.
The rebel is wrong, but human yet;
He's got a heart, and thrusts a bayonet.
fie gives us battle with wondrous will—
This bluff's a perverted Bunker Hill.

The stillness stealing through the throng
The silent thought and dismal fear revealed;

They turned and went,
   musing on right and wrong
   And mysteries dimly sealed—
Breasting the storm in daring discontent;
The storm, whose black flag showed in heaven,
As if to say no quarter there was given
     To wounded men in wood,
  Or true hearts yearning for the good—
All fatherless seemed the human soul.
But next day brought a bitterer bowl—
  On the bulletin-board this stood:

Saturday morning at 3 A.M.
  A stir within the Fort betrayed
That the rebels were getting under arms;
  Some plot these early birds had laid.
But a lancing sleet cut him who stared
Into the storm. After some vague alarms,
Which left our lads unscared,
Out sallied the enemy at dint of dawn,
   With cavalry and artillery, and went
   In fury at our environment.
Under cover of shot and shell
   Three columns of infantry rolled on,
   Vomited out of Donelson—
Rolled down the slopes like rivers of hell,
   Surged at our line, and swelled and poured
Like breaking surf. But unsubmerged
   Our men stood up, except where roared
The enemy through one gap. We urged
Our all of manhood to the stress,
But still showed shattered in our desperateness.
   Back set the tide,
But soon afresh rolled in;
  And so it swayed from side to side—
Far batteries joining in the din,
Though sharing in another fray—
  Till all became an Indian fight,
Intricate, dusky, stretching far away,
Yet not without spontaneous plan

However tangled showed the plight:
Duels all over 'tween man and man,
Duels on cliff-side, and down in ravine,
    Duels at long range, and bone to bone;
Duels every where flitting and half unseen.
    Only by courage good as their own,
And strength outlasting theirs,
    Did our boys at last drive the rebels off
Yet they went not back to their distant lairs
    In strong-hold, but loud in scoff
Maintained themselves on conquered ground—
Uplands; built works, or stalked around.
Our night wing bore this onset. Noon
Brought calm to Donelson.

The reader ceased; the storm beat hard;
    'Twas day, but the office-gas was lit;
Nature retained her sulking-fit,
        In her hand the shard.

Flitting faces took the hue
Of that washed bulletin-board in view,
And seemed to bear the public grief
As private, and uncertain of relief,
Yea, many an earnest heart was won,
    As broodingly he plodded on,
To find in himself some bitter thing,
Some hardness in his lot as narrowing
        As Donelson.
That night the board stood barren there,
    Oft eyed by wistful people passing,
    Who nothing saw but the rain-beads chasing
Each other down the watered square,
As down some storm-beat grave-yard stone.
But next day showed—
MORE NEWS LAST NIGHT.

STORY OF SATURDAY AFTERNOON.

VICISSITUDES OF THE WAR.

The damaged gun-boats can't wage fight
For days; so says the Commodore.
Thus no diversion can be had.
Under a sunless sky of lead
    Our grim-faced boys in blackened plight
Gaze toward the ground they held before,
And then on Grant. He marks their mood,
And hails it, and will turn the same to good.
Spite all that they have undergone,
Their desperate hearts are set upon
This winter fort, this stubborn fort,
This castle of the last resort,
    This Donelson.

1 P.M.

            An order given
    Requires withdrawal from the front
    Of regiments that bore the brunt
    Of morning's fray. Their ranks all riven
Are being replaced by fresh, strong men.
Great vigilance in the foeman's Den;
He snuffs the stormers. Need it is
That for that fell assault of his,
That rout inflicted, and self-scorn—
Immoderate in noble natures, torn
By sense of being through slackness overborne—
The rebel be given a quick return;
The kindest face looks now half stern.
Balked of their prey in airs that freeze,
Some fierce ones glare like savages.
And yet, and yet, strange moments are—
Well—blood, and tears, and anguished War!
The morning's battle-ground is seen
    In lifted glades, like meadows rare;
    The blood-drops on the snow-crust there
Like clover in the white-weed show—
    Flushed fields of death, that call again—
    Call to our men, and not in vain,
For that way must the stormers go.

3 P.M.
                        The work begins.
        Light drifts of men thrown forward, fade
        In skirmish-line along the slope,
        Where some dislodgments must be made
        Ere the stormer with the strong-hold cope.

        Lew Wallace, moving to retake
        The heights late lost—
                                (Herewith a break.
            Storms at the West derange the wires.
        Doubtless, ere morning, we shall hear
        The end; we look for news to cheer—
        Let Hope fan all her fires.)

Next day in large bold hand was seen
The closing bulletin:

VICTORY!

            Our troops have retrieved the day
        By one grand surge along the line;
        The spirit that urged them was divine.
            The first works flooded, naught could stay
        The stormers: on! still on!
        Bayonets for Donelson!
        Over the ground that morning lost
        Rolled the blue billows, tempest-tossed,
            Following a hat on the point of a sword.
        Spite shell and round-shot, grape and canister,
        Up they climbed without rail or banister
            Up the steep hill-sides long and broad,
        Driving the rebel deep within his works.
        'Tis nightfall; not an enemy lurks.
            In sight. The chafing men
                Fret for more fight:
            "To-night, to-night let us take the Den!"
        But night is treacherous, Grant is wary;
        Of brave blood be a little chary.

Patience! The Fort is good as won;
To-morrow, and into Donelson.

LATER AND LAST.

THE FORT IS OURS.

A flag came out at early morn
Bringing surrender. From their towers
   Floats out the banner late their scorn.
In Dover, hut and house are full
    Of rebels dead or dying.
    The National flag is flying
From the cramed courthouse pinnacle.
Great boatloads of our wounded go
To-day to Nashville. The sleet-winds blow;
But all is right: the fight is won,
The winter-fight for Donelson.
       Hurrah!
The spell of old defeat is broke,
   The habit of victory begun;
Grant strikes the war's first sounding stroke
      At Donelson.
For lists of killed and wounded, see
The morrow's dispatch: to-day 'tis victory.

The man who read this to the crowd
   Shouted as the end he gained;
    And though the unflagging tempest rained,
      They answered him aloud.
And hand grasped hand, and glances met
In happy triumph; eyes grew wet.
O, to the punches brewed that night
Went little water. Windows bright
Beamed rosy on the sleet without,
And from the deep street came the frequent shout;
While some in prayer, as these in glee,
Blessed heaven for the winter-victory.
But others were who wakeful laid

In midnight beds, and early rose,
    And, feverish in the foggy snows,
Snatched the damp paper—wife and maid.
    The death-list like a river flows
       Down the pale sheet,
And there the whelming waters meet.

Ah God! may Time with happy haste
Bring wail and triumph to a waste,
    And war be done;
The battle flag-staff fall athwart
The curs'd ravine, and wither; naught
    Be left of trench or gun;
The bastion, let it ebb away,
Washed with the river bed; and Day
    In vain seek Donelson.

THE CUMBERLAND
(MARCH, 1862)

Some names there are of telling Sound,
    Whose voweled syllables free
Are pledge that they shall ever live renowned;
    Such seems to be
A Frigate's name (by present glory spanned)—
    The Cumberland.
         Sounding name as ere was sung,
         Flowing, rolling on the tongue—
         Cumberland! Cumberland!

She warred and sunk. There's no denying
    That she was ended—quelled;
And yet her flag above her fate is flying,
    As when it swelled
Unswallowed by the swallowing sea: so grand—
    The Cumberland.
         Goodly name as ere was Sung,
         Roundly rolling on the tongue—
         Cumberland! Cumberland!

What need to tell how she was fought—
    The sinking flaming gun—
The gunner leaping out the port—
      Washed back, undone!
Her dead unconquerably manned
      The Cumberland.
             Noble name as ere was sung,
             Slowly roll it on the tongue—
             Cumberland! Cumberland!

Long as hearts shall share the flame
    Which burned in that brave crew,
Her fame shall live—outlive the victor's name;
      For this is due.
Your flag and flag-staff shall in story stand—
      Cumberland!
             Sounding name as ere was sung,
             Long they'll roll it on the tongue—
             Cumberland! Cumberland!

IN THE TURRET
(MARCH, 1862)

Your honest heart of duty, Worden,
    So helped you that in fame you dwell;
Your bore the first iron battle's burden
    Sealed as in a diving-bell
Alcides, groping into haunted hell
To bring forth King Admetus' bride,
Braved naught more vaguely direful and untried.
    What poet shall uplift his charm,
Bold Sailor, to your height of daring,
    And interblend therewith the calm,
And build a goodly style upon your bearing.

Escaped the gale of outer ocean—
    Cribbed in a craft which like a log
Was washed by every billow's motion—
    By night you heard of Og

The huge; nor felt your courage clog
    At tokens of his onset grim:
You marked the sunk ship's flag-staff slim,
    Lit by her burning sister's heart;
You marked, and mused: "Day brings the trial:
    Then be it proved if I have part
With men whose manhood never took denial."

A prayer went up—a champion's. Morning
    Beheld you in the Turret walled
By adamant, where a spirit forewarning
    And all-deriding called:
"Man, darest thou—desperate, unappalled—
Be first to lock thee in the armored tower?
I have thee now; and what the battle-hour
    To me shall bring—heed well—thou'lt share;
This plot-work, planned to be the foeman's terror,
    To thee may prove a goblin-snare;
Its very strength and cunning—monstrous error!"

"Stand up, my hear; be strong; what matter
    If here thou seest thy welded tomb:
And let huge Og with thunders batter—
    Duty be still my doom,
Though drowning come in liquid gloom;
First duty, duty next, and duty last;
Ay, Turret, rivet me here to duty fast!"—
    So nerved, you fought, wisely and well;
And live, twice live in life and story;
    But over your Monitor dirges swell,
In wind and wave that keep the rites of glory.

THE TEMERAIRE[c]
(supposed to have been suggested to an Englishman of the old order
by the fight of the Monitor and Merrimac)

The gloomy hulls, in armor grim,
    Like clouds o'er moors have met,
And prove that oak, and iron, and man
    Are tough in fibre yet.

But Splendors wane. The sea-fight yields
    No front of old display;
The garniture, emblazonment,
    And heraldry all decay.

Towering afar in parting light,
    The fleets like Albion's forelands shine—
The full-sailed fleets, the shrouded show
    Of Ships-of-the-Line.

The fighting *Temeraire,*
    Built of a thousand trees,
Lunging out her lightnings,
    And beetling o'er the seas—
O Ship, how brave and fair,
    That fought so oft and well,
On open decks you manned the gun
    Armorial.[d]
What cheerings did you share,
    Impulsive in the van,
When down upon leagued France and Spain
    We English ran—

The freshet at your bowsprit
    Like the foam upon the can.
Bickering, your colors
    Licked up the Spanish air,
You flapped with flames of battle-flags—
    Your challenge, *Temeraire!*
The rear ones of your fleet
    They yearned to share your place,
Still vying with the Victory
    Throughout that earnest race—
The Victory, whose Admiral,
    With orders nobly won,
Shone in the globe of the battle glow—
    The angel in that sun.
Parallel in story,
    Lo, the stately pair,
As late in grapple ranging,
    The foe between them there—

When four great hulls lay tiered
    And the fiery tempest cleared,
And your prizes twain appeared,
      Temeraire!

But Trafalgar is over now,
    The quarter-deck undone;
The carved and castled navies fire
    Their evening-gun
O, Titan *Temeraire,*
    Your stern-lights fade away;
Your bulwarks to the years must yield,
    And heart-of-oak decay.
A pigmy steam-tug tows you,
    Gigantic, to the shore—
Dismantled of your guns and spars,
    And sweeping wings of war.
The rivets clinch the iron-clads,
    Men learn a deadlier lore;
But Fame has nailed your battle-flags—
    Your ghost it sails before:
O, the navies old and oaken,
    O, the *Temeraire* no more!

A UTILITARIAN VIEW
OF THE MONITOR'S FIGHT

Plain be the phrase, yet apt the verse,
    More ponderous than nimble;
For since grimed War here laid aside
His painted pomp, 'twould ill befit
    Overmuch to ply
The rhyme's barbaric cymbal.

Hail to victory without the gaud
    Of glory; zeal that needs no fans
Of banners; plain mechanic power
Plied cogently in War now placed—
    Where War belongs—
Among the trades and artisans.

Yet this was battle, and intense—
    Beyond the strife of fleets heroic;
Deadlier, closer, calm 'mid storm;
No passion; all went on by crank,
      Pivot, and screw,
    And calculations of caloric.

Needless to dwell; the story's known.
    The ringing of those plates on plates
Still ringeth round the world—
The clangor of that blacksmith's fray.
      The anvil-din
    Resounds this message from the Fates:

War shall yet be, and to the end;
    But war-paint shows the streaks of weather;
War yet shall be, but warriors
Are now but operatives; War's made
      Less grand than Peace,
    And a singe runs through lace and feather.

SHILOH
a requiem
(APRIL, 1862)

Skimming lightly, wheeling still,
    The swallows fly low
Over the field in clouded days,
    The forest-field of Shiloh—
Over the field where April rain
Solaced the parched ones stretched in pain
Through the pause of night
That followed the Sunday fight
    Around the church of Shiloh—
The church so lone, the log-built one,
That echoed to many a parting groan
      And natural prayer
    Of dying foemen mingled there—
Foemen at morn, but friends at eve—
    Fame or country least their care:

(What like a bullet can undeceive!)
  But now they lie low
While over them the swallows skim,
  And all is hushed at Shiloh.

THE BATTLE FOR THE MISSISSIPPI
(APRIL, 1862)

When Israel camped by Migdol hoar,
  Down at her feet her shawm she threw,
But Moses sung and timbrels rung
  For Pharaoh's stranded crew.
So God appears in apt events—
  The Lord is a man of war!
So the strong wing to the muse is given
   In victory's roar.

Deep be the ode that hymns the fleet—
  The fight by night—the fray
Which bore our Flag against the powerful stream,
  And led it up to day.
Dully through din of larger strife
  Shall bay that warring gun;
But none the less to us who live
  It peals—an echoing one.

The shock of ships, the jar of walls,
  The rush through thick and thin—
The flaring fire-rafts, glare and gloom—
  Eddies, and shells that spin—
The boom-chain burst, the hulks dislodged,
  The jam of gun-boats driven,
Or fired, or sunk—made up a war
  Like Michael's waged with leven.

The manned Varuna stemmed and quelled
  The odds which hard beset;
The oaken flagship, half ablaze,

Passed on and thundered yet;
While foundering, gloomed in grimy flame,
    The Ram Manassas—hark the yell!—
Plunged, and was gone; in joy or fright,
    The River gave a startled swell.

They fought through lurid dark till dawn;
    The war-smoke rolled away
With clouds of night, and showed the fleet
    In scarred yet firm array,
Above the forts, above the drift
    Of wrecks which strife had made;
And Farragut sailed up to the town
    And anchored—sheathed the blade.

The moody broadsides, brooding deep,
    Hold the lewd mob at bay,
While o'er the armed decks' solemn aisles
    The meek church-pennons play;
By shotted guns the sailors stand,
    With foreheads bound or bare;
The captains and the conquering crews
    Humble their pride in prayer.

They pray; and after victory, prayer
    Is meet for men who mourn their slain;
The living shall unmoor and sail,
    But Death's dark anchor secret deeps detain.
Yet Glory slants her shaft of rays
    Far through the undisturbed abyss;
There must be other, nobler worlds for them
    Who nobly yield their lives in this.

MALVERN HILL
(JULY, 1862)

Ye elms that wave on Malvern Hill
    In prime of morn and May,

Recall ye how McClellan's men
        Here stood at bay?
While deep within yon forest dim
    Our rigid comrades lay—
Some with the cartridge in their mouth,
Others with fixed arms lifted south—
      Invoking so
The cypress glades? Ah wilds of woe!

The spires of Richmond, late beheld
    Through rifts in musket-haze,
Were closed from view in clouds of dust
      On leaf-walled ways,
Where streamed our wagons in caravan;
    And the Seven Nights and Days
Of march and fast, retreat and fight,
Pinched our grimed faces to ghastly plight—
      Does the elm wood
Recall the haggard beards of blood?

The battle-smoked flag, with stars eclipsed,
    We followed (it never fell!)—
In silence husbanded our strength—
      Received their yell;
Till on this slope we patient turned
    With cannon ordered well;
Reverse we proved was not defeat;
But ah, the sod what thousands meet!—
      Does Malvern Wood
Bethink itself, and muse and brood?

> *We elms of Malvern Hill*
>   *Remember every thing;*
> *But sap the twig will fill;*
> *Wag the world how it will,*
>   *Leaves must be green in Spring.*

When tempest winnowed grain from bran,
And men were looking for a man,
Authority called you to the van,
      McClellan;
Along the line the plaudit ran,
As later when Antietam's cheers began.

Through storm-cloud and eclipse must move
Each Cause and Man, dear to the stars and Jove;
Nor always can the wisest tell
Deferred fulfillment from the hopeless knell—
The struggler from the floundering ne'er-do-well.
A pall-cloth on the Seven Days fell,
      McClellan—
Unprosperously heroical!
Who could Antietam's wreath foretell?

Authority called you; then, in mist
And loom of jeopardy—dismissed.
But staring peril soon appalled;
You, the Discarded, she recalled—
Recalled you, nor endured delay;
And forth you rode upon a blasted way,
Arrayed Pope's rout, and routed Lee's array,
      McClellan:
Your tent was choked with captured flags that day,
      McClellan.
Antietam was a telling fray.

Recalled you; and she heard your drum
Advancing through the ghastly gloom.
You manned the wall, you propped the Dome,
You stormed the powerful stormer home,
      McClellan:
Antietam's cannon long shall boom.

At Alexandria, left alone,
        McClellan—
Your veterans sent from you, and thrown
To fields and fortunes all unknown—
What thoughts were yours, revealed to none
While faithful still you labored on—
Hearing the far Manassas gun!
        McClellan,
Only Antietam could atone.

You fought in the front (an evil day,
        McClellan)—
The fore-front of the first assay;
The Cause went sounding, groped its way;
The leadsmen quarrelled in the bay;
Quills thwarted swords; divided sway;
The rebel flushed in his lusty May:
You did your best, as in you lay,
        McClellan.
Antietam's sun-burst sheds a ray.

Your medalled soldiers love you well,
        McClellan:
Name your name, their true hearts swell;
With you they shook dread Stonewall's spell,[f]
With you they braved the blended yell
Of rebel and maligner fell;
With you in shame or fame they dwell,
        McClellan
Antietam-braves a brave can tell.

And when your comrades (now so few,
        McClellan—
Such ravage in deep files they rue)
Meet round the board, and sadly view
The empty places; tribute due
They render to the dead—and you!
Absent and silent o'er the blue;
The one-armed lift the wine to you,
        McClellan,
And great Antietam's cheers renew.

A View from Oxford Cloisters

With Tewksbury and Barnet heath
    In days to come the field shall blend,
The story dim and date obscure;
    In legend all shall end.
Even now, involved in forest shade
    A Druid-dream the strife appears,
The fray of yesterday assumes
      The haziness of years.
          In North and South still beats the vein
          Of Yorkist and Lancastrian.

Our rival Roses warred for Sway—
    For Sway, but named the name of Right;
And Passion, scorning pain and death,
    Lent sacred fervor to the fight.
Each lifted up a broidered cross,
    While crossing blades profaned the sign;
Monks blessed the fratricidal lance,
    And sisters scarfs could twine.
          Do North and South the sin retain
          Of Yorkist and Lancastrian?

But Rosecrans in the cedarn glade,
    And, deep in denser cypress gloom,
Dark Breckinridge, shall fade away
      Or thinly loom.
The pale throngs who in forest cowed
    Before the spell of battle's pause,
Forefelt the stillness that shall dwell
      On them and on their wars.
          North and South shall join the train
          Of Yorkist and Lancastrian.

But where the sword has plunged so deep,
    And then been turned within the wound
By deadly Hate; where Climes contend
      On vasty ground—

No warning Alps or seas between,
    And small the curb of creed or law,
And blood is quick, and quick the brain;
    Shall North and South their rage deplore,
        And reunited thrive amain
        Like Yorkist and Lancastrian?

RUNNING THE BATTERIES
As Observed from the Anchorage above Vicksburgh
(APRIL, 1863)

A moonless night—a friendly one;
    A haze dimmed the shadowy shore
As the first lampless boat slid silent on;
    Hist! and we spake no more;
We but pointed, and stilly, to what we saw.

We felt the dew, and seemed to feel
    The secret like a burden laid.
The first boat melts; and a second keel
    Is blent with the foliaged shade—
Their midnight rounds have the rebel officers made?

Unspied as yet. A third—a fourth—
    Gunboat and transport in Indian file
Upon the war-path, smooth from the North;
    But the watch may they hope to beguile?
The manned river-batteries stretch for mile on mile.

A flame leaps out; they are seen;
    Another and another gun roars;
We tell the course of the boats through the screen
    By each further fort that pours,
And we guess how they jump from their beds on those
        shrouded shores.

Converging fires. We speak, though low:
    "That blastful furnace can they thread?"

"Why, Shadrach, Meshach, and Abed-nego
  Came out all right, we read;
The Lord, be sure, he helps his people, Ned."

How we strain our gaze. On bluffs they shun
  A golden growing flame appears—
Confirms to a silvery steadfast one:
  "The town is afire!" crows Hugh: "three cheers!"
Lot stops his mouth: "Nay, lad, better three tears."

A purposed light; it shows our fleet;
  Yet a little late in its searching ray,
So far and strong, that in phantom cheat
  Lank on the deck our shadows lay;
The shining flag-ship stings their guns to furious play.

How dread to mark her near the glare
  And glade of death the beacon throws
Athwart the racing waters there;
  One by one each plainer grows,
Then speeds a blazoned target to our gladdened foes.

The impartial cresset lights as well
  The fixed forts to the boats that run;
And, plunged from the ports, their answers swell
  Back to each fortress dun:
Ponderous words speaks every monster gun.

Fearless they flash through gates of flame,
  The salamanders hard to hit,
Though vivid shows each bulky frame;
  And never the batteries intermit,
Nor the boat's huge guns; they fire and flit.

Anon a lull. The beacon dies:
  "Are they out of that strait accurst?"
But other flames now dawning rise,
  Not mellowly brilliant like the first,
But rolled in smoke, whose whitish volumes burst.

A baleful brand, a hurrying torch
 Whereby anew the boats are seen—
A burning transport all alurch!
 Breathless we gaze; yet still we glean
Glimpses of beauty as we eager lean.

The effulgence takes an amber glow
 Which bathes the hill-side villas far;
Affrighted ladies mark the show
 Painting the pale magnolia—
The fair, false, Circe light of cruel War.

The barge drifts doomed, a plague-struck one.
 Shoreward in yawls the sailors fly.
But the gauntlet now is nearly run,
 The spleenful forts by fits reply,
And the burning boat dies down in morning's sky.

All out of range. Adieu, Messieurs!
 Jeers, as it speeds, our parting gun.
So burst we through their barriers
 And menaces every one:
So Porter proves himself a brave man's son.[g]

STONEWALL JACKSON
Mortally Wounded at Chancellorsville
(MAY, 1863)

The Man who fiercest charged in fight,
 Whose sword and prayer were long—
    Stonewall!
 Even him who stoutly stood for Wrong,
How can we praise? Yet coming days
 Shall not forget him with this song.

Dead is the Man whose Cause is dead,
 Vainly he died and set his seal—
    Stonewall!

Earnest in error, as we feel;
True to the thing he deemed was due,
    True as John Brown or steel.

Relentlessly he routed us;
    But *we* relent, for he is low—
            Stonewall!
    Justly his fame we outlaw; so
We drop a tear on the bold Virginian's bier,
    Because no wreath we owe.

STONEWALL JACKSON
(Ascribed to a Virginian)

One man we claim of wrought renown
    Which not the North shall care to slur;
A Modern lived who sleeps in death,
    Calm as the marble Ancients are:
        'Tis he whose life, though a vapor's wreath,
        Was charged with the lightning's burning breath—
            Stonewall, stormer of the war.

But who shall hymn the Roman heart?
    A stoic he, but even more:
The iron will and lion thew
    Were strong to inflict as to endure:
        Who like him could stand, or pursue?
        His fate the fatalist followed through:
        In all his great soul found to do
            Stonewall followed his star.

He followed his star on the Romney march
    Through the sleet to the wintry war;
And he followed it on when he bowed the grain—
    The Wind of the Shenandoah;
        At Gaines's Mill in the giants' strain—
        On the fierce forced stride to Manassas-plain,
        Where his sword with thunder was clothed again,
            Stonewall followed his star.

His star he followed athwart the flood
    To Potomac's Northern shore,
When midway wading, his host of braves
    "My Maryland!" loud did roar—
        To red Antietam's field of graves,
        Through mountain-passes, woods and waves,
        They followed their pagod with hymns and glaives,
        For Stonewall followed a star.

Back it led him to Marye's slope,
    Where the shock and the fame he bore;
And to green Moss-Neck it guided him—
    Brief respite from throes of war:
        To the laurel glade by the Wilderness grim,
        Through climaxed victory naught shall dim,
        Even unto death it piloted him—
        Stonewall followed his star.

Its lead he followed in gentle ways
    Which never the valiant mar;
A cap we sent him, bestarred, to replace
    The sun-scorched helm of war:
        A fillet he made of the shining lace
        Childhood's laughing brow to grace—
        Not his was a goldsmith's star.

O, much of doubt in after days
    Shall cling, as now, to the war;
Of the right and the wrong they'll still debate,
    Puzzled by Stonewall's star:
        "Fortune went with the North elate,"
        "Ay, but the South had Stonewall's weight,
        And he fell in the South's vain war."

The Check

O pride of the days in prime of the months
    Now trebled in great renown,
When before the ark of our holy cause
        Fell Dagon down—
Dagon foredoomed, who, armed and targed,
Never his impious heart enlarged
Beyond that hour; God walled his power,
And there the last invader charged.

He charged, and in that charge condensed
    His all of hate and all of fire;
He sought to blast us in his scorn,
        And wither us in his ire.
Before him went the shriek of shells—
Aerial screamings, taunts and yells;
Then the three waves in flashed advance
    Surged, but were met, and back they set:
Pride was repelled by sterner pride,
    And Right is a stronghold yet.

Before our lines it seemed a beach
    Which wild September gales have strown
With havoc on wreck, and dashed therewith
        Pale crews unknown—
Men, arms, and steeds. The evening sun
Died on the face of each lifeless one,
And died along the winding marge of fight
        And searching-parties lone.

Sloped on the hill the mounds were green,
    Our centre held that place of graves,
And some still hold it in their swoon,
    And over these a glory waves.
The warrior-monument, crashed in fight,[h]
Shall soar transfigured in loftier light,
        A meaning ampler bear;

Soldier and priest with hymn and prayer
Have laid the stone, and every bone
      Shall rest in honor there.

THE HOUSE-TOP
A Night Piece
(JULY, 1863)

No sleep. The sultriness pervades the air
And binds the brain—a dense oppression, such
As tawny tigers feel in matted shades,
Vexing their blood and making apt for ravage.
Beneath the stars the roofy desert spreads
Vacant as Libya. All is hushed near by.
Yet fitfully from far breaks a mixed surf
Of muffled sound, the Atheist roar of riot.
Yonder, where parching Sirius set in drought,
Balefully glares red Arson—there—and there.
The Town is taken by its rats—ship-rats
And rats of the wharves. All civil charms
And priestly spells which late held hearts in awe—
Fear-bound, subjected to a better sway
Than sway of self; these like a dream dissolve,
And man rebounds whole aeons back in nature.[i]
Hail to the low dull rumble, dull and dead,
And ponderous drag that shakes the wall.
Wise Draco comes, deep in the midnight roll
Of black artillery; he comes, though late;
In code corroborating Calvin's creed
And cynic tyrannies of honest kings;
He comes, nor parties; and the Town, redeemed,
Gives thanks devout; nor, being thankful, heeds
The grimy slur on the Republic's faith implied,
Which holds that Man is naturally good,
And—more—is Nature's Roman, never to be scourged.

Who inhabiteth the Mountain
  That it shines in lurid light,
And is rolled about with thunders,
  And terrors, and a blight,
Like Kaf the peak of Eblis—
  Kaf, the evil height?
Who has gone up with a shouting
  And a trumpet in the night?

There is battle in the Mountain—
  Might assaulteth Might;
'Tis the fastness of the Anarch,
  Torrent-torn, an ancient height;
The crags resound the clangor
  Of the war of Wrong and Right;
And the armies in the valley
  Watch and pray for dawning light.

Joy, joy, the day is breaking,
  And the cloud is rolled from sight;
There is triumph in the Morning
  For the Anarch's plunging flight;
God has glorified the Mountain
  Where a Banner burneth bright,
And the armies in the valley
  They are fortified in right.

Chattanooga

(NOVEMBER, 1863)

A kindling impulse seized the host
  Inspired by Heaven's elastic air;[j]
Their hearts outran their General's plan,
  Though Grant commanded there—
  Grant, who without reserve can dare;

And, "Well, go on and do your will,"
    He said, and measured the mountain then:
So master-riders fling the rein—
    But you must know your men.

On yester-morn in grayish mist,
    Armies like ghosts on hills had fought
And rolled from the cloud their thunders loud
    The Cumberlands far had caught:
    To-day the sunlit steeps are sought.
Grant stood on cliffs whence all was plain,
    And smoked as one who feels no cares;
But mastered nervousness intense
    Alone such calmness wears.

The summit-cannon plunge their flame
    Sheer down the primal wall,
But up and up each linking troop
    In stretching festoons crawl—
    Nor fire a shot. Such men appall
The foe, though brave. He, from the brink,
    Looks far along the breadth of slope,
And sees two miles of dark dots creep,
    And knows they mean the cope.

He sees them creep. Yet here and there
    Half hid 'mid leafless groves they go;
As men who ply through traceries high
    Of turreted marbles show—
    So dwindle these to eyes below.
But fronting shot and flanking shell
    Sliver and rive the inwoven ways;
High tops of oaks and high hearts fall,
    But never the climbing stays.

From right to left, from left to right
    They roll the rallying cheer—
Vie with each other, brother with brother,
    Who shall the first appear—

What color-bearer with colors clear
In sharp relief, like sky-drawn Grant,
   Whose cigar must now be near the stump—
While in solicitude his back
   Heaps slowly to a hump.

Near and more near; till now the flags
   Run like a catching flame;
And one flares highest, to peril nighest—
   He means to make a name:
   Salvos! they give him his fame.
The staff is caught, and next the rush,
   And then the leap where death has led;
Flag answered flag along the crest,
   And swarms of rebels fled.

But some who gained the envied Alp,
   And—eager, ardent, earnest there—
Dropped into Death's wide-open arms,
   Quelled on the wing like eagles struck in air—
   Forever they slumber young and fair,
The smile upon them as they died;
   Their end attained, that end a height:
Life was to these a dream fulfilled,
   And death a starry night.

THE ARMIES OF THE WILDERNESS

(1863–64)

I

Like snows the camps on Southern hills
   Lay all the winter long,
Our levies there in patience stood—
   They stood in patience strong.
On fronting slopes gleamed other camps
   Where faith as firmly clung:
Ah, forward kin! so brave amiss—
The zealots of the Wrong.

In this strife of brothers
(God, hear their country call),
However it be, whatever betide,
Let not the just one fall.

Through the pointed glass our soldiers saw
    The base-ball bounding sent:
They could have joined them in their sport
    But for the vale's deep rent.
And others turned the reddish soil,
    Like diggers of graves they bent;
The reddish soil and trenching toil
    Begat presentiment.

Did the Fathers feel mistrust?
    Can no final good be wrought?
Over and over, again and again
    Must the fight for the Right be fought?

They lead a Gray-back to the crag:
    "Your earth-works yonder—tell us, man!"
"A prisoner—no deserter, I,
    Nor one of the tell-tale clan."
His rags they mark: "True-blue like you
    Should wear the color—your Country's, man!"
He grinds his teeth: "However that be,
    Yon earth-works have their plan."

Such brave ones, foully snared
    By Belial's wily plea,
Were faithful unto the evil end—
    Feudal fidelity.

"Well, then, your camps—come, tell the names!"
    Freely he leveled his finger then:
"Yonder—see—are our Georgians; on the crest,
    The Carolinians; lower, past the glen,
Virginians—Alabamians—Mississippians—Kentuckians
    (Follow my finger)—Tennesseans; and the ten
Camps *there*—ask your grave-pits; they'll tell.

Halloa! I see the picket-hut, the den
　　Where I last night lay." "Where's Lee?"
　　"In the hearts and bayonets of all yon men!"

　　　　The tribes swarm up to war
　　　　　As in ages long ago,
　　　　Ere the palm of promise leaved
　　　　　And the lily of Christ did blow.

Their mounted pickets for miles are spied
　　Dotting the lowland plain,
The nearer ones in their veteran-rags—
　　Loutish they loll in lazy disdain.
But ours in perilous places bide
　　With rifles ready and eyes that strain
Deep through the dim suspected wood
Where the Rapidan rolls amain.

　　　　The Indian has passed away,
　　　　　But creeping comes another—
　　　　Deadlier far. Picket,
　　　　　Take heed—take heed of thy brother!

From a wood-hung height, an outpost lone,
　　Crowned with a woodman's fort,
The sentinel looks on a land of dole,
　　Like Paran, all amort.
Black chimneys, gigantic in moor-like wastes,
　　The scowl of the clouded sky retort;
The hearth is a houseless stone again—
　　Ah! where shall the people be sought?

　　　　Since the venom such blastment deals,
　　　　　The South should have paused, and thrice,
　　　　Ere with heat of her hate she hatched
　　　　　The egg with the cockatrice.

A path down the mountain winds to the glade
　　Where the dead of the Moonlight Fight lie low;
A hand reaches out of the thin-laid mould

As begging help which none can bestow.
But the field-mouse small and busy ant
   Heap their hillocks, to hide if they may the woe:
By the bubbling spring lies the rusted canteen,
   And the drum which the drummer-boy dying let go.

> *Dust to dust, and blood for blood—*
>   *Passion and pangs! Has Time*
> *Gone back? or is this the Age*
>   *Of the world's great Prime?*

The wagon mired and cannon dragged
   Have trenched their scar; the plain
Tramped like the cindery beach of the damned—
   A site for the city of Cain.
And stumps of forests for dreary leagues
   Like a massacre show. The armies have lain
By fires where gums and balms did burn,
   And the seeds of Summer's reign.

> *Where are the birds and boys?*
>   *Who shall go chestnutting when*
> *October returns? The nuts—*
>   *O, long ere they grow again.*

They snug their huts with the chapel-pews,
   In court-houses stable their steeds—
Kindle their fires with indentures and bonds,
   And old Lord Halifax's parchment deeds;
And Virginian gentlemen's libraries old—
   Books which only the scholar heeds—
Are flung to his kennel. It is ravage and range,
   And gardens are left to weeds.

> *Turned adrift into war*
>   *Man runs wild on the plain,*
> *Like the jennets let loose*
>   *On the Pampas—zebras again.*

Like the Pleiads dim, see the tents through the storm—
    Aloft by the hill-side hamlet's graves,
On a headstone used for a hearth-stone there
    The water is bubbling for punch for our braves.
What if the night be drear, and the blast
    Ghostly shrieks? their rollicking staves
Make frolic the heart; beating time with their swords,
    What care they if Winter raves?

> *Is life but a dream? and so,*
>   *In the dream do men laugh aloud?*
> *So strange seems mirth in a camp,*
>   *So like a white tent to a shroud.*

II

The May-weed springs; and comes a Man
    And mounts our Signal Hill;
A quiet Man, and plain in garb—
    Briefly he looks his fill,
Then drops his gray eye on the ground,
    Like a loaded mortar he is still:
Meekness and grimness meet in him—
    The silent General.

> *Were men but strong and wise,*
>   *Honest as Grant, and calm,*
> *War would be left to the red and black ants,*
>   *And the happy world disarm.*

That eve a stir was in the camps,
    Forerunning quiet soon to come
Among the streets of beechen huts
    No more to know the drum.
The weed shall choke the lowly door,
    And foxes peer within the gloom,
Till scared perchance by Mosby's prowling men,
    Who ride in the rear of doom.

Far West, and farther South,
  Wherever the sword has been,
Deserted camps are met,
  And desert graves are seen.

The livelong night they ford the flood;
  With guns held high they silent press,
Till shimmers the grass in their bayonets' sheen—
  On Morning's banks their ranks they dress;
Then by the forests lightly wind,
  Whose waving boughs the pennons seem to bless,
Borne by the cavalry scouting on—
  Sounding the Wilderness.

    Like shoals of fish in spring
      That visit Crusoe's isle,
    The host in the lonesome place—
      The hundred thousand file.

The foe that held his guarded hills
  Must speed to woods afar;
For the scheme that was nursed by the Culpepper hearth
  With the slowly-smoked cigar—
The scheme that smouldered through winter long
  Now bursts into act—into war—
The resolute scheme of a heart as calm
  As the Cyclone's core.

    The fight for the city is fought
      In Nature's old domain;
    Man goes out to the wilds,
      And Orpheus' charm is vain.

In glades they meet skull after skull
  Where pine-cones lay—the rusted gun,
Green shoes full of bones, the mouldering coat
  And cuddled-up skeleton;
And scores of such. Some start as in dreams,
  And comrades lost bemoan:
By the edge of those wilds Stonewall had charged—
  But the Year and the Man were gone.

> At the height of their madness
>> The night winds pause,
> Recollecting themselves;
>> But no lull in these wars.

A gleam!—a volley! And who shall go
　　Storming the swarmers in jungles dread?
No cannon-ball answers, no proxies are sent—
　　They rush in the shrapnel's stead.
Plume and sash are vanities now—
　　Let them deck the pall of the dead;
They go where the shade is, perhaps into Hades,
　　Where the brave of all times have led.

> There's a dust of hurrying feet,
>> Bitten lips and bated breath,
> And drums that challenge to the grave,
>> And faces fixed, forefeeling death.

What husky huzzahs in the hazy groves—
　　What flying encounters fell;
Pursuer and pursued like ghosts disappear
　　In gloomed shade—their end who shall tell?
The crippled, a ragged-barked stick for a crutch,
　　Limp to some elfin dell—
Hobble from the sight of dead faces—white
　　As pebbles in a well.

> Few burial rites shall be;
>> No priest with book and band
> Shall come to the secret place
>> Of the corpse in the foeman's land.

Watch and fast, march and fight—clutch your gun!
　　Day-fights and night-fights; sore is the stress;
Look, through the pines what line comes on?
　　Longstreet slants through the hauntedness!
'Tis charge for charge, and shout for yell:
　　Such battles on battles oppress—
But Heaven lent strength, the Right strove well,
　　And emerged from the Wilderness.

> Emerged, for the way was won;
>   But the Pillar of Smoke that led
> Was brand-like with ghosts that went up
>   Ashy and red.

None can narrate that strife in the pines,
    A seal is on it—Sabaean lore!
Obscure as the wood, the entangled rhyme
    But hints at the maze of war—
Vivid glimpses or livid through peopled gloom,
    And fires which creep and char—
A riddle of death, of which the slain
        Sole solvers are.

> Long they withhold the roll
>   Of the shroudless dead. It is right;
> Not yet can we bear the flare
>   Of the funeral light.

ON THE PHOTOGRAPH OF A CORPS COMMANDER

Ay, man is manly. Here you see
    The warrior-carriage of the head,
And brave dilation of the frame;
    And lighting all, the soul that led
In Spottsylvania's charge to victory,
    Which justifies his fame.

A cheering picture. It is good
    To look upon a Chief like this,
In whom the spirit moulds the form.
    Here favoring Nature, oft remiss,
With eagle mien expressive has endued
    A man to kindle strains that warm.

Trace back his lineage, and his sires,
    Yeoman or noble, you shall find
Enrolled with men of Agincourt,
    Heroes who shared great Harry's mind.

Down to us come the knightly Norman fires,
     And front the Templars bore.

Nothing can lift the heart of man
     Like manhood in a fellow-man.
The thought of heaven's great King afar
     But humbles us—too weak to scan;
But manly greatness men can span,
     And feel the bonds that draw.

THE SWAMP ANGEL[k]

There is a coal-black Angel
     With a thick Afric lip,
And he dwells (like the hunted and harried)
     In a swamp where the green frogs dip.
But his face is against a City
     Which is over a bay of the sea,
And he breathes with a breath that is blastment,
     And dooms by a far decree.

By night there is fear in the City,
     Through the darkness a star soareth on;
There's a scream that screams up to the zenith,
     Then the poise of a meteor lone—
Lighting far the pale fright of the faces,
     And downward the coming is seen;
Then the rush, and the burst, and the havoc,
     And wails and shrieks between.

It comes like the thief in the gloaming;
     It comes, and none may foretell
The place of the coming—the glaring;
     They live in a sleepless spell
That wizens, and withers, and whitens;
     It ages the young, and the bloom
Of the maiden is ashes of roses—
     The Swamp Angel broods in his gloom.

Swift is his messengers' going,
> But slowly he saps their halls,
As if by delay deluding.
> They move from their crumbling walls
Farther and farther away;
> But the Angel sends after and after,
By night with the flame of his ray—
> By night with the voice of his screaming—
Sends after them, stone by stone,
> And farther walls fall, farther portals,
And weed follows weed through the Town.

Is this the proud City? the scorner
> Which never would yield the ground?
Which mocked at the coal-black Angel?
> The cup of despair goes round.
Vainly she calls upon Michael
> (The white man's seraph was he),
For Michael has fled from his tower
> To the Angel over the sea.

Who weeps for the woeful City
> Let him weep for our guilty kind;
Who joys at her wild despairing—
> Christ, the Forgiver, convert his mind.

THE BATTLE FOR THE BAY
(AUGUST, 1864)

O mystery of noble hearts,
> To whom mysterious seas have been
In midnight watches, lonely calm and storm,
>> A stern, sad discipline,
And rooted out the false and vain,
> And chastened them to aptness for
> Devotion and the deeds of war,
And death which smiles and cheers in spite of pain.

Beyond the bar the land-wind dies,
    The prow becharmed at anchor swim:
A summer night; the stars withdrawn look down—
        Fair eve of battle grim.
The sentries pace, bonetas glide;
    Below, the sleeping sailors swing,
    And in their dreams to quarters spring,
Or cheer their flag, or breast a stormy tide.

But drums are beat: *Up anchor all!*
    The triple lines steam slowly on;
Day breaks; along the sweep of decks each man
        Stands coldly by his gun—
As cold as it. But he shall warm—
    Warm with the solemn metal there,
    And all its ordered fury share,
In attitude a gladiatorial form.

The Admiral—yielding to the love
    Which held his life and ship so dear—
Sailed second in the long fleet's midmost line;
        Yet thwarted all their care:
He lashed himself aloft, and shone
    Star of the fight, with influence sent
    Throughout the dusk embattlement;
And so they neared the strait and walls of stone.

No sprightly fife as in the field,
    The decks were hushed like fanes in prayer;
Behind each man a holy angel stood—
        He stood, though none was 'ware.
Out spake the forts on either hand,
    Back speak the ships when spoken to,
    And set their flags in concert true,
And *On and in!* is Farragut's command.

But what delays?'mid wounds above
    Dim buoys give hint of death below—
Sea-ambuscades, where evil art had aped

Hecla that hides in snow.
The centre-van, entangled, trips;
    The starboard leader holds straight on:
    A cheer for the Tecumseh!—nay,
Before their eyes the turreted ship goes down!

The fire redoubles. While the fleet
    Hangs dubious—ere the horror ran—
The Admiral rushes to his rightful place—
                Well met! apt hour and man!—
Closes with peril, takes the lead,
    His action is a stirring call;
    He strikes his great heart through them all,
And is the genius of their daring deed.

The forts are daunted, slack their fire,
    Confounded by the deadlier aim
And rapid broadsides of the speeding fleet,
                And fierce denouncing flame.
Yet shots from four dark hulls embayed
    Come raking through the loyal crews,
    Whom now each dying mate endues
With his last look, anguished yet undismayed.

A flowering time to guilt is given,
    And traitors have their glorying hour;
A late, but sure, the righteous Paramount comes—
                Palsy is on their power!
So proved it with the rebel keels,
    The strong-holds past: assailed, they run;
    The Selma strikes, and the work is done:
The dropping anchor the achievement seals.

But no, she turns—the Tennessee!
    The solid Ram of iron and oak,
Strong as Evil, and bold as Wrong, though lone—
                A pestilence in her smoke.
The flagship is her singled mark,
    The wooden Hartford. Let her come;

She challenges the planet of Doom,
And naught shall save her—not her iron bark.

Slip anchor, all! and at her, all!
    Bear down with rushing beaks—and now!
First the Monongahela struck—and reeled;
            The Lackawana's prow
Next crashed—crashed, but not crashing; then
    The Admiral rammed, and rasping nigh
    Sloped in a broadside, which glanced by:
The Monitors battered at her adamant den.

The Chickasaw plunged beneath the stern
    And pounded there; a huge wrought orb
From the Manhattan pierced one wall, but dropped;
            Others the seas absorb.
Yet stormed on all sides, narrowed in,
    Hampered and cramped, the bad one fought—
    Spat ribald curses from the port
Whose shutters, jammed, locked up this Man-of-Sin.

No pause or stay. They made a din
    Like hammers round a boiler forged;
Now straining strength tangled itself with strength,
            Till Hate her will disgorged.
The white flag showed, the fight was won—
    Mad shouts went up that shook the Bay;
    But pale on the scarred fleet's decks there lay
A silent man for every silenced gun.

And quiet far below the wave,
    Where never cheers shall move their sleep,
Some who did boldly, nobly earn them, lie—
            Charmed children of the deep.
But decks that now are in the seed,
    And cannon yet within the mine,
    Shall thrill the deeper, gun and pine,
Because of the Tecumseh's glorious deed.

SHERIDAN AT CEDAR CREEK
(OCTOBER, 1864)

Shoe the steed with silver
      That bore him to the fray,
When he heard the guns at dawning—
            Miles away;
When he heard them calling, calling—
      Mount! nor stay:
                  Quick, or all is lost;
                  They've surprised and stormed the post,
                  They push your routed host—
Gallop! retrieve the day.

House the horse in ermine—
      For the foam-flake blew
White through the red October;
      He thundered into view;
They cheered him in the looming,
      Horseman and horse they knew.
                  The turn of the tide began,
                  The rally of bugles ran,
                  He swung his hat in the van;
The electric hoof-spark flew.

Wreathe the steed and lead him—
      For the charge he led
Touched and turned the cypress
      Into amaranths for the head
Of Philip, king of riders,
      Who raised them from the dead.
                  The camp (at dawning lost),
                  By eve, recovered—forced,
                  Rang with laughter of the host
At belated Early fled.

Shroud the horse in sable—
      For the mounds they heap!
There is firing in the Valley,

And yet no strife they keep;
It is the parting volley,
   It is the pathos deep.
      There is glory for the brave
      Who lead, and nobly save,
      But no knowledge in the grave
Where the nameless followers sleep.

IN THE PRISON PEN
(1864)

Listless he eyes the palisades
   And sentries in the glare;
'Tis barren as a pelican-beach—
   But his world is ended there.

Nothing to do; and vacant hands
   Bring on the idiot-pain;
He tries to think—to recollect,
   But the blur is on his brain.

Around him swarm the plaining ghosts
   Like those on Virgil's shore—
A wilderness of faces dim,
   And pale ones gashed and hoar.

A smiting sun. No shed, no tree;
   He totters to his lair—
A den that sick hands dug in earth
   Ere famine wasted there,

Or, dropping in his place, he swoons,
   Walled in by throngs that press,
Till forth from the throngs they bear him dead—
   Dead in his meagreness.

He rides at their head;
     A crutch by his saddle just slants in view,
One slung arm is in splints, you see,
     Yet he guides his strong steed—how coldly too.

He brings his regiment home—
     Not as they filed two years before,
But a remnant half-tattered, and battered, and worn,
Like castaway sailors, who—stunned
          By the surf's loud roar,
     Their mates dragged back and seen no more—
Again and again breast the surge,
     And at last crawl, spent, to shore.

A still rigidity and pale—
     An Indian aloofness lones his brow;
He has lived a thousand years
Compressed in battle's pains and prayers,
     Marches and watches slow.

There are welcoming shouts, and flags;
     Old men off hat to the Boy,
Wreaths from gay balconies fall at his feet,
     But to *him*—there comes alloy.

It is not that a leg is lost,
     It is not that an arm is maimed,
It is not that the fever has racked—
     Self he has long disclaimed.

But all through the Seven Days' Fight,
     And deep in the Wilderness grim,
And in the field-hospital tent,
     And Petersburg crater, and dim
Lean brooding in Libby, there came—
     Ah heaven!—what *truth* to him.

Aloft he guards the starry folds
    Who is the brother of the star;
The bird whose joy is in the wind
    Exulteth in the war.

No painted plume—a sober hue,
    His beauty is his power;
That eager calm of gaze intent
    Forsees the Sibyl's hour.

Austere, he crowns the swaying perch,
    Flapped by the angry flag;
The hurricane from the battery sings,
    But his claw has known the crag.

Amid the scream of shells, his scream
    Runs shrilling; and the glare
Of eyes that brave the blinding sun
    The volleyed flame can bear.

The pride of quenchless strength is his—
    Strength which, though chained, avails;
The very rebel looks and thrills—
    The anchored Emblem hails.

Though scarred in many a furious fray,
    No deadly hurt he knew;
Well may we think his years are charmed—
    The Eagle of the Blue.

A DIRGE FOR MCPHERSON[m]
killed in front of Atlanta
(JULY, 1864)

Arms reversed and banners craped—
    Muffled drums;

Snowy horses sable-draped—
    McPherson comes.

       But, tell us, shall we know him more,
       Lost-Mountain and lone Kenesaw?

Brave the sword upon the pall—
    A gleam in gloom;
So a bright name lighteth all
    McPherson's doom.

Bear him through the chapel-door—
    Let priest in stole
Pace before the warrior
    Who led. Bell-toll!

Lay him down within the nave,
    The Lesson read—
Man is noble, man is brave,
    But man's—a weed.

Take him tip again and wend
    Graveward, nor weep:
There's a trumpet that shall rend
    This Soldier's sleep.

Pass the ropes the coffin round,
    And let descend;
Prayer and volley—let it sound
    McPherson's end.

       True fame is his, for life is o'er—
       Sarpedon of the mighty war.

AT THE CANNON'S MOUTH
destruction of the Ram Albemarle by the torpedo-launch
(OCTOBER, 1864)

Palely intent, he urged his keel
    Full on the guns, and touched the spring;

Himself involved in the bolt he drove
Timed with the armed hull's shot that stove
His shallop-die or do!
Into the flood his life he threw,
    Yet lives—unscathed—a breathing thing
To marvel at.

            He has his fame;
But that mad dash at death, how name?

Had Earth no charm to stay in the Boy
    The martyr-passion? Could he dare
Disdain the Paradise of opening joy
Which beckons the fresh heart every where?
Life has more lures than any girl
    For youth and strength; puts forth a share
Of beauty, hinting of yet rarer store;
And ever with unfathomable eyes,
            Which bafflingly entice,
Still strangely does Adonis draw.
And life once over, who shall tell the rest?
Life is, of all we know, God's best.
What imps these eagles then, that they
Fling disrespect on life by that proud way
In which they soar above our lower clay.

Pretence of wonderment and doubt unblest:
    In Cushing's eager deed was shown
    A spirit which brave poets own—
That scorn of life which earns life's crown;
    Earns, but not always wins; but *he*—
    The star ascended in his nativity.

THE MARCH TO THE SEA
(DECEMBER, 1864)

Not Kenesaw high-arching,
    Nor Allatoona's glen—
Though there the graves lie parching—
    Stayed Sherman's miles of men;

From charred Atlanta marching
　　They launched the sword again.
　　　　The columns streamed like rivers
　　　　　Which in their course agree,
　　And they streamed until their flashing
　　　　Met the flashing of the sea:
　　　　　It was glorious glad marching,
　　　　　That marching to the sea.

They brushed the foe before them
　　(Shall gnats impede the bull?);
Their own good bridges bore them
　　Over swamps or torrents full,
And the grand pines waving o'er them
　　Bowed to axes keen and cool.
　　　　The columns grooved their channels,
　　　　　Enforced their own decree,
　　　　And their power met nothing larger
　　　　　Until it met the sea:
　　　　　It was glorious glad marching,
　　　　　A marching glad and free.

Kilpatrick's snare of riders
　　In zigzags mazed the land,
Perplexed the pale Southsiders
　　With feints on every hand;
Vague menace awed the hiders
　　In fort beyond command.
　　　　To Sherman's shifting problem
　　　　　No foeman knew the key;
　　　　But onward went the marching
　　　　　Unpausing to the sea:
　　　　　It was glorious glad marching,
　　　　　The swinging step was free.

The flankers ranged like pigeons
　　In clouds through field or wood;
The flocks of all those regions,
　　The herds and horses good,
Poured in and swelled the legions,

For they caught the marching mood.
  A volley ahead! They hear it;
   And they hear the repartee:
  Fighting was but frolic
   In that marching to the sea:
    It was glorious glad marching,
    A marching bold and free.

All nature felt their coming,
 The birds like couriers flew,
And the banners brightly blooming
 The slaves by thousands drew,
And they marched beside the drumming,
 And they joined the annies blue.
   The cocks crowed from the cannon
    (Pets named from Grant and Lee),
   Plumed fighters and campaigners
    In that marching to the sea:
    It was glorious glad marching,
    For every man was free.

The foragers through calm lands
 Swept in tempest gay,
And they breathed the air of balm-lands
 Where rolled savannas lay,
And they helped themselves from farm-lands—
 As who should say them nay?
   The regiments uproarious
    Laughed in Plenty's glee;
   And they marched till their broad laughter
    Met the laughter of the sea:
    It was glorious glad marching,
    That marching to the sea.

The grain of endless acres
 Was threshed (as in the East)
By the trampling of the Takers,
 Strong march of man and beast;
The flails of those earth-shakers
 Left a famine where they ceased.

          The arsenals were yielded;
              The sword (that was to be),
          Arrested in the forging,
              Rued that marching to the sea:
                  It was glorious glad marching,
                  But ah, the stern decree!

For behind they left a wailing,
    A terror and a ban,
And blazing cinders sailing,
    And houseless households wan,
Wide zones of counties paling,
    And towns were maniacs ran,
            Was Treason's retribution?
            Necessity the plea?
        They will long remember Sherman
            And his streaming columns free—
                They will long remember Sherman
                Marching to the sea.

THE FRENZY IN THE WAKE[n]
Sherman's advance through the Carolinas
(FEBRUARY, 1865)

So strong to suffer, shall we be
    Weak to contend, and break
The sinews of the Oppressor's knee
    That grinds upon the neck?
        O, the garments rolled in blood
           Scorch in cities wrapped in flame,
        And the African—the imp!
        He gibbers, imputing shame.

Shall Time, avenging every woe,
    To us that joy allot
Which Israel thrilled when Sisera's brow
    Showed gaunt and showed the clot?
        Curse on their foreheads, cheeks, and eyes—
        The Northern faces—true

To the flag we hate, the flag whose stars
    Like planets strike us through.

From frozen Maine they come,
    Far Minnesota too;
They come to a sun whose rays disown—
    May it wither them as the dew!
        The ghosts of our slain appeal:
          "Vain shall our victories be?"
        But back from its ebb the flood recoils—
        Back in a whelming sea.

With burning woods our skies are brass,
    The pillars of dust are seen;
The live-long day their cavalry pass—
    No crossing the road between.
        We were sore deceived—an awful host!
         They move like a roaring wind,
        Have we gamed and lost? but even despair
        Shall never our hate rescind.

THE FALL OF RICHMOND
the tidings received in the Northern metropolis
(APRIL, 1865)

What mean these peals from every tower,
    And crowds like seas that sway?
The cannon reply; they speak the heart
    Of the People impassioned, and say—
A city in flags for a city in flames,
Richmond goes Babylon's way—
        Sing and pray.

O weary years and woeful wars,
    And armies in the grave;
But hearts unquelled at last deter
The helmed dilated Lucifer—
    Honor to Grant the brave,
Whose three stars now like Orion's rise

When wreck is on the wave—
  Bless his glaive.

Well that the faith we firmly kept,
  And never our aim forswore
For the Terrors that trooped from each recess
When fainting we fought in the Wilderness,
  And Hell made loud hurrah;
But God is in Heaven, and Grant in the Town,
  And Right through might is Law—
    God's way adore.

THE SURRENDER AT APPOMATTOX
(APRIL, 1865)

As billows upon billows roll,
  On victory victory breaks;
Ere yet seven days from Richmond's fall
  And crowning triumph wakes
The loud joy-gun, whose thunders run
  By sea-shore, streams, and lakes.
    The hope and great event agree
    In the sword that Grant received from Lee.

The warring eagles fold the wing,
  But not in Caesar's sway;
Not Rome o'ercome by Roman arms we sing
  As on Pharsalia's day,
But Treason thrown, though a giant grown,
  And Freedom's larger play.
    All human tribes glad token see
    In the close of the wars of Grant and Lee.

A CANTICLE
*significant of the national exaltation of enthusiasm
at the close of the war*

O the precipice Titanic
  Of the congregated Fall,

And the angle oceanic
     Where the deepening thunders call—
       And the Gorge so grim,
       And the firmamental rim!
Multitudinously thronging
    The waters all converge,
Then they sweep adown in sloping
    Solidity of surge.

      The Nation, in her impulse
        Mysterious as the Tide,
      In emotion like an ocean
        Moves in power, not in pride;
      And is deep in her devotion
        As Humanity is wide.

      Thou Lord of hosts victorious,
        The confluence Thou hast twined;
      By a wondrous way and glorious
        A passage Thou dost find—
        A passage Thou dost find:
      Hosanna to the Lord of hosts,
        The hosts of human kind.

Stable in its baselessness
    When calm is in the air,
The Iris half in tracelessness
    Hovers faintly fair.
Fitfully assailing it
    A wind from heaven blows,
Shivering and paling it
    To blankness of the snows;
While, incessant in renewal,
    The Arch rekindled grows,
Till again the gem and jewel
    Whirl in blinding overthrows—
Till, prevailing and transcending,
    Lo, the Glory perfect there,
And the contest finds an ending,
    For repose is in the air.

But the foamy Deep unsounded,
    And the dim and dizzy ledge,
And the booming roar rebounded,
    And the gull that skims the edge!
        The Giant of the Pool
        Heaves his forehead white as wool—
Toward the Iris ever climbing
    From the Cataracts that call—
Irremovable vast arras
    Draping all the Wall.

        The Generations pouring
          From times of endless date,
    In their going, in their flowing
    Ever form the steadfast State;
        And Humanity is growing
    Toward the fullness of her fate.

        Thou Lord of hosts victorious,
          Fulfill the end designed;
    By a wondrous way and glorious
        A passage Thou dost find—
        A passage Thou dost find:
    Hosanna to the Lord of Hosts,
        The hosts of human kind.

THE MARTYR
*indicative of the passion of the people
on the 15th day of April, 1865*

Good Friday was the day
    Of the prodigy and crime,
When they killed him in his pity,
    When they killed him in his prime
Of clemency and calm—
        When with yearning he was filled
        To redeem the evil-willed,
And, though conqueror, be kind;

But they killed him in his kindness,
In their madness and their blindness,
And they killed him from behind.

There is sobbing of the strong,
And a pall upon the land;
But the people in their weeping
Bare the iron hand;
Beware the People weeping
When they bare the iron hand.

He lieth in his blood—
The father in his face;
They have killed him, the Forgiver—
The Avenger takes his place,°
The Avenger wisely stern,
Who in righteousness shall do
What the heavens call him to,
And the parricides remand;
For they killed him in his kindness,
In their madness and their blindness,
And his blood is on their hand.

There is sobbing of the strong,
And a pall upon the land;
But the People in their weeping
Bare the iron hand:
Beware the People weeping
When they bare the iron hand.

"The Coming Storm"
a picture by S. R. Gifford, and owned by E. B. included in the
N. A. exhibition, April 1865

All feeling hearts must feel for him
Who felt this picture. Presage dim—
Dim inklings from the shadowy sphere
Fixed him and fascinated here.

A demon-cloud like the mountain one
    Burst on a spirit as mild
As this urned lake, the home of shades,
    But Shakespeare's pensive child.

Never the lines had lightly scanned,
    Steeped in fable, steeped in fate;
The Hamlet in his heart was 'ware,
    Such hearts can antedate.

No utter surprise can come to him
    Who reaches Shakespeare's core;
That which we seek and shun is there—
        Man's final lore.

REBEL COLOR-BEARERS AT SHILOH[P]
*a plea against the vindictive cry raised by civilians shortly after the
surrender at Appomattox*

The color-bearers facing death
White in the whirling sulphurous wreath,
    Stand boldly out before the line;
Right and left their glances go,
Proud of each other, glorying in their show;
Their battle-flags about them blow,
    And fold them as in flame divine:
Such living robes are only seen
Round martyrs burning on the green—
And martyrs for the Wrong have been.

Perish their Cause! but mark the men—
Mark the planted statues, then
Draw trigger on them if you can.

The leader of a patriot-band
Even so could view rebels who so could stand;
    And this when peril pressed him sore,
Left aidless in the shivered front of war—
    Skulkers behind, defiant foes before,

And fighting with a broken brand.
The challenge in that courage rare—
Courage defenseless, proudly bare—
Never could tempt him; he could dare
Strike up the leveled rifle there.

Sunday at Shiloh, and the day
When Stonewall charged—McClellan's crimson May,
And Chickamauga's wave of death,
And of the Wilderness the cypress wreath—
    All these have passed away.
The life in the veins of Treason lags,
Her daring color-bearers drop their flags,
    And yield. *Now* shall we fire?
        Can poor spite be?
Shall nobleness in victory less aspire
Than in reverse? Spare Spleen her ire,
    And think how Grant met Lee.

THE MUSTER[q]
suggested by two days review at Washington
(MAY, 1865)

The Abrahamic river—
    Patriarch of floods,
Calls the roll of all his streams
    And watery multitudes:
        Torrent cries to torrent,
          The rapids hail the fall;
        With shouts the inland freshets
        Gather to the call.

The quotas of the Nation,
    Like the water-shed of waves,
Muster into union—
    Eastern warriors, Western braves.

Martial strains are mingling,
    Though distant far the bands,

And the wheeling of the squadrons
    Is like surf upon the sands.

The bladed guns are gleaming—
    Drift in lengthened trim,
Files on files for hazy miles—
    Nebulously dim.

O Milky Way of armies—
    Star rising after star,
New banners of the Commonwealths,
    And eagles of the War.

The Abrahamic river
    To sea-wide fullness fed,
Pouring from the thaw-lands
    By the God of floods is led:
        His deep enforcing current
            The streams of ocean own,
        And Europe's marge is evened
            By rills from Kansas lone.

AURORA-BOREALIS
commemorative of the dissolution of armies at the peace
(MAY, 1865)

What power disbands the Northern Lights
    After their steely play?
The lonely watcher feels an awe
    Of Nature's sway,
        As when appearing,
        He marked their flashed uprearing
    In the cold gloom—
    Retreatings and advancings,
(Like dallyings of doom),
        Transitions and enhancings,
            And bloody ray.

The phantom-host has failed quite,
    Splendor and Terror gone—
Portent or promise—and gives way
    To pale, meek Dawn;
        The coming, going,
        Alike in wonder showing—
Alike the God,
    Decreeing and commanding
The million blades that glowed,
    The muster and disbanding—
        Midnight and Morn.

THE RELEASED REBEL PRISONER[r]
(JUNE, 1865)

Armies he's seen—the herds of war,
    But never such swarms of men
As now in the Nineveh of the North—
    How mad the Rebellion then!

And yet but dimly he divines
    The depth of that deceit,
And superstition of vast pride
    Humbled to such defeat.

Seductive shone the Chiefs in arms—
    His steel the nearest magnet drew;
Wreathed with its kind, the Gulf-weed drives—
    'Tis Nature's wrong they rue.

His face is hidden in his beard,
    But his heart peers out at eye—
And such a heart! like a mountain-pool
    Where no man passes by.

He thinks of Hill—a brave soul gone;
    And Ashby dead in pale disdain,
And Stuart with the Rupert-plume,
    Whose blue eye never shall laugh again.

He hears the drum; he sees our boys
    From his wasted fields return;
Ladies feast them on strawberries,
    And even to kiss them yearn.

He marks them bronzed, in soldier-trim,
    The rifle proudly borne;
They bear it for an heir-loom home,
    And he—disarmed—jail-worn.

Home, home—his heart is full of it:
    But home he never shall see,
Even should he stand upon the spot;
    'Tis gone!—where his brothers be.

The cypress-moss from tree to tree
    Hangs in his Southern land;
As drear, from thought to thought of his
    Run memories hand in hand.

And so he lingers—lingers on
    In the City of the Foe—
His cousins and his countrymen
    Who see him listless go.

A GRAVE NEAR PETERSBURG, VIRGINIA[5]

Head-board and foot-board duly placed—
    Grassed is the mound between;
Daniel Drouth is the slumberer's name—
    Long may his grave be green!

Quick was his way—a flash and a blow,
    Full of his fire was he—
A fire of hell—'tis burnt out now—
    Green may his grave long be!

May his grave be green, though he
    Was a rebel of iron mould:

Many a true heart—true to the Cause,
  Though the blaze of his wrath lies cold.

May his grave be green—still green
  While happy years shall run;
May none come nigh to disinter
  The—*Buried Gun*.

"FORMERLY A SLAVE"
an idealized portrait, by E. Vedder, in the spring exhibition of the National Academy, 1865

The sufferance of her race is shown,
  And retrospect of life,
Which now too late deliverance dawns upon;
  Yet is she not at strife.

Her children's children they shall know
  The good withheld from her;
And so her reverie takes prophetic cheer—
  In spirit she sees the stir

Far down the depth of thousand years,
  And marks the revel shine;
Her dusky face is lit with sober light,
  Sibylline, yet benign.

THE APPARITION
(a retrospect)

Convulsions came; and, where the field
  Long slept in pastoral green,
A goblin-mountain was upheaved
(Sure the scared sense was all deceived),
  Marl-glen and slag-ravine.

The unreserve of Ill was there,
  The clinkers in her last retreat;

But, ere the eye could take it in,
or mind could comprehension win,
    It sunk!—and at our feet.

So, then, Solidity's a crust—
    The core of fire below;
All may go well for many a year,
But who can think without a fear
    Of horrors that happen so?

MAGNANIMITY BAFFLED

"Sharp words we had before the fight;
    But—now the fight is done—
Look, here's my hand," said the Victor bold,
    "Take it—an honest one!
What, holding back? I mean you well;
    Though worsted, you strove stoutly, man;
The odds were great; I honor you;
    Man honors man.

"Still silent, friend? can grudges be?
    Yet am I held a foe?—
Turned to the wall, on his cot he lies—
    Never I'll leave him so!
Brave one! I here implore your hand;
    Dumb still? all fellowship fled?
Nay, then, I'll have this stubborn hand!"
    He snatched it—it was dead.

ON THE SLAIN COLLEGIANS[t]

Youth is the time when hearts are large,
    And stirring wars
Appeal to the spirit which appeals in turn
    To the blade it draws.
If woman incite, and duty show
    (Though made the mask of Cain),

Or whether it be Truth's sacred cause,
     Who can aloof remain
That shares youth's ardor, uncooled by the snow
     Of wisdom or sordid gain?

The liberal arts and nurture sweet
Which give his gentleness to man—
     Train him to honor, lend him grace
Through bright examples meet—
That culture which makes never wan
With underminings deep, but holds
     The surface still, its fitting place,
     And so gives sunniness to the face
And bravery to the heart; what troops
     Of generous boys in happiness thus bred—
     Saturnians through life's Tempe led,
Went from the North and came from the South,
With golden mottoes in the mouth,
     To lie down midway on a bloody bed.

Woe for the homes of the North,
And woe for the seats of the South:
All who felt life's spring in prime,
And were swept by the wind of their place and time—
     All lavish hearts, on whichever side,
Of birth urbane or courage high,
Armed them for the stirring wars—
Armed them—some to die.
     Apollo-like in pride,
Each would slay his Python—caught
The maxims in his temple taught—
     Aflame with sympathies whose blaze
Perforce enwrapped him—social laws,
     Friendship and kin, and by-gone days—
Vows, kisses—every heart unmoors,
And launches into the seas of wars.
What could they else—North or South?
Each went forth with blessings given
By priests and mothers in the name of Heaven;
     And honor in all was chief.

Warred one for Right, and one for Wrong?
So put it; but they both were young—
Each grape to his cluster clung,
All their elegies are sung.

The anguish of maternal hearts
    Must search for balm divine;
But well the striplings bore their fated parts
    (The heavens all parts assign)—
Never felt life's care or cloy.
Each bloomed and died an unabated Boy;
Nor dreamed what death was—thought it mere
Sliding into some vernal sphere.
They knew the joy, but leaped the grief,
Like plants that flower ere comes the leaf—
Which storms lay low in kindly doom,
And kill them in their flush of bloom.

AMERICA

I

Where the wings of a sunny Dome expand
I saw a Banner in gladsome air—
Starry, like Berenice's Hair—
Afloat in broadened bravery there;
With undulating long-drawn flow,
As rolled Brazilian billows go
Voluminously o'er the Line.
The Land reposed in peace below;
    The children in their glee
Were folded to the exulting heart
    Of young Maternity.

II

Later, and it streamed in fight
    When tempest mingled with the fray,
And over the spear-point of the shaft
    I saw the ambiguous lightning play.

Valor with Valor strove, and died:
Fierce was Despair, and cruel was Pride;
And the lorn Mother speechless stood,
Pale at the fury of her brood.

III

Yet later, and the silk did wind
    Her fair cold form;
Little availed the shining shroud,
    Though ruddy in hue, to cheer or warm,
A watcher looked upon her low, and said—
She sleeps, but sleeps, she is not dead.
    But in that sleep contortion showed
The terror of the vision there—
    A silent vision unavowed,
Revealing earth's foundation bare,
    And Gorgon in her hidden place.
It was a thing of fear to see
    So foul a dream upon so fair a face,
And the dreamer lying in that starry shroud.

IV

But from the trance she sudden broke-
    The trance, or death into promoted life;
At her feet a shivered yoke,
And in her aspect turned to heaven
    No trace of passion or of strife—
A clear calm look. It spake of pain,
But such as purifies from stain—
Sharp pangs that never come again—
    And triumph repressed by knowledge meet,
Power dedicate, and hope grown wise,
    And youth matured for age's seat—
Law on her brow and empire in her eyes.
    So she, with graver air and lifted flag;
While the shadow, chased by light,
Fled along the far-drawn height,
    And left her on the crag.

ON THE HOME GUARDS
who perished in the defense of Lexington, Missouri

The men who here in harness died
 Fell not in vain, though in defeat.
They by their end well fortified
 The Cause, and built retreat
(With memory of their valor tried)
For emulous in many an after fray—
Hearts sore beset, which died at bay.

INSCRIPTION
for the graves at Pea Ridge, Arkansas

Let none misgive we died amiss
 When here we strove in furious fight:
Furious it was; nathless was this
 Better than tranquil plight,
And tame surrender of the Cause
Hallowed by hearts and by the laws.
 We here who warred for Man and Right,
The choice of warring never laid with us.
 There we were ruled by the traitor's choice.
 Nor long we stood to trim and poise,
But marched, and fell—victorious!

THE FORTITUDE OF THE NORTH
under the disaster of the Second Manassas

No shame they take for dark defeat
 While prizing yet each victory won,
Who fight for the Right through all retreat,
 Nor pause until their work is done.
The Cape-of-Storms is proof to every throe;
 Vainly against that foreland beat
Wild winds aloft and wilder waves below:
The black cliffs gleam through rents in sleet
When the livid Antarctic storm-clouds glow.

killed in the victory of Baton Rouge, Louisiana

Afar they fell. It was the zone
   Of fig and orange, cane and lime
(A land how all unlike their own,
With the cold pine-grove overgrown),
   But still their Country's clime.
And there in youth they died for her—
          The Volunteers,
For her went up their dying prayers:
   So vast the Nation, yet so strong the tie.
What doubt shall come, then, to deter
   The Republic's earnest faith and courage high.

AN EPITAPH

When Sunday tidings from the front
   Made pale the priest and people,
And heavily the blessing went,
   And bells were dumb in the steeple;
The Soldier's widow (summering sweetly here,
   In shade by waving beeches lent)
   Felt deep at heart her faith content,
And priest and people borrowed of her cheer.

INSCRIPTION
for Marye's Heights, Fredericksburg

To them who crossed the flood
And climbed the hill, with eyes
   Upon the heavenly flag intent,
   And through the deathful tumult went
Even unto death: to them this Stone—
Erect, where they were overthrown—
   Of more than victory the monument.

The grass shall never forget this grave.
When homeward footing it in the sun
    After the weary ride by rail
The stripling soldiers passed her door,
    Wounded perchance, or wan and pale,
She left her household work undone—
Duly the wayside table spread,
    With evergreens shaded, to regale
Each travel-spent and grateful one.
So warm her heart—childless—unwed,
Who like a mother comforted.

ON THE SLAIN AT CHICKAMAUGA

Happy are they and charmed in life
    Who through long wars arrive unscarred
At peace. To such the wreath be given,
If they unfalteringly have striven—
    In honor, as in limb, unmarred.
Let cheerful praise be rife,
    And let them live their years at ease,
Musing on brothers who victorious died—
    Loved mates whose memory shall ever please.

And yet mischance is honorable too—
    Seeming defeat in conflict justified
Whose end to closing eyes is hid from view.
The will, that never can relent—
The aim, survivor of the bafflement,
    Make this memorial due.

AN UNINSCRIBED MONUMENT
on one of the battle-fields of the Wilderness

Silence and Solitude may hint
    (Whose home is in yon piny wood)

What I, though tableted, could never tell—
The din which here befell,
   And striving of the multitude.
The iron cones and spheres of death
    Set round me in their rust,
      These, too, if just,
Shall speak with more than animated breath.
    Thou who beholdest, if thy thought,
Not narrowed down to personal cheer,
Take in the import of the quiet here—
    The after-quiet—the calm full fraught;
Thou too wilt silent stand—
Silent as I, and lonesome as the land.

On Sherman's Men
who fell in the assault of Kenesaw Mountain, Georgia

They said that Fame her clarion dropped
   Because great deeds were done no more—
That even Duty knew no shining ends,
And Glory—'twas a fallen star!
   But battle can heroes and bards restore.
      Nay, look at Kenesaw:
Perils the mailed ones never knew
Are lightly braved by the ragged coats of blue,
And gentler hearts are bared to deadlier war.

On the Grave of a Young Cavalry Officer Killed in the Valley of Virginia

Beauty and youth, with manners sweet, and friends—
   Gold, yet a mind not unenriched had he
Whom here low violets veil from eyes.
   But all these gifts transcended be:
His happier fortune in this mound you see.

A REQUIEM
for soldiers lost in ocean transports

When, after storms that woodlands rue,
    To valleys comes atoning dawn,
The robins blithe their orchard-sports renew;
    And meadow-larks, no more withdrawn,
Caroling fly in the languid blue;
The while, from many a hid recess,
Alert to partake the blessedness,
The pouring mites their airy dance pursue.
    So, after ocean's ghastly gales,
When laughing light of hoyden morning breaks,
        Every finny hider wakes—
    From vaults profound swims up with glittering scales;
    Through the delightsome sea he sails,
With shoals of shining tiny things
Frolic on every wave that flings
    Against the prow its showery spray;
All creatures joying in the morn,
Save them forever from joyance torn,
    Whose bark was lost where now the dolphins play;
Save them that by the fabled shore,
    Down the pale stream are washed away,
Far to the reef of bones are borne;
    And never revisits them the light,
Nor sight of long-sought land and pilot more;
    Nor heed they now the lone bird's flight
Round the lone spar where mid-sea surges pour.

ON A NATURAL MONUMENT
in a field of Georgia[u]

No trophy this—a Stone unhewn,
    And stands where here the field immures
The nameless brave whose palms are won.
Outcast they sleep; yet fame is nigh—
    Pure fame of, deeds, not doers;
Nor deeds of men who bleeding die
    In cheer of hymns that round them float:

In happy dreams such close the eye.
But withering famine slowly wore,
 And slowly fell disease did gloat.
Even Nature's self did aid deny;
In horror they choked the pensive sigh.
 Yea, off from home sad Memory bore
(Though anguished Yearning heaved that way),
Lest wreck of reason might befall.
 As men in gales shun the lee shore,
Though there the homestead be, and call,
And thitherward winds and waters sway—
As such lorn mariners, so fared they.
But naught shall now their peace molest.
 Their fame is this: they did endure—
Endure, when fortitude was vain
To kindle any approving strain
Which they might hear. To these who rest,
 This healing sleep alone was sure.

COMMEMORATIVE OF A NAVAL VICTORY

Sailors there are of gentlest breed,
 Yet strong, like every goodly thing;
The discipline of arms refines,
 And the wave gives tempering.
 The damasked blade its beam can fling;
It lends the last grave grace:
The hawk, the hound, and sworded nobleman
 In Titian's picture for a king,
Are of hunter or warrior race.

In social halls a favored guest
 In years that follow victory won,
How sweet to feel your festal fame
 In woman's glance instinctive thrown:
 Repose is yours—your deed is known,
It musks the amber wine;
It lives, and sheds a light from storied days
 Rich as October sunsets brown,
Which make the barren place to shine.

But seldom the laurel wreath is seen
    Unmixed with pensive pansies dark;
There's a light and a shadow on every man
    Who at last attains his lifted mark—
    Nursing through night the ethereal spark.
Elate he never can be;
He feels that spirit which glad had hailed his worth,
    Sleep in oblivion.—The shark
Glides white through the phosphorus sea.

PRESENTATION TO THE AUTHORITIES
*by privates, of colors captured in battles
ending in the surrender of Lee*

These flags of armies overthrown—
Flags fallen beneath the sovereign one
In end foredoomed which closes war;
We here, the captors, lay before
    The altar which of right claims all—
Our Country. And as freely we,
    Revering ever her sacred call,
Could lay our lives down—though life be
Thrice loved and precious to the sense
Of such as reap the recompense
    Of life imperiled for just cause—
Imperiled, and yet preserved;
While comrades, whom Duty as strongly nerved,
Whose wives were all as dear, lie low.
But these flags given, glad we go
    To waiting homes with vindicated laws.

THE RETURNED VOLUNTEER TO HIS RIFLE

Over this hearth—my father's seat—
    Repose, to patriot-memory dear,
Thou tried companion, whom at last I greet
    By steepy banks of Hudson here.
How oft I told thee of this scene—

The Highlands blue—the river's narrowing sheen.
Little at Gettysburg we thought
To find such haven; but God kept it green.
Long rest! with belt, and bayonet, and canteen.

THE SCOUT TOWARD ALDIE

The cavalry-camp lies on the slope
    Of what was late a vernal hill,
But now like a pavement bare—
An outpost in the perilous wilds
    Which ever are lone and still;
        But Mosby's men are there—
        Of Mosby best beware.

Great trees the troopers felled, and leaned
    In antlered walls about their tents;
Strict watch they kept; 'twas *Hark!* and *Mark!*
Unarmed none cared to stir abroad
    For berries beyond their forest-fence:
        As glides in seas the shark,
        Rides Mosby through green dark.

All spake of him, but few had seen
    Except the maimed ones or the low;
Yet rumor made him every thing—
A farmer—woodman—refugee—
    The man who crossed the field but now;
        A spell about his life did cling—
        Who to the ground shall Mosby bring?

The morning-bugles lonely play,
    Lonely the evening-bugle calls—
Unanswered voices in the wild;
The settled hush of birds in nest
    Becharms, and all the wood enthralls:
        Memory's self is so beguiled
        That Mosby seems a satyr's child.

They lived as in the Eerie Land—
    The fire-flies showed with fairy gleam;
And yet from pine-tops one might ken
The Capitol Dome—hazy—sublime—
    A vision breaking on a dream:
        So strange it was that Mosby's men
        Should dare to prowl where the Dome was seen.

A ride toward Aldie broke the spell.—
    The Leader lies before his tent
Gazing at heaven's all-cheering lamp
Through blandness of a morning rare;
    His thoughts on bitter-sweets are bent:
        His sunny bride is in the camp—
        But Mosby—graves are beds of damp!

The trumpet calls; he goes within;
    But none the prayer and sob may know:
Her hero he, but bridegroom too.
Ah, love in a tent is a queenly thing,
    And fame, be sure, refines the vow;
        But fame fond wives have lived to rue,
        And Mosby's men fell deeds can do.

Tan-tara! tan-tara! tan-tara!
    Mounted and armed he sits a king;
For pride she smiles if now she peep—
Elate he rides at the head of his men;
    He is young, and command is a boyish thing:
        They file out into the forest deep—
        Do Mosby and his rangers sleep?

The sun is gold, and the world is green,
    Opal the vapors of morning roll;
The champing horses lightly prance—
Full of caprice, and the riders too
    Curving in many a caricole.
        But marshaled soon, by fours advance—
        Mosby had checked that airy dance.

By the hospital-tent the cripples stand—
    Bandage, and crutch, and cane, and sling,
And palely eye the brave array;
The froth of the cup is gone for them
    (Caw! caw! the crows through the blueness wing):
        Yet these were late as bold, as gay;
        But Mosby—a clip, and grass is bay.

How strong they feel on their horses free,
    Tingles the tendoned thigh with life;
Their cavalry jackets make boys of all—
With golden breasts like tile oriole;
    The chat, the jest, and laugh are rife.
        But word is passed from the front—a call
        For order; the wood is Mosby's hall.

To which behest one rider sly
    (Spurred, but unarmed) gave little heed—
Of dexterous fun not slow or spare,
He teased his neighbors of touchy mood,
    Into plungings he pricked his steed:
        A black-eyed man on a coal-black mare,
        Alive as Mosby in mountain air.

His limbs were long, and large, and round;
    He whispered, winked—did all but shout:
A healthy man for the sick to view;
The taste in his mouth was sweet at morn;
    Little of care he cared about.
        And yet of pains and pangs he knew—
        In others, maimed by Mosby's crew.

The Hospital Steward—even he
    (Sacred in person as a priest),
And on his coat—sleeve broidered nice
Wore the caduceus, black and green.
    No wonder he sat so light on his beast;
        This cheery man in suit of price
        Not even Mosby dared to slice.

They pass the picket by the pine
    And hollow log—a lonesome place;
His horse adroop, and pistol clean;
'Tis cocked—kept leveled toward the wood;
    Strained vigilance ages his childish face.
        Since midnight has that stripling been
        Peering for Mosby through the green.

Splashing they cross the freshet-flood,
    And up the muddy bank they strain;
A horse at a spectral white-ash shies—
One of the span of the ambulance,
    Black as a hearse. They give the rein:
        Silent speed on a scout were wise,
        Could cunning baffle Mosby's spies.

Rumor had come that a band was lodged
    In green retreats of hills that peer
By Aldie (famed for the swordless charge[v]).
Much store they'd heaped of captured arms
    And, peradventure, pilfered cheer;
        For Mosby's lads oft hearts enlarge
        In revelry by some gorge's marge.

"Don't let your sabres rattle and ring;
    To his oat-bag let each man give heed—
There now, that fellow's bag's untied,
Sowing the road with the precious grain.
    Your carbines swing at hand—you need!
        Look to yourselves, and your nags beside,
        Men who after Mosby ride."

Picked lads and keen went sharp before—
    A guard, though scarce against surprise;
And rearmost rode an answering troop,
But flankers none to right or left.
    No bugle peals, no pennon flies:
        Silent they sweep, and fain would swoop
        On Mosby with an Indian whoop.

On, right on through the forest land,
    Nor man, nor maid, nor child was seen—
Not even a dog. The air was still;
The blackened hut they turned to see,
    And spied charred benches on the green;
        A squirrel sprang from the rotting mill
        Whence Mosby sallied late, brave blood to spill.

By worn-out fields they cantered on—
    Drear fields amid the woodlands wide;
By cross-roads of some olden time,
In which grew groves; by gate-stones down—
    Grassed ruins of secluded pride:
        A strange lone land, long past the prime,
        Fit land for Mosby or for crime.

The brook in the dell they pass. One peers
    Between the leaves: "Ay, there's the place—
There, on the oozy ledge—'twas there
We found the body (Blake's, you know);
    Such whirlings, gurglings round the face—
        Shot drinking! Well, in war all's fair—
        So Mosby says. The bough—take care!"

Hard by, a chapel. Flower-pot mould
    Danked and decayed the shaded roof;
The porch was punk; the clapboards spanned
With ruffled lichens gray or green;
    Red coral-moss was not aloof;
        And mid dry leaves green dead-man's-hand
        Groped toward that chapel in Mosby-land.

They leave the road and take the wood,
    And mark the trace of ridges there—
A wood where once had slept the farm—
A wood where once tobacco grew
    Drowsily in the hazy air,
        And wrought in all kind things a calm—
        Such influence, Mosby! bids disarm.

To ease even yet the place did woo—
    To ease which pines unstirring share,
For ease the weary horses sighed:
Halting, and slackening girths, they feed,
    Their pipes they light, they loiter there;
        Then up, and urging still the Guide,
        On, and after Mosby ride.

This Guide in frowzy coat of brown,
    And beard of ancient growth and mould,
Bestrode a bony steed and strong,
As suited well with bulk he bore—
    A wheezy man with depth of hold
        Who jouncing went. A staff he swung—
        A wight whom Mosby's wasp had stung.

Burnt out and homeless—hunted long!
    That wheeze he caught in autumn-wood
Crouching (a fat man) for his life,
And spied his lean son 'mong the crew
    That probed the covert. Ah! black blood
        Was his 'gainst even child and wife—
        Fast friends to Mosby. Such the strife.

A lad, unhorsed by sliding girths,
    Strains hard to readjust his seat
Ere the main body show the gap
'Twixt them and the rear-guard; scrub-oaks near
    He sidelong eyes, while hands move fleet;
        Then mounts and spurs. One drops his cap—
        "Let Mosby find!" nor heeds mishap.

A gable time-stainedpeeps through trees:
    "You mind the fight in the haunted house?
That's it; we clenched them in the room—
An ambuscade of ghosts we thought,
    But proved sly rebels on a bouse!
        Luke lies in the yard." The chimneys loom:
        Some muse on Mosby—some on doom.

Less nimbly now through brakes they wind,
    And ford wild creeks where men have drowned;
The pool they skirt, avoid the fen,
And so till night, when down they lie,
    Their steeds still saddled, in wooded ground:
        Rein in hand they slumber then,
        Dreaming of Mosby's cedarn den.

But Colonel and Major friendly sat
    Where boughs deformed low made a seat.
The Young Man talked (all sworded and spurred)
Of the partisan's blade he longed to win,
    And frays in which he meant to beat.
        The grizzled Major smoked, and heard:
        "But what's that—Mosby?" "No, a bird."

A contrast here like sire and son,
    Hope and Experience sage did meet;
The Youth was brave, the Senior too;
But through the Seven Days one had served,
    And gasped with the rear-guard in retreat:
        So he smoked and smoked, and the wreath he blew—
        "Any *sure* news of Mosby's crew?"

He smoked and smoked, eyeing the while
    A huge tree hydra-like in growth—
Moon-tinged—with crook'd boughs rent or lopped—
Itself a haggard forest. "Come!"
    The Colonel cried, "to talk you're loath;
        D'ye hear? I say he must be stopped,
        This Mosby—caged, and hair close cropped."

"Of course; but what's that dangling there?"
    "Where?" "From the tree—that gallows-bough
"A bit of frayed bark, is it not?"
"Ay—or a rope; did *we* hang last?—
    Don't like my neckerchief any how;"
        He loosened it: "O ay, we'll stop
        This Mosby—but that vile jerk and drop!"^w

By peep of light they feed and ride,
　　Gaining a grove's green edge at morn,
And mark the Aldie hills uprear
And five gigantic horsemen carved
　　Clear-cut against the sky withdrawn;
　　　　Are more behind? an open snare?
　　　　Or Mosby's men but watchmen there?

The ravaged land was miles behind,
　　And Loudon spread her landscape rare;
Orchards in pleasant lowlands stood,
Cows were feeding, a cock loud crew,
　　But not a friend at need was there;
　　　　The valley-folk were only good
　　　　To Mosby and his wandering brood.

What best to do? what mean yon men?
　　Colonel and Guide their minds compare;
Be sure some looked their Leader through;
Dismounted, on his sword he leaned
　　As one who feigns an easy air;
　　　　And yet perplexed he was they knew—
　　　　Perplexed by Mosby's mountain-crew.

The Major hemmed as he would speak,
　　But checked himself, and left the ring
Of cavalrymen about their Chief—
Young courtiers mute who paid their court
　　By looking with confidence on their king;
　　　　They knew him brave, foresaw no grief—
　　　　But Mosby—the time to think is brief.

The Surgeon (sashed in sacred green)
　　Was glad 'twas not for *him* to say
What next should be; if a trooper bleeds,
Why he will do his best, as wont,
　　And his partner in black will aid and pray;
　　　　But judgment bides with him who leads,
　　　　And Mosby many a problem breeds.

This Surgeon was the kindliest man
    That ever a callous trade professed;
He felt for him, that Leader young,
And offered medicine from his flask:
    The Colonel took it with marvelous zest.
        For such fine medicine good and strong,
        Oft Mosby and his foresters long.

A charm of proof. "Ho, Major, come—
    Pounce on yon men! Take half your troop,
Through the thickets wind—pray speedy be—
And gain their rear. And, Captain Morn,
    Picket these roads—all travelers stop;
        The rest to the edge of this crest with me,
        That Mosby and his scouts may see."

Commanded and done. Ere the sun stood steep,
    Back came the Blues, with a troop of Grays,
Ten riding double—luckless ten!—
Five horses gone, and looped hats lost,
    And love-locks dancing in a maze—
        Certes, but sophomores from the glen
        Of Mosby—not his veteran men.

"Colonel," said the Major, touching his cap,
    "We've had our ride, and here they are."
"Well done! how many found you there?"
"As many as I bring you here."
    "And no one hurt?" "There'll be no scar—
        One fool was battered." "Find their lair?"
        "Why, Mosby's brood camp every where."

He sighed, and slid down from his horse,
    And limping went to a spring-head nigh.
"Why, bless me, Major, not hurt, I hope?"
"Battered my knee against a bar
    When the rush was made; all right by-and-by.—
        Halloa! they gave you too much rope—
        Go back to Mosby, eh? elope?"

Just by the low-hanging skirt of wood
    The guard, remiss, had given a chance
For a sudden sally into the cover—
But foiled the intent, nor fired a shot,
    Though the issue was a deadly trance;
        For, hurled 'gainst an oak that humped low over,
        Mosby's man fell, pale as a lover.

They pulled some grass his head to ease
    (Lined with blue shreds a ground-nest stirred).
The Surgeon came—"Here's a to-do!"
"Ah!" cried the Major, darting a glance,
    "This fellow's the one that fired and spurred
        Down hill, but met reserves below—
        My boys, not Mosby's—so we go!"

The Surgeon—bluff, red, goodly man—
    Kneeled by the hurt one; like a bee
He toiled. The pale young Chaplain too—
(Who went to the wars for cure of souls,
    And his own student-ailments)—he
        Bent over likewise; spite the two
        Mosby's poor man more pallid grew.

Meanwhile the mounted captives near
    Jested; and yet they anxious showed;
Virginians; some of family-pride,
And young, and full of fire, and fine
    In open feature and cheek that glowed;
        And here thralled vagabonds now they ride—
        But list! one speaks for Mosby's side.

"Why, three to one—your horses strong—
    Revolvers, rifles, and a surprise—
Surrender we account no shame!
We live, are gay, and life is hope;
    We'll fight again when fight is wise.
        There are plenty more from where we came;
        But go find Mosby—start the game!"

Yet one there was who looked but glum;
    In middle-age, a father he,
And this his first experience too:
"They shot at my heart when my hands were up—
    This fighting's crazy work, I see!"
        But noon is high; what next to do?
        The woods are mute, and Mosby is the foe.

"Save what we've got," the Major said;
    "Bad plan to make a scout too long;
The tide may turn, and drag them back,
And more beside. These rides I've been,
    And every time a mine was sprung.
        To rescue, mind, they won't be slack—
        Look out for Mosby's rifle-crack."

"We welcome it! give crack for crack!
    Peril, old lad, is what I seek."
"O then, there's plenty to be had—
By all means on, and have our fill!"
    With that, grotesque, he writhed his neck,
        Showing a scar by buck-shot made—
        Kind Mosby's Christmas gift, he said.

"But, Colonel, my prisoners-let a guard
    Make sure of them, and lead to camp.
That done, we're free for a dark-room fight
If so you say." The other laughed;
    "Trust me, Major, nor throw a damp.
        But first to try a little sleight—
        Sure news of Mosby would suit me quite."

Herewith he turned—"Reb, have a dram?"
    Holding the Surgeon's flask with a smile
To a young scapegrace from the glen.
"Oh yes!" he eagerly replied,
    "And thank you, Colonel, but—any guile?
        For if you think we'll blab—why, then
        You don't know Mosby or his men."

The Leader's genial air relaxed.
    "Best give it up," a whisperer said.
"By heaven, I'll range their rebel den!"
"They'll treat you well," the captive cried;
    "They're all like us—handsome—well-bred;
        In wood or town, with sword or pen,
        Polite is Mosby, bland his men."

"Where were you, lads, last night?—come, tell!"
    "We?—at a wedding in the Vale—
The bridegroom our comrade; by his side
Belisent, my cousin—O, so proud
    Of her young love with old wounds pale—
        A Virginian girl! God bless her pride—
        Of a crippled Mosby-man the bride!"

"Four walls shall mend that saucy mood,
    And moping prisons tame him down,"
Said Captain Cloud. "God help that day,"
Cried Captain Morn, "and he so young.
    But hark, he sings—a madcap one!"
        "O, we multiply merrily in the May,
        The birds and Mosby's men, they say!"

While echoes ran, a wagon old,
    Under stout guard of Corporal Chew
Came up; a lame horse, dingy white,
With clouted harness; ropes in hand,
    Cringed the humped driver, black in hue;
        By him (for Mosby's band a sight)
        A sister-rebel sat, her veil held tight.

"I picked them up," the Corporal said,
    "Crunching their way over stick and root,
Through yonder wood. The man here—Cuff—
Says they are going to Leesburg town."
    The Colonel's eye took in the group;
        The veiled one's hand he spied—enough!
        Not Mosby's. Spite the gown's poor stuff,

Off went his hat: "Lady, fear not;
    We soldiers do what we deplore—
I must detain you till we march."
The stranger nodded. Nettled now,
    He grew politer than before:—
        "'Tis Mosby's fault, this halt and search:"
        The lady stiffened in her starch.

"My duty, madam, bids me now
    Ask what may seem a little rude.
Pardon—that veil—withdraw it, please
(Corporal! make every man fall back);
    Pray, now, I do but what I should;
        Bethink you, 'tis in masks like these
        That Mosby haunts the villages."

Slowly the stranger drew her veil,
    And looked the Soldier in the eye—
A glance of mingled foul and fair;
Sad patience in a proud disdain,
    And more than quietude. A sigh
        She heaved, as if all unaware,
        And far seemed Mosby from her care.

She came from Yewton Place, her home,
    So ravaged by the war's wild play—
Campings, and foragings, and fires—
That now she sought an aunt's abode.
    Her kinsmen? In Lee's army, they.
        The black? A servant, late her sire's.
        And Mosby? Vainly he inquires.

He gazed, and sad she met his eye;
    "In the wood yonder were you lost?"
No; at the forks they left the road
Because of hoof-prints (thick they were—
    Thick as the words in notes thrice crossed),
        And fearful, made that episode.
        In fear of Mosby? None she showed.

Her poor attire again he scanned:
    "Lady, once more; I grieve to jar
On all sweet usage, but must plead
To have what peeps there from your dress;
    That letter—'tis justly prize of war."
        She started—gave it—she must need.
        "'Tis not from Mosby? May I read?"

And straight such matter he perused
    That with the Guide he went apart.
The Hospital Steward's turn began:
"Must squeeze this darkey; every tap
    Of knowledge we are bound to start."
        "Garry," she said, "tell all you can
        Of Colonel Mosby—that brave man."

"Dun know much, sare; and missis here
    Know less dan me. But dis I know—"
"Well, what?" "I dun know what I know."
"A knowing answer!" The hump-back coughed,
    Rubbing his yellowish wool like tow.
        "Come—Mosby—tell!" "O dun look so!
        My gal nursed missis—let we go."

"Go where?" demanded Captain Cloud;
    Back into bondage? Man, you're free!"
"Well, *let* we free!" The Captain's brow
Lowered; the Colonel came—had heard:
    "Pooh! pooh! his simple heart I see—
        A faithful servant.—Lady" (a bow),
        "Mosby's abroad—with us you'll go.

"Guard! look to your prisoners; back to camp!
    The man in the grass—can he mount and away?
Why, how he groans!" "Bad inward bruise—
Might lug him along in the ambulance."
    "Coals to Newcastle! let him stay.
        Boots and saddles!—our pains we lose,
        Nor care I if Mosby hear the news!"

But word was sent to a house at hand,
    And a flask was left by the hurt one's side.
They seized in that same house a man,
Neutral by day, by night a foe—
    So charged his neighbor late, the Guide.
        A grudge? Hate will do what it can;
        Along he went for a Mosby-man.

No secrets now; the bugle calls;
    The open road they take, nor shun
The hill; retrace the weary way.
But one there was who whispered low,
    "This is a feint—we'll back anon;
        Young Hair-Brains don't retreat, they say;
        A brush with Mosby is the play!"

They rode till eve. Then on a farm
    That lay along a hill-side green,
Bivouacked. Fires were made, and then
Coffee was boiled; a cow was coaxed
    And killed, and savory roasts were seen;
        And under the lee of a cattle-pen
        The guard slipped freely with Mosby's men.

The ball was bandied to and fro;
    Hits were given and hits were met:
"Chickamauga, Feds—take off your hat!"
"But the Fight in the Clouds repaid you, Rebs!"
    "Forgotten about Manassas yet?"
        Chatting and chaffing, and tit for tat,
        Mosby's clan with the troopers sat.

"Here comes the moon!" a captive cried;
    "A song." what say? Archy, my lad!"
Hailing the still one of the clan
(A boyish face with girlish hair),
    "Give us that thing poor Pansy made
        Last year." He brightened, and began;
        And this was the song of Mosby's man:

Spring is come; she shows her pass—
    Wild violets cool!
South of woods a small close grass—
    A vernal wool!
Leaves are a'bud on the sassafras—
    They'll soon be full:
Blessings on the friendly screen—
    I'm for the South! says the leafage green.

Robins! fly, and take your fill
    of out-of-doors—
Garden, orchard, meadow, hill,
    Barns and bowers;
Take your fill, and have your will—
    Virginia's yours!
But, bluebirds! keep away, and fear
    The ambuscade in bushes here.

"A green song that," a sergeant said;
    "But where's poor Pansy? gone, I fear."
"Ay, mustered out at Ashby's Gap."
    "I see; now for a live man's song;
    Ditty for ditty—prepare to cheer.
        Comrades, you can fling a cap!
        You barehead Mosby-boys—why—clap!"

Nine Blue-coats went a-nutting
    Slyly in Tennessee—
Not for chestnuts—better than that—
    Hush, you bumblebee!
        Nutting, nutting—
        All through the year there's nutting!

A tree they spied so yellow,
    Rustling in motion queer;
In they fired, and down they dropped—
    Butternuts, my dear!
        Nutting, nutting—
        Who'll 'list to go a-nutting?

Ah! why should good fellows foemen be?
    And who would dream that foes they were—
Larking and singing so friendly then—
A family likeness in every face.
    But Captain Cloud made sour demur:
        "Guard! keep your prisoners *in* the pen,
        And let none talk with Mosby's men."

That captain was a valorous one
    (No irony, but honest truth),
Yet down from his brain cold drops distilled,
Making stalactites in his heart—
    A conscientious soul, forsooth;
        And with a formal hate was filled
        Of Mosby's band; and some he'd killed.

Meantime the lady rueful sat,
    Watching the flicker of a fire
Where the Colonel played the outdoor host
In brave old hall of ancient Night.
    But ever the dame grew shyer and shyer,
        Seeming with private grief engrossed—
        Grief far from Mosby, housed or lost.

The ruddy embers showed her pale.
    The Soldier did his best devoir:
"Some coffee?—no?—a cracker?—one?"
Cared for her servant—sought to cheer.
    "I know, I know—a cruel war!
        But wait—even Mosby'll eat his bun;
        The Old Hearth—back to it anon!"

But cordial words no balm could bring;
    She sighed, and kept her inward chafe,
And seemed to hate the voice of glee—
Joyless and tearless. Soon he called
    An escort: "See this lady safe
        In yonder house.—Madam, you're free.
        And now for Mosby.—Guide! with me."

("A night-ride, eh") "Tighten your girths!
   But, buglers! not a note from you.
Fling more rails on the fires—a blaze!"
("Sergeant, a feint—I told you so—
   Toward Aldie again, Bivouac, adieu!")
     After the cherry flames they gaze,
     Then back for Mosby through the maze.

The moon looked through the trees, and tipped
   The scabbards with her elfin beam;
The Leader backward cast his glance,
Proud of the cavalcade that came—
   A hundred horses, bay and cream:
     "Major! look how the lads advance—
     Mosby we'll have in the ambulance!"

"No doubt, no doubt:—was that a hare?—
   First catch, then cook; and cook him brown."
"Trust me to catch," the other cried—
"The lady's letter!—a dance, man, dance
   This night is given in Leesburg town!"
     "He'll be there, too!" wheezed out the Guide;
     "That Mosby loves a dance and ride!"

"The lady, ah!—the lady's letter—
   A *lady* then, is in the case,"
Muttered the Major. "Ay, her aunt
Writes her to come by Friday eve
   (To-night), for people of the place,
     At Mosby's last fight jubilant,
     A party give, though table-cheer be scant."

The Major hemmed. "Then this night-ride
   We owe to her?—One lighted house
In a town else dark.—The moths, begar!
Are not quite yet all dead!" "How? how?"
     "A mute, meek, mournful little mouse!—
     Mosby has wiles which subtle are—
     But woman's wiles in wiles of war!"

"Tut, Major! by what craft or guile "
    "Can't tell! but he'll be found in wait.
Softly we enter, say, the town—
Good! pickets post, and all so sure—
    When-crack! the rifles from every gate,
        The Grey-backs fire—dash up and down—
        Each alley unto Mosby known!"

"Now, Major, now—you take dark views
    Of a moonlight night." "Well, well, we'll see,"
And smoked as if each whiff were gain.
The other mused; then sudden asked,
    "What would you do in grand decree?"
        "I'd beat, if I could, Lee's armies—then
        Send constables after Mosby's men."

"Ay, ay!—you're odd." The moon sailed up;
    On through the shadowy land they went.
"Names must be made and printed be!"
Hummed the blithe Colonel. "Doc, your flask!
    Major, I drink to your good content.
        My pipe is out—enough for me!
        One's buttons shine—does Mosby see?

"But what comes here?" A man from the front
    Reported a tree athwart the road.
"Go round it, then, no time to bide;
All right go on! Were one to stay
    For each distrust of a nervous mood,
        Long miles we'd make in this our ride
        Through Mosby-land.—On! with the Guide!"

Then sportful to the Surgeon turned:
    "Green sashes hardly serve by night!"
"Nor bullets nor bottles," the Major sighed,
"Against these moccasin-snakes—such foes
    As seldom come to solid fight:
        They kill and vanish; through grass they glide;
        Devil take Mosby!"—his horse here shied.

"Hold! look—the tree, like a dragged balloon;
   A globe of leaves—some trickery here;
My nag is right—best now be shy."
A movement was made, a hubbub and snarl;
   Little was plain—they blindly steer.
      The Pleiads, as from ambush sly,
      Peep out—Mosby's men in the sky!

As restive they turn, how sore they feel,
   And cross, and sleepy, and full of spleen,
And curse the war. "Fools, North and South!"
Said one right out. "O for a bed!
   O now to drop in this woodland green!"
      He drops as the syllables leave his mouth
      Mosby speaks from the undergrowth—

Speaks in a volley! out jets the flame!
   Men fall from their saddles like plums from trees;
Horses take fright, reins tangle and bind;
"Steady—dismount—form—and into the wood!"
   They go, but find what scarce can please:
      Their steeds have been tied in the field behind,
      And Mosby's men are off like the wind.

Sound the recall! vain to pursue—
   The enemy scatters in wilds he knows,
To reunite in his own good time;
And, to follow, they need divide—
   To come lone and lost on crouching foes;
      Maple ind hemlock, beech and lime,
      Are Mosby's confederates, share the crime.

"Major," burst in a bugler small,
   "The fellow we left in Loudon grass—
Sir Slyboots with the inward bruise,
His voice I heard—the very same—
   Some watchword in the ambush pass;
      Ay, sir, we had him in his shoes—
      We caught him—Mosby—but to lose!"

"Go, go!—these saddle-dreamers! Well,
   And here's another.—Cool, sir, cool!"
"Major, I saw them mount and sweep,
And one was bumped, or I mistake,
   And in the skurry dropped his wool."
      "A wig! go fetch it:—the lads need sleep;
      They'll next see Mosby in a sheep!

"Come, come, fall back! reform your ranks—
   All's jackstraws here! Where's Captain Morn?—
We've parted like boats in a raging tide!
But stay—the Colonel—did he charge?
   And comes he there? 'Tis streak of dawn;
      Mosby is off, the woods are wide—
      Hist! there's a groan—this crazy ride!"

As they searched for the fallen, the dawn grew chill;
   They lay in the dew: "Ah, hurt much, Mink?
And-yes-the Colonel!" Dead! but so calm
That death seemed nothing—even death,
   The thing we deem every thing heart can think;
      Amid wilding roses that shed their balm,
      Careless of Mosby he lay—in a charm!

The Major took him by the hand—
   Into the friendly clasp it bled
(A ball through heart and hand he rued):
"Good-bye!" and gazed with humid glance;
   Then in a hollow revery said,
      "The weakest thing is lustihood;
      But Mosby"—and he checked his mood.

"Where's the advance?—cut off, by heaven!
   Come, Surgeon, how with your wounded there?"
"The ambulance will carry all."
"Well, get them in; we go to camp.
   Seven prisoners gone? for the rest have care."
      Then to himself, "This grief is gall;
      That Mosby!—I'll cast a silver ball!"

"Ho!" turning—"Captain Cloud, you mind
    The place where the escort went—so shady?
Go, search every closet low and high,
And barn, and bin, and hidden bower—
    Every covert—find that lady!
      And yet I may misjudge her—ay,
      Women (like Mosby) mystify.

"We'll see. Ay, Captain, go—with speed!
    Surround and search; each living thing
Secure; that done, await us where
We last turned off. Stay! fire the cage
    If the birds be flown." By the cross-road spring
      The bands rejoined; no word; the glare
      Told all. Had Mosby plotted there?

The weary troop that wended now—
    Hardly it seemed the same that pricked
Forth to the forest from the camp:
Foot-sore horses, jaded men;
    Every backbone felt as nicked,
      Each eye dim as a sick-room lamp,
      All faces stamped with Mosby's stamp.

In order due the Major rode—
    Chaplain and Surgeon on either hand;
A riderless horse a negro led;
In a wagon the blanketed sleeper went;
    Then the ambulance with the bleeding band;
      And, an emptied oat-bag on each head,
      Went Mosby's men, and marked the dead.

What gloomed them? what so cast them down,
    And changed the cheer that late they took,
As double-guarded now they rode
Between the files of moody men?
    Some sudden consciousness they brook,
      Or dread the sequel. That night's blood
      Disturbed even Mosby's brotherhood.

The flagging horses stumbled at roots,
 Floundered in mires, or clinked the stones;
No ride spake except aside;
But the wounded cramped in the ambulance,
 It was horror to hear their groans—
  Jerked along in the woodland ride,
  While Mosby's clan their revery hide.

The Hospital Steward—even he—
 Who on the sleeper kept his glance,
Was changed; late bright-black beard and eye
Looked now hearse-black; his heavy heart,
 Like his fagged mare, no more could dance;
  His grape was now a raisin dry:
  'Tis Mosby's homily—*Man must die.*

The amber sunset flushed the camp
 As on the hill their eyes they fed;
The pickets dumb looks at the wagon dart;
A handkerchief waves from the bannered tent—
 As white, alas! the face of the dead:
  Who shall the withering news impart?
  The bullet of Mosby goes through heart to heart!

They buried him where the lone ones lie
 (Lone sentries shot on midnight post)—
A green-wood grave-yard hid from ken,
Where sweet-fern flings an odor nigh—
 Yet held in fear for the gleaming ghost!
  Though the bride should see threescore and ten,
  She will dream of Mosby and his men.

Now halt the verse, and turn aside—
 The cypress falls athwart the way;
No joy remains for bard to sing;
And heaviest dole of all is this,
 That other hearts shall be as gay
  As hers that now no more shall spring:
  To Mosby-land the dirges cling.

LEE IN THE CAPITOL[x]
(APRIL, 1866)

Hard pressed by numbers in his strait
    Rebellion's soldier-chief no more contends—
Feels that the hour is come of Fate,
    Lays down one sword, and widened warfare ends.
The captain who fierce armies led
Becomes a quiet seminary's head—
Poor as his privates, earns his bread.
In studious cares and aims engrossed,
    Strives to forget Stuart and Stonewall dead—
Comrades and cause, station and riches lost,
    And all the ills that flock when fortune's fled.
No word he breathes of vain lament,
    Mute to reproach, nor hears applause—
His doom accepts, perforce content,
    And acquiesces in asserted laws;
Secluded now would pass his life,
And leave to time the sequel of the strife.
    But missives from the Senators ran;
Not that they now would gaze upon a swordless foe,
And power made powerless and brought low:
    Reasons of state, 'tis claimed, require the man.
Demurring not, promptly he comes
By ways which show the blackened homes,
    And—last—the seat no more his own,
But Honor's; patriot grave-yards fill
The forfeit slopes of that patrician hill,
    And fling a shroud on Arlington.
The oaks ancestral all are low;
No more from the porch his glance shall go
Ranging the varied landscape o'er,
Far as the looming Dome—no more.
One look he gives, then turns aside,
Solace he summons from his pride:
"So be it! They await me now
Who wrought this stinging overthrow;
They wait me; not as on the day

Of Pope's impelled retreat in disarray—
By me impelled—when toward yon Dome
The clouds of war came rolling home."
The burst, the bitterness was spent,
The heart-burst bitterly turbulent,
And on he fared.

In nearness now
He marks the Capitol—a show
Lifted in amplitude, and set
With standards flushed with the glow of Richmond yet;
    Trees and green terraces sleep below.
Through the clear air, in sunny light,
The marble dazes—a temple white.

Intrepid soldier! had his blade been drawn
For yon starred flag, never as now
Bid to the Senate-house had he gone,
But freely, and in pageant borne,
As when brave numbers without number, massed,
Plumed the broad way, and pouring passed—
Bannered, beflowered—between the shores
Of faces, and the dinn'd huzzas,
And balconies kindling at the sabre-flash,
'Mid roar of drums and guns, and cymbal-crash,
While Grant and Sherman shone in blue—
Close of the war and victory's long review.

Yet pride at hand still aidful swelled,
And tip the hard ascent he held.
The meeting follows. In his mien
The victor and the vanquished both are seen—
All that he is, and what he late had been.
Awhile, with curious eyes they scan
The Chief who led invasion's van—
Allied by family to one,
Founder of the Arch the Invader warred upon:
Who looks at Lee must think of Washington;
In pain must think, and hide the thought,
So deep with grievous meaning it is fraught.

Secession in her soldier shows
Silent and patient; and they feel
      (Developed even in just success)
Dim inklings of a hazy future steal;
      Their thoughts their questions well express:
"Does the sad South still cherish hate?
Freely will Southern men with Northern mate?
The blacks—should we our arm withdraw,
Would that betray them? some distrust your law.
And how if foreign fleets should come—
Would the South then drive her wedges home?"
And more hereof. The Virginian sees—
Replies to such anxieties.
Discreet his answers run—appear
Briefly straightforward, coldly clear.

"If now," the Senators, closing, say,
"Aught else remain, speak out, we pray."
Hereat he paused; his better heart
Strove strongly then; prompted a worthier part
Than coldly to endure his doom.
Speak out? Ay, speak, and for the brave,
Who else no voice or proxy have;
Frankly their spokesman here become,
And the flushed North from her own victory save.
That inspiration overrode—
Hardly it quelled the galling load
Of personal ill. The inner feud
He, self-contained, a while withstood;
They waiting. In his troubled eye
Shadows from clouds unseen they spy;
They could not mark within his breast
The pang which pleading thought oppressed:
He spoke, nor felt the bitterness die.

"My word is given—it ties my sword;
Even were banners still abroad,
Never could I strive in arms again
While you, as fit, that pledge retain.
Our cause I followed, stood in field and gate—

All's over now, and now I follow Fate.
But this is naught. A People call—
A desolated land, and all
The brood of ills that press so sore,
The natural offspring of this civil war,
Which ending not in fame, such as might rear
Fitly its sculptured trophy here,
Yields harvest large of doubt and dread
To all who have the heart and head
To feel and know. How shall I speak?
Thoughts knot with thoughts, and utterance check.
Before my eyes there swims a haze,
Through mists departed comrades gaze—
First to encourage, last that shall upbraid!
How shall I speak? The South would fain
Feel peace, have quiet law again—
Replant the trees for homestead-shade.

    You ask if she recants: she yields.
Nay, and would more; would blend anew,
As the bones of the slain in her forests do,
Bewailed alike by us and you.

    A voice comes out from those charnel-fields,
A plaintive yet unheeded one:
'Died all in vain? both sides undone?'
Push not your triumph; do not urge
Submissiveness beyond the verge.
Intestine rancor would you bide,
Nursing eleven sliding daggers in your side?
Far from my thought to school or threat;
I speak the things which hard beset.
Where various hazards meet the eyes,
To elect in magnanimity is wise.
Reap victory's fruit while sound the core;
What sounder fruit than re-established law?
I know your partial thoughts do press
Solely on us for war's unhappy stress;
But weigh—consider—look at all,
And broad anathema you'll recall.
The censor's charge I'll not repeat,
That meddlers kindled the war's white heat—

Vain intermeddlers or malign,
Both of the palm and of the pine;
I waive the thought—which never can be rife—
Common's the crime in every civil strife:
But this I feel, that North and South were driven
By Fate to arms. For *our* unshriven,
    As never may any be again—
All those who stemmed Secession's pride
But at last were swept bv the urgent tide
    Into the chasm. I know their pain.
A story here may be applied:
"In Moorish lands there lived a maid
    Brought to confess by vow the creed
    Of Christians. Fain would priests persuade
That now she must approve by deed
    The faith she kept. "What deed?" she asked.
"Your old sire leave, nor deem it sin,
    And come with us." Still more they tasked
The sad one: "If heaven you'd win—
Far from the burning pit withdraw,
Then must you learn to bate your kin,
    Yea, side against them—such the law,
For Moor and Christian are at war."
"Then will I never quit my sire,
But here with him through every trial go,
Nor leave him though in flames below—
God help me in his fire!"
So in the South; vain every plea
'Gainst Nature's strong fidelity;
    True to the home and to the heart,
Throngs cast their lot with kith and kin,
    Foreboding, cleaved to the natural part—
Was this the unforgivable sin?
These noble spirits are yet yours to win.
Shall the great North go Sylla's way?
Proscribe? prolong the evil day?
Confirm the curse? infix the hate?
In Union's name forever alienate?

From reason who can urge the plea—
Freemen conquerors of the free?
When blood returns to the shrunken vein,
Shall the wound of the Nation bleed again?
Well may the wars wan thought supply,
And kill the kindling of the hopeful eye,
Unless you do what even kings have done
In leniency—unless you shun
To copy Europe in her worst estate—
Avoid the tyranny you reprobate."

He ceased. His earnestness unforeseen
Moved, but not swayed their former mien;
    And they dismissed him. Forth he went
Through vaulted walks in lengthened line
Like porches erst upon the Palatine:
    Historic reveries their lesson lent,
    The Past tier shadow through the Future sent.

But no. Brave though the Soldier, grave his plea—
    Catching the light in the future's skies,
Instinct disowns each darkening prophecy:
    Faith in America never dies;
Heaven shall the end ordained fulfill.
We march with Providence cheery still.

A MEDITATION

How often in the years that close,
    When truce had stilled the sieging gun,
The soldiers, mounting on their works,
    With mutual curious glance have run
From face to face along the fronting show,
And kinsman spied, or friend—even in a foe.

What thoughts conflicting then were shared,
    While sacred tenderness perforce
Welled from the heart and wet the eye;

And something of a strange remorse
Rebelled against the sanctioned sin of blood,
And Christian wars of natural brotherhood.

Then stirred the god within the breast—
    The witness that is man's at birth;
A deep misgiving undermined
    Each plea and subterfuge of earth;
They felt in that rapt pause, with warning rife,
Horror and anguish for the civil strife.

Of North or South they reeked not then,
    Warm passion cursed the cause of war:
Can Africa pay back this blood
    Spilt on Potomac's shore?
Yet doubts, as pangs, were vain the strife to stay,
And hands that fain had clasped again could slay.

How frequent in the camp was seen
    The herald from the hostile one,
A guest and frank companion there
    When the proud formal talk was done;
The pipe of peace was smoked even 'mid the war,
And fields in Mexico again fought o'er.

In Western battle long they lay
    So near opposed in trench or pit,
That foeman unto foeman called
    As men who screened in tavern sit:
"You bravely fight" each to the other said—
"Toss us a biscuit!" o'er the wall it sped.

And pale on those same slopes, a boy—
    A stormer, bled in noonday glare;
No aid the Blue-coats then could bring,
    He cried to them who nearest were,
And out there came 'mid howling shot and shell
A daring foe who him befriended well.

Mark the great Captains on both sides,
    The soldiers with the broad renown—

They all were messmates on the Hudson's marge,
    Beneath one roof they laid them down;
And, free from hate in many an after pass,
Strove as in school-boy rivalry of the class.

A darker side there is; but doubt
    In Nature's charity hovers there:
If men for new agreement yearn,
    Then old upbraiding best forbear:
"The South's the sinner!" Well, so let it be;
But shall the North sin worse, and stand the Pharisee?

O, now that brave men yield the sword,
    Mine be the manful soldier-view;
By how much more they boldly warred,
    By so much more is mercy due:
When Vicksburg fell, and the moody files marched out,
Silent the victors stood, scorning to raise a shout.

NOTES

Note[a]

The gloomy lull of the early part of the winter of 1860–1, seeming big with final disaster to our institutions, affected some minds that believed them to constitute one of the great hopes of mankind, much as the eclipse which came over the promise of the first French Revolution affected kindred natures, throwing them for the time into doubts and misgivings universal.

Note[b]

'The terrible Stone Fleet, on a mission as pitiless as the granite that freights it, sailed this morning from Port Royal, and before two days are past will have made Charleston an inland city. The ships are all old whalers, and cost the Government from \$2500 to \$5000 each. Some of them were once famous ships.'—(From Newspaper Correspondence of the day.)

Sixteen vessels were accordingly sunk on the bar at the river entrance. Their names were as follows:—

Amazon	Leonidas
America	Maria Theresa
American	Potomac
Archer	Rebecca Simms
Courier	L. C. Richmond
Fortune	Robin Hood
Herald	Tenedos
Kensington	William Lee

All accounts seem to agree that the object proposed was not accomplished. The channel is even said to have become ultimately benefited by the means employed to obstruct it.

Note[c]

The *Temeraire*, that storied ship of the old English fleet, and the subject of the well-known painting by Turner, commends itself to the mind seeking for some one craft to stand for the poetic ideal of those great historic wooden warships, whose gradual displacement is lamented by none more than by regularly educated navy officers, and of all nations.

Note[d]

Some of the cannon of old times, especially the brass ones, unlike the more effective ordnance of the present day, were cast in shapes which Cellini might have designed, were gracefully enchased, generally with the arms of the country. A few of them—field-pieces—captured in our earlier wars, are preserved in arsenals and navy-yards.

Note[e]

Whatever just military criticism, favorable or otherwise, has at any time been made upon General McClellan's campaigns, will stand. But if, during the excitement of the conflict, aught was spread abroad tending to unmerited disparagement of the man, it must necessarily die out, though not perhaps without leaving some traces, which may or may not prove enduring. Some there are whose votes aided in the re-election of Abraham Lincoln, who yet believed, and retain the belief, that General McClellan, to say the least, always proved himself a patriotic and honorable soldier. The feeling which surviving comrades entertain for their

late commander is one which, from its passion, is susceptible of
versified representation, and such it receives.

Note[f]

At Antietam Stonewall Jackson led one wing of Lee's army,
consequently sharing that day in whatever may be deemed to
have been the fortunes of his superior.

Note[g]

Admiral Porter is a son of the late Commander Porter, commander of the frigate *Essex* on that Pacific cruise which ended in
the desperate fight off Valparaiso with the English frigates *Cherub*
and *Phoebe*, in the year 1814.

Note[h]

Among numerous head-stones or monuments on Cemetery
Hill, marred or destroyed by the enemy's concentrated fire, was
one, somewhat conspicuous, of a Federal officer killed before
Richmond in 1862.

On the 4th of July, 1865, the Gettysburg National Cemetery,
on the same height with the original burial-ground, was consecrated, and the corner-stone laid of a commemorative pile.

Note[i]

'I dare not write the horrible and inconceivable atrocities
committed,' says Froissart, in alluding to the remarkable sedition
in France during his time. The like may be hinted of some proceedings of the draft-rioters.

Note[j]

Although the month was November, the day was in character
an October one—cool, clear, bright, intoxicatingly invigorating;
one of those days peculiar to the ripest hours of our American
autumn. This weather must have had much to do with the spontaneous enthusiasm which seized the troops—an enthusiasm aided, doubtless, by glad thoughts of the victory of Lookout Mountain won the day previous, and also by the elation attending the
capture, after a fierce struggle, of the long ranges of rifle-pits at
the mountain's base, where orders for the time should have stopped
the advance. But there and then it was that the army took the bit

between its teeth, and ran away with the generals to the victory commemorated. General Grant, at Culpepper, a few weeks prior to crossing the Rapidan for the Wilderness, expressed to a visitor his impression of the impulse and the spectacle: Said he, 'I never saw anything like it:' language which seems curiously under-toned, considering its application; but from the taciturn Commander it was equivalent to a superlative or hyperbole from the talkative.

The height of the Ridge, according to the account at hand, varies along its length from six to seven hundred feet above the plain; it slopes at an angle of about forty-five degrees.

Note[k]

The great Parrott gun, planted in the marshes of James Island, and employed in the prolonged, though at times intermitted bombardment of Charleston, was known among our soldiers as the Swamp Angel.

St. Michael's, characterized by its venerable tower, was the historic and aristocratic church of the town.

Note[l]

Among the North-western regiments there would seem to have been more than one which carried a living eagle as an added ensign. The bird commemorated here was, according to the account, borne aloft on a perch beside the standard; went through successive battles and campaigns; was more than once under the surgeon's hands; and at the close of the contest found honorable repose in the capital of Wisconsin, from which state he had gone to the wars.

Note[m]

The late Major-General McPherson, commanding the Army of the Tennessee, a native of Ohio and a West Pointer, was one of the foremost spirits of the war. Young, though a veteran; hardy, intrepid, sensitive in honour, full of engaging qualities, with manly beauty, possessed of genius, a favourite with the army, and with Grant and Sherman. Both Generals have generously acknowledged their professional obligations to the able engineer and admirable soldier, their subordinate and junior.

In an informed account written by the Achilles to this Sarpe-don, he says:

"On that day we avenged his death. Near twenty-two hun-dred of the enemy's dead remained on the ground when night closed upon the scene of action."

It is significant of the scale on which the war was waged that the engagement thus written of goes solely (so far as can be learned) under the vague designation of one of the battles before Atlanta.

Note[n]

This piece was written while yet the reports were coming north of Sherman's homeward advance from Savannah. It is need-less to point out its purely dramatic character.

Though the sentiment ascribed in the beginning of the sec-ond stanza must, in the present reading, suggest the historic trag-edy of the 14th of April, nevertheless, as intimated, it was written prior to that event, and without any distinct application in the writer's mind. After consideration, it is allowed to remain.

Few need be reminded that, by the less intelligent classes of the South, Abraham Lincoln, by nature the most kindly of men, was regarded as a monster wantonly warring upon liberty. He stood for the personification of tyrannic power. Each Union sol-dier was called a Lincolnite.

Undoubtedly Sherman, in the devastation he inflicted after leaving Atlanta, acted not in contravention of orders; and all, in a military point of view, is by military judges deemed to have been expedient and nothing can abate General Sherman's shining re-nown; his claims to it rest on no single campaign. Still, there are those who cannot but contrast some of the scenes enacted in Georgia and the Carolinas, and also in the Shenandoah, with a circumstance in a great civil war of heathen antiquity. Plutarch relates that in a military council held by Pompey and the chiefs of that party which stood for the Commonwealth, it was decided that under no plea should any city be sacked that was subject to the people of Rome. There was this difference, however, between the Roman civil conflict and the American one. The war of Pompey and Caesar divided the Roman people promiscuously; that of the North and South ran a frontier line between what for the time were distinct communities or nations. In this circumstance, possibly, and some others, may be found both the cause and the justification of some of the sweeping measures adopted.

Note°

At this period of excitement the thought was by some passionately welcomed that the Presidential successor had been raised up by heaven to wreak vengeance on the South. The idea originated in the remembrance that Andrew Johnson by birth belonged to that class of Southern whites who never cherished love for the dominant one; that he was a citizen of Tennessee, where the contest at times and in places had been close and bitter as a Middle Age feud; that himself and family had been hardly treated by the Secessionists.

But the expectations built hereon (if, indeed, ever soberly entertained), happily for the country, have not been verified.

Likewise, the feeling which would have held the entire South chargeable with the crime of one exceptional assassin, this too has died away with the natural excitement of the hour.

Note^P

The incident on which this piece is based is narrated in a newspaper account of the battle to be found in the "Rebellion Record." During the disaster to the National forces on the first day, a brigade on the extreme left found itself isolated. The perils it encountered are given in detail. Among others, the following sentences occur—

'Under cover of the fire from the bluffs, the rebels rushed down, crossing the ford, and in a moment were seen forming this side the creek in open fields, and within close musket-range. Their colour-bearers stepped defiantly to the front as the engagement opened furiously; the rebels pouring in sharp, quick volleys of musketry, and their batteries above continuing to support them with a destructive fire. Our sharpshooters wanted to pick off the audacious rebel colour-bearers, but Colonel Stuart interposed: "No, no, they're too brave fellows to be killed."'

Note^q

According to a report of the Secretary of War, there were on the first day of March, 1865, 965,000 men on the army pay-rolls.

Of these, some 200,000—artillery, cavalry, and infantry—made up from the larger portion of the veterans of Grant and Sherman, marched by the President. The total number of Union troops enlisted during the war was 2,668,000.

Note[r]

For a month or two after the completion of peace, some thousands of released captives from the military prisons of the North, natives of all parts of the South, passed through the city of New York, sometimes waiting farther transportation for days, during which interval they wandered penniless about the streets, or lay in their worn and patched grey uniforms under the trees of the Battery, near the barracks where they were lodged and fed. They were transported and provided for at the charge of the Government.

Note[s]

Shortly prior to the evacuation of Petersburg, the enemy, with a view to ultimate repossession, interred some of his heavy guns in the same field with his dead, and with every circumstance calculated to deceive. Subsequently the negroes exposed the stratagem.

Note[t]

The records of Northern colleges attest what numbers of our noblest youth went from them to the battle-field. Southern members of the same classes arrayed themselves on the side of Secession; while Southern seminaries contributed large quotas. Of all these, what numbers marched who never returned except on the shield.

Note[u]

Written prior to the founding of the National Cemetery at Andersonville, where 15,000 of the re-interred captives now sleep, each beneath his personal head-board, inscribed from records found in the prison hospital. Some hundreds rest apart and without name. A glance at the published pamphlet containing the list of the buried at Andersonville conveys a feeling mournfully impressive. Seventy-four large double-columned pages in fine print. Looking through them is like getting lost among the old turbaned head-stones and cypresses in the interminable Black Forest of Scutari, over against Constantinople.

Note[v]

In one of Kilpatrick's earlier cavalry fights near Aldie, a Colonel who, being under arrest, had been temporarily deprived of his sword, nevertheless, unarmed, insisted upon charging at the head of his men, which he did, and the onset proved victorious.

Note[w]

Certain of Mosby's followers, on the charge of being unlicensed foragers or fighters, being hung by order of a Union cavalry commander, the Partisan promptly retaliated in the woods. In turn, this also was retaliated, it is said. To what extent such deplorable proceedings were carried it is not easy to learn.

South of the Potomac in Virginia and within a gallop of the Long Bridge at Washington, is the confine of a country, in some places wild, which throughout the war it was unsafe for a Union man to traverse except with an armed escort. This was the chase of Mosby, the scene of many of his exploits or those of his men. In the heart of this region at least one fortified camp was maintained by our cavalry, and from time to time expeditions were made therefrom. Owing to the nature of the country and the embittered feeling of its inhabitants, many of these expeditions ended disastrously. Such results were helped by the exceeding cunning of the enemy, born of his woodcraft, and, in some instances, by undue confidence on the part of our men. A body of cavalry, starting from camp with the view of breaking up a nest of rangers, and absent say three days, would return with a number of their own forces killed and wounded (ambushed), without being able to retaliate farther than by foraging on the country, destroying a house or two reported to be haunts of the guerillas, or capturing non-combatants accused of being secretly active in their behalf.

In the verse the name of Mosby is invested with some of those associations with which the popular mind is familiar. But facts do not warrant the belief that every clandestine attack of men who passed for Mosby's was made under his eye, or even by his knowledge.

In partisan warfare he proved himself shrewd, able, and enterprising, and always a wary fighter. He stood well in the confi-

dence of his superior officers, and was employed by them at times
in furtherance of important movements. To our wounded on more
than one occasion he showed considerate kindness. Officers and
civilians captured by forces under his immediate command were,
so long as remaining under his orders, treated with civility. These
things are well known to those personally familiar with the irreg-
ular fighting in Virginia.

Battle-Pieces

Note[x]

Among those summoned during the spring just passed to
appear before the Reconstruction Committee of Congress was
Robert E. Lee. His testimony is deeply interesting, both in itself
and as coming from him. After various questions had been put
and briefly answered, these words were addressed to him:—

"If there be any other matter about which you wish to speak
on this occasion, do so freely." Waiving this invitation, he re-
sponded by a short personal explanation of some point in a previous answer, and after a few more brief questions and replies, the
interview closed.

In the verse a poetical liberty has been ventured. Lee is not
only represented as responding to the invitation, but also as at last
renouncing his cold reserve, doubtless the cloak to feelings more
or less poignant. If for such freedom warrant be necessary, the
speeches in ancient histories, not to speak of those in Shakespeare's historic plays, may not unfitly perhaps be cited.

The character of the original measures proposed about this
time in the National Legislature for the treatment of the (as yet)
Congressionally excluded South, and the spirit in which these
measures were advocated—these are circumstances which it is
fairly supposable would have deeply influenced the thoughts,
whether spoken or withheld, of a Southerner placed in the position of Lee before the Reconstruction Committee.

SUPPLEMENT

Were I fastidiously anxious for the symmetry of this book, it
would close with the notes. But the times are such that patriotism—not free from solicitude—urges a claim overriding all literary scruples.

It is more than a year since the memorable surrender, but

events have not yet rounded themselves into completion. Not justly can we complain of this. There has been an upheaval affecting the basis of things; to altered circumstances complicated adaptations are to be made; there are difficulties great and novel. But is Reason still waiting for Passion to spend itself? We have sung of the soldiers and sailors, but who shall hymn the politicians?

In view of the infinite desirableness of Re-establishment, and considering that, so far as feeling is concerned, it depends not mainly on the temper in which the South regards the North, but rather conversely; one who never was a blind adherent feels constrained to submit some thoughts, counting on the indulgence of his countrymen.

And, first, it may be said that, if among the feelings and opinions growing immediately out of a great civil convulsion, there are any which time shall modify or do away, they are presumably those of a less temperate and charitable cast.

There seems no reason why patriotism and narrowness should go together, or why intellectual impartiality should be confounded with political trimming, or why serviceable truth should keep cloistered because not partisan. Yet the work of Reconstruction, if admitted to be feasible at all, demands little but common sense and Christian charity. Little but these? These are much.

Some of us are concerned because as yet the South shows no penitence. But what exactly do we mean by this? Since down to the close of the war she never confessed any for braving it, the only penitence now left her is that which springs solely from the sense of discomfiture; and since this evidently would be a contrition hypocritical, it would be unworthy in us to demand it. Certain it is that penitence, in the sense of voluntary humiliation, will never be displayed. Nor does this afford just ground for unreserved condemnation. It is enough, for all practical purposes, if the South have been taught by the terrors of civil war to feel that Secession, like Slavery, is against Destiny; that both now lie buried in one grave; that her fate is linked with ours; and that together we comprise the Nation.

The clouds of heroes who battled for the Union it is needless to eulogize here. But how of the soldiers on the other side? And when of a free community we name the soldiers, we thereby name the people. It was in subserviency to the slave-interest that Secession was plotted; but it was under the plea, plausibly urged, that certain inestimable rights guaranteed by the Constitution were directly menaced that the people of the South were cajoled into revolution. Through the arts of the conspirators and the perversity of fortune, the most sensitive love of liberty was entrapped into the support of a war whose implied end was the erecting in our advanced century of an Anglo-American empire based upon the systematic degradation of man.

Spite this clinging reproach, however, signal military virtues and achievements have conferred upon the Confederate arms historic fame, and upon certain of the commanders a renown extending beyond the sea—a renown which we of the North could not suppress, even if we would. In personal character, also, not a few of the military leaders of the South enforce forbearance; the memory of others the North refrains from disparaging; and some, with more or less reluctance, she can respect. Posterity, sympathizing with our convictions, but removed from our passions, may perhaps go farther here. If George IV could, out of the graceful instinct of a gentleman, raise an honourable monument in the great fane of Christendom over the remains of the enemy of his dynasty, Charles Edward, the invader of England and victor in the rout at Preston Pans—upon whose head the king's ancestor but one reign removed had set a price—is it probable that the grandchildren of General Grant will pursue with rancor, or slur by sour neglect, the memory of Stonewall Jackson?

But the South herself is not wanting in recent histories and biographies which record the deeds of her chieftains—writings freely published at the North by loyal houses, widely read here, and with a deep though saddened interest. By students of the war such works are hailed as welcome accessories, and tending to the completeness of the record.

Supposing a happy issue of present perplexities, then, in the generation next to come, Southerners there will be yielding allegiance to the Union, feeling all their interests bound up in it, and yet cherishing unrebuked that kind of feeling for the memory of the soldiers of the fallen Confederacy that Burns, Scott, and the Ettrick Shepherd felt for the memory of the gallant clansmen ruined through their fidelity to the Stuarts—a feeling whose passion was tempered by the poetry imbuing it, and which in no wise affected their loyalty to the Georges, and which, it may be added, indirectly contributed excellent things to literature.

But, setting this view aside, dishonourable would it be in the South were she willing to abandon to shame the memory of brave men who with signal personal disinterestedness warred in her behalf, though from motives, as we believe, so deplorably astray.

Patriotism is not baseness, neither is it inhumanity. The mourners who this summer bear flowers to the mounds of the Virginian and Georgian dead are, in their domestic bereavement and proud affection, as sacred in the eye of Heaven as are those who go with similar offerings of tender grief and love into the cemeteries of our Northern martyrs. And yet, in one aspect, how needless to point that contrast.

Cherishing such sentiments, it will hardly occasion surprise that, in looking over the battle-pieces in the foregoing collection, I have been tempted to withdraw or modify some of them, fearful lest in presenting, though but dramatically and by way of a poetic record, the passions and epithets of civil war, I might be contributing to a bitterness which every sensible American must wish at an end. So, too, with the emotion of victory as reproduced on some pages, and particularly toward the close. It should not be construed into an exultation misapplied—an exultation as ungenerous as unwise, and made to minister, however indirectly, to that kind of censoriousness too apt to be produced in certain natures by success after trying reverses. Zeal is not of necessity religion, neither is it always of the same essence with poetry or patriotism.

There were excesses which marked the conflict, most of which are perhaps inseparable from a civil strife so intense and prolonged, and involving warfare in some border countries new and imperfectly civilized. Barbarities also there were, for which the Southern people collectively can hardly be held responsible, though perpetrated by ruffians in their name. But surely other qualities— exalted ones—courage and fortitude matchless, were likewise displayed, and largely; and justly may these be held the characteristic traits, and not the former.

In this view, what Northern writer, however patriotic, but must revolt from acting on paper a part any way akin to that of the live dog to the dead lion; and yet it is right to rejoice for our triumph, so far as it may justly imply an advance for our whole country and for humanity.

Let it be held no reproach to any one that he pleads for reasonable consideration for our late enemies, now stricken down and unavoidably debarred, for the time, from speaking through authorized agencies for themselves. Nothing has been urged here in the foolish hope of conciliating those men—few in number, we trust—who have resolved never to be reconciled to the Union. On such hearts everything is thrown away except it be religious commiseration, and the sincerest. Yet let them call to mind that unhappy Secessionist, not a military man, who with impious alacrity fired the first shot of the Civil War at Sumter, and a little more than four years after fired the last one into his own heart at Richmond.

Noble was the gesture into which patriotic passion surprised the people in a utilitarian time and country; yet the glory of the war falls short of its pathos—a pathos which now at last ought to disarm all animosity.

How many and earnest thoughts still rise, and how hard to repress them. We feel what past years have been, and years, unretarded years, shall come. May we all have moderation; may we all show candor. Though, perhaps, nothing could ultimately have averted the strife, and though to treat of human actions is to deal wholly with second causes, nevertheless, let us not cover up or try to extenuate what, humanly speaking, is the truth—namely, that those unfraternal denunciations, continued through years, and which at last inflamed to deeds that ended in bloodshed, were reciprocal; and that, had the preponderating strength and the prospect of its unlimited increase lain on the other side, on ours might have lain those actions which now in our late opponents we stigmatize in the name of Rebellion. As frankly let us own— what it would be unbecoming to parade were foreigners concerned—that our triumph was won not more by skill and bravery than by superior resources and crushing numbers; that it was a triumph, too, over a people for years politically misled by designing men, and also by some honestly-erring men, who from their position could not have been otherwise than broadly influential; a people who, though, indeed, they sought to perpetuate the curse of slavery, and even extend it, were not the authors of it, but (less fortunate, not less righteous than we) were the fated inheritors; a people who, having a like origin with ourselves, share essentially in whatever worthy qualities we may possess. No one can add to the lasting reproach which hopeless defeat has now cast upon Secession by withholding the recognition of these verities.

Surely we ought to take it to heart that that kind of pacification, based upon principles operating equally all over the land, which lovers of their country yearn for, and which our arms, though signally triumphant, did not bring about, and which law-making, however anxious, or energetic, or repressive, never by itself can achieve, may yet be largely aided by generosity of sentiment public and private. Some revisionary legislation and adaptive is indispensable; but with this should harmoniously work another kind of prudence, not unallied with entire magnanimity. Benevolence and policy—Christianity and Machiavelli—dissuade from penal severities toward the subdued. Abstinence here is as obligatory as considerate care for our unfortunate fellow-men late in bonds, and, if observed, would equally prove to be wise forecast. The great qualities of the South, those attested in the War, we can perilously alienate, or we may make them nationally available at need.

The blacks, in their infant pupilage to freedom, appeal to the sympathies of every humane mind. The paternal guardianship which for the interval Government exercises over them was prompted equally by duty and benevolence. Yet such kindliness should not be allowed to exclude kindliness to communities who stand nearer to us in nature. For the future of the freed slaves we may well be concerned; but the future of the whole country, involving the future of the blacks, urges a paramount claim upon our anxiety. Effective benignity, like the Nile, is not narrow in its bounty, and true policy is always broad. To be sure, it is vain to seek to glide, with moulded words, over the difficulties of the situation. And for them who are neither partisans, nor enthusiasts, nor theorists, nor cynics, there are some doubts not readily to be solved. And there are fears. Why is not the cessation of war now at length attended with the settled calm of peace? Wherefore in a clear sky do we still turn our eyes toward the South, as the Neapolitan, months after the eruption, turns his toward Vesuvius? Do we dread lest the repose may be deceptive? In the recent convulsion has the crater but shifted? Let us revere that sacred uncertainty which forever impends over men and nations. Those of us who always abhorred slavery as an atheistical iniquity, gladly we join in the exulting chorus of humanity over its downfall. But we should remember that emancipation was accomplished not by deliberate legislation; only through agonized violence could so mighty a result be effected. In our natural solicitude to confirm the benefit of liberty to the blacks, let us forbear from measures of dubious constitutional rightfulness toward our white countrymen—measures of a nature to provoke, among other of the last evils, exterminating hatred of race toward race. In imagination let us place ourselves in the unprecedented position of the Southerners—their position as regards the millions of ignorant manumitted slaves in their midst, for whom some of us now claim the suffrage. Let us be Christians toward our fellow-whites, as well as philanthropists toward the blacks, our fellow-men. In all things, and toward all, we are enjoined to do as we would be done by. Nor should we forget that benevolent desires, after passing a certain point, cannot undertake their own fulfilment without incurring the risk of evils beyond those sought to be remedied. Something may well be left to the graduated care of future legislation, and to heaven. In one point of view the coexistence of the two races in the South—whether the negro be bond or free— seems (even as it did to Abraham Lincoln) a grave evil. Emancipation has ridded the country of the reproach, but not wholly of the calamity. Especially in the present transition period for both races in the South, more or less of trouble may not unreasonably be anticipated; but let us not hereafter be too swift to charge the blame exclusively in any one quarter. With certain evils men must be more or less patient. Our institutions have a potent digestion, and may in time convert and assimilate to good all elements thrown in, however originally alien.

But, so far as immediate measures looking toward permanent Re-establishment are concerned, no consideration should tempt us to pervert the national victory into oppression for the vanquished. Should plausible promise of eventual good, or a deceptive or spurious sense of duty, lead us to essay this, count we must on serious consequences, not the least of which would be divisions among the Northern adherents of the Union. Assuredly, if any honest Catos there be who thus far have gone with us, no longer will they do so, but oppose us, and as resolutely as hitherto they have supported. But this path of thought leads toward those waters of bitterness from which one can only turn aside and be silent.

But supposing Re-establishment so far advances that the Southern seats in Congress are occupied, and by men qualified in accordance with those cardinal principles of representative government which hitherto have prevailed in the land—what then? Why, the Congressmen elected by the people of the South will—represent the people of the South. This may seem a flat conclusion; but, in view of the last five years, may there not be latent significance in it? What will be the temper of those Southern members? And, confronted by them, what will be the mood of our own representatives? In private life true reconciliation seldom follows a violent quarrel; but, if subsequent intercourse be unavoidable, nice observances and mutual are indispensable to the prevention of a new rupture. Amity itself can only be maintained by reciprocal respect, and true friends are punctilious equals. On the floor of Congress North and South are to come together after a passionate duel, in which the South, though proving her valor, has been made to bite the dust. Upon differences in debate shall acrimonious recriminations be exchanged? Shall censorious superiority assumed by one section provoke defiant self-assertion on the other? Shall Manassas and Chickamauga be retorted for Chattanooga and Richmond? Under the supposition that the full Congress will be composed of gentlemen, all this is impossible. Yet, if otherwise, it needs no prophet of Israel to foretell the end. The maintenance of Congressional decency in the future will rest mainly with the North. Rightly will more forbearance be required from the North than the South, for the North is victor.

But some there are who may deem these latter thoughts inapplicable, and for this reason: Since the test-oath operatively excludes from Congress all who in any way participated in Secession, therefore none but Southerners wholly in harmony with the North are eligible to seats. This is true for the time being. But the oath is alterable; and in the wonted fluctuations of parties not improbably it will undergo alteration, assuming such a form, perhaps, as not to bar the admission into the National Legislature of men who represent the populations lately in revolt. Such a result would involve no violation of the principles of democratic government. Not readily can one perceive how the political existence of the millions of late Secessionists can permanently be ignored by this Republic. The years of the war tried our devotion to the Union; the time of peace may test the sincerity of our faith in democracy.

In no spirit of opposition, not by way of challenge, is anything here thrown out. These thoughts are sincere ones; they seem natural—inevitable. Here and there they must have suggested themselves to many thoughtful patriots. And, if they be just thoughts, ere long they must have that weight with the public which already they have had with individuals.

For that heroic band—those children of the furnace who, in regions like Texas and Tennessee, maintained their fidelity through terrible trials—we of the North felt for them, and profoundly we honor them. Yet passionate sympathy, with resentments so close as to be almost domestic in their bitterness, would hardly in the present juncture tend to discreet legislation. Were the Unionists and Secessionists but as Guelphs and Ghibellines? If not, then far be it from a great nation now to act in the spirit that animated a triumphant town-faction in the Middle Ages. But crowding thoughts must at last be checked; and, in times like the present, one who desires to be impartially just in the expression of his views, moves as among sword-points presented on every side.

Let us pray that the terrible historic tragedy of our time may not have been enacted without instructing our whole beloved country through terror and pity; and may fulfilment verify in the end those expectations which kindle the bards of Progress and Humanity.

THE END.

Editor's Notes

The best account of Melville's activities during the war and his writing and publishing of the book is Stanton Garner's *The Civil War World of Herman Melville*, a crucial companion to any reading of the poems. In addition to its very full biographical treatment of the period, it contains much information about battles, raids, and the reactions of the civilian population that sometimes helped and sometimes hindered the progress of the war. Its treatment of individual poems and the structure of the book is accurate and perceptive. Shurr gives an excellent reading of the poems, and articles by Fogle and Milder add much to our knowledge. *Battle-Pieces and Aspects of the War,* with an introduction by Lee Rust Brown, contains a photographic reproduction of the 1866 edition. Useful notes on the backgrounds of the poems can be found in Hennig Cohen, ed., *The Battle-Pieces of Herman Melville* and in Robert Penn Warren's introduction to his *Selected Poems of Herman Melville.*

Melville's Civil War poems should be compared with Walt Whitman's poems in the "Drum-Taps" and "Memories of President Lincoln" sequences of *Leaves of Grass.* Unlike Melville's pieces, Whitman's do not identify specific battles, but poems like "The Wound-Dresser," "Cavalry Crossing a Ford," "An Army Corps on the March," and "A Sight in Camp in the Daybreak Gray and Dim" do offer vivid pictures of the war.

"THE PORTENT." John Brown's raid at Harpers Ferry took place on October 16, 1859. Brown was wounded and captured; tried for treason, he was hanged on December 2. Although there were many illustrations in journals, some showing Brown ascending the gallows or standing above the trapdoor, hood over his head as the executioners prepared him, Melville's poem describes a scene—the moment after execution—that was not reproduced for readers. The importance of the word "weird" (l. 13) lies in its multiple suggestions of meaning, including "supernatural" or "uncanny," but the word is adapted from the Anglo-Saxon "wyrd," a name for fate.

"THE STONE FLEET: AN OLD SAILOR'S LAMENT (DECEMBER, 1861)." In his whaling days Melville had sailed aboard ships like these, and he must have felt keenly the fruitless destruction of these familiar ships with their "great bluff bows, and broad in the beam." For him, this was an early sign of the terrible destruction the war would bring.

"IN THE TURRET." Lieutenant John Worden, commander of the Union ironclad *Monitor,* engaged the Confederate ironclad *Merrimac* in an inconclusive battle on March 9, 1862. The courage of Worden is likened to that of Hercules (Alcides) descending into Hades to rescue Alcestis.

"THE TEMERAIRE." Melville found one "aspect" of the war in the change from the naval engagements of the old wooden ships to the technologically advanced battles between ships shielded by metal. The "Englishman of the old order" describes the painting by J. M. W. Turner entitled *The Fighting "Temeraire." Tugged to her Last Berth to be broken up,* 1838, dwelling upon its "garniture, emblazonment, / And heraldry," as well as its armament, "the gun /Armorial." Melville was moved to annotate the word "armorial" with a comment on the cannons as artworks "cast in shapes which Cellini might have designed." In one of his unpublished poems, "At the Hostelry" (Section V, ll. 18–22), Melville alludes to the building of an ironclad ship, the *Dunderberg,* by the Union forces, a piece of work never completed.

"BATTLE OF STONE RIVER RIVER, TENNESSEE: A VIEW FROM OXFORD CLOISTERS (JANUARY, 1863)." The battle took place in December 1862 and was inconclusive. The poem is of great interest in that it illustrates what Melville meant by "aspects of the war." Its speaker, an Englishman, views the battle from his cloistered retreat in Oxford and recalls scenes from battles during the War of the Roses in the year 1471. The speaker notes the likenesses between these engagements, so distant in time and place. Both sides war in "the name of Right," battling that profanes the sign of the cross. "Do North and South the sin retain / Of Yorkist and Lancastrian?" the Oxford scholar asks.

"THE MARTYR." Melville's poem on the assassination of President Lincoln is, perhaps, one of the pieces that he needed to compose to round out, to some degree, the narrative "aspects" of the war. As Garner perceptively notes, Melville was mostly interested in how the North reacted to Lincoln's death, and this interest led him away from any expression of a personal grief at the event (385). The resulting poem is weaker than it might have been, merely taking note of another dreadful outcome of the war. It should be compared with Whitman's great poem on the same subject, "When Lilacs Last in the Dooryard Bloom'd." Whitman's "O Captain! My Captain!" was a great popular success as a public poem about the assassination and a much less effective piece than the splendid elegy.

"'THE COMING STORM.'" This is one of the poems in the volume inspired by a painting by Sanford R. Gifford, which, as Melville notes in his epigraph to the poem, he saw at the April 1865 exhibition at the National Academy of Design. The property of Edwin Booth, this painting was a reminder of the assassination of Lincoln by Booth's brother on April 12 and the ways in which the picture, by its subject and title, was a "presage dim" of the coming storm of conflict.

"FORMERLY A SLAVE." Another poem based upon a picture, by Elihu Vedder (1836–1923), the poem uses ekphrasis to serve as a prophetic view of what will become of slavery and its victims at some distant point in the future. Melville often drew upon his knowledge of paintings and sculpture in his literary work. He greatly admired the paintings and other artworks of Elihu Vedder and, in 1891, dedicated his last published book of poems, *Timoleon*, to Vedder.

"THE SCOUT TOWARD ALDIE." During his visits to the scenes of war in 1864, Melville accompanied a scouting party on one of its missions. His lengthy note on Mosby gives some information in setting the background for his poem, a story in verse handled with great narrative skill. Garner's excellent treatment describes both Melville's adventures with the scouting party and his poetic license in dealing with Mosby, a "mythic figure" and a "shape-changer" (320).

"VERSES INSCRIPTIVE AND MEMORIAL." The group of poems, beginning with "On the Home Guards Who Perished in the Defense of Lexington, Missouri" and running through "The Returned Volunteer to His Rifle," forms a moving coda to the poems of battle, for here are inscriptions, sometimes made for uninscribed or natural monuments, epitaphs, memorials, a requiem, and the commemoration of a naval battle. All are quiet, reflective poems that recall bravery, loss, and the terrible price of war.

"NOTES." Melville clearly felt that the book required the twenty-four notes that he appended to the volume, with their information about the names of the whaling ships scuttled in Charleston Harbor, the numbers of soldiers in the army in March 1865, the burial sites at Andersonville and elsewhere, and the testimony of Robert E. Lee before the Reconstruction Committee of Congress. This is a first case of his trying to work with both prose and poetry in the same volume. His choice of materials to include and leave out of the poems is an index of his deep feelings about the war and its burdens, but his notes offer a different ground for interpretation of his writings. He was discovering that poetry, for all its possibilities, had some limitations as well. Within the large framework of an epic poem about the war, he might have been able to make a poetic catalogue of the ships' names or have the muse tell about numbers of troops and locations of burial sites. But the brief lyrics, ballads, and narratives did not offer room for examples.

"SUPPLEMENT." (For a good summary statement, see Garner 436–38.) As Melville pointed out, he was aware that this prose conclusion did some violence to "the symmetry of this book," but he felt that there were overriding reasons for attaching it to the poems. Concerned for the success of the Union, he asks for "reasonable consideration" for the defeated South and for pacification of the country, for decent treatment of the blacks, and for political moves by the Congress that will make the transition from war to peace an easy one. "Amity itself," he observes, "can only be maintained by reciprocal respect."

Excerpts from *Clarel* —

29. THE RECLUSE   *Excerpts from*
                                                   Clarel

Ere yet they win that verge and line,
Reveal the stranger. Name him—Vine.
His home to tell—kin, tribe, estate—
Would naught avail. Alighting grow,
As on the tree the mistletoe,
All gifts unique. In seeds of fate
Borne on the winds these emigrate
And graft the stock.

              Vine's manner shy
A clog, a hindrance might imply;
A lack of parlor-wont. But grace   10
Which is in substance deep and grain
May, peradventure, well pass by
The polish of veneer. No trace
Of passion's soil or lucre's stain,
Though life was now half ferried o'er.
If use he served not, but forbore—
Such indolence might still but pine
In dearth of rich incentive high:
Apollo slave in Mammon's mine?
Better Admetus' shepherd lie.   20
    A charm of subtle virtue shed
A personal influence coveted,
Whose source was difficult to tell
As ever was that perfumed spell
Of Paradise-flowers invisible
Which angels round Cecilia bred.
    A saint then do we here unfold?
Nay, the ripe flush, Venetian mould
Evinced no nature saintly fine,
But blood like swart Vesuvian wine.   30
What cooled the current? Under cheer
Of opulent softness, reigned austere
Control of self. Flesh, but scarce pride,
Was curbed: desire was mortified;
But less indeed by moral sway

Than doubt if happiness thro' clay
Be reachable. No sackclothed man;
Howbeit, in sort Carthusian
Tho' born a Sybarite. And yet
Not beauty might he all forget,
The beauty of the world, and charm   40
He prized it tho' it scarce might warm.
    Like to the nunnery's denizen
His virgin soul communed with men
But thro' the wicket. Was it clear
This coyness bordered not on fear—
Fear or an apprehensive sense?
Not wholly seemed it diffidence
Recluse. Nor less did strangely wind
Ambiguous elfishness behind
All that: an Ariel unknown.   50
It seemed his very speech in tone
Betrayed disuse. Thronged streets astir
To Vine but ampler cloisters were.
Cloisters? No monk he was, allow;
But gleamed the richer for the shade
About him, as in sombre glade
Of Virgil's wood the Sibyl's Golden Bough.

30. THE SITE OF THE PASSION

And wherefore by the convents be
Gardens? Ascetics roses twine?
Nay, but there is a memory.
Within a garden walking see
The angered God. And where the vine
And olive in the darkling hours
Inweave green sepulchers of bowers—
Who, to defend us from despair,
Pale undergoes the passion there
In solitude? Yes, memory
Links Eden and Gethsemane;   10
So that not meaningless in sway
Gardens adjoin the convents gray.

On Salem's hill in Solomon's years
Of gala, o the happy town!
In groups the people sauntered down,
And, Kedron crossing, lightly wound
Where now the tragic grove appears,
Then palmy, and a pleasure-ground.

The student and companions win   20
The wicket—pause, and enter in.
By roots strapped down in fold on fold—
Gnarled into wens and knobs and knees—
In olives, monumental trees,
The Pang's survivors they behold.
A wizened blue fruit drops from them,
Nipped harvest of Jerusalem.
Wistful here Clarel turned toward Vine,
And would have spoken; but as well
Hail Dathan swallowed in the mine—   30
Tradition, legend, lent such spell
And rapt him in remoteness so.
     Meanwhile, in shade the olives throw,
Nehemiah pensive sat him down
And turned the chapter in St John.
     What frame of mind may Clarel woo?
He the night-scene in picture drew—
The band which came for sinless blood
With swords and staves, a multitude.
They brush the twigs, small birds take wing,   40
The dead boughs crackle, lanterns swing,
Till lo, they spy them thro' the wood.
"Master!"—'Tis Judas. Then the kiss.
And He, He falters not at this—
Speechless, unspeakably submiss:
The fulsome serpent on the cheek
Sliming: endurance more than meek—
Endurance of the fraud foreknown,
And fiend-heart in the human one.
Ah, now the pard on Clarel springs: 50
The Passion's narrative plants stings.
     To break away, he turns and views

The white-haired under olive bowed
Immersed in Scripture; and he woos—
"Whate'er the chapter, read aloud."
The saint looked up, but with a stare
Absent and wildered, vacant there.

　　As part to kill time, part for task
Some shepherd old pores over book—
Shelved farm-book of his life forepast　　　　60
When he bestirred him and amassed;
If chance one interrupt, and ask—
What read you? he will turn a look
Which shows he knows not what he reads,
Or knowing, he but weary heeds,
Or scarce remembers; here much so
With Nehemiah, dazed out and low.
And presently—to intercept—
Over Clarel, too, strange numbness crept.

　　A monk, custodian of the ground,　　　　70
Drew nigh, and showed him by the steep
The rock or legendary mound
Where James and Peter fell asleep.
Dully the pilgrim scanned the spot,
Nor spake.—"Signor, and think'st thou not
'Twas sorrow brought their slumber on?
St. Luke avers no sluggard rest:
Nay, but excess of feeling pressed
Till ache to apathy was won."
To Clarel 'twas no hollow word.　　　　80
Experience did proof afford.
For Vine, aloof he loitered—shrunk
In privity and shunned the monk.
Clarel awaited him. He came—
The shadow of his previous air
Merged in a settled neutral frame—
Assumed, may be. Would Vine disclaim
All sympathy the youth might share?

　　About to leave, they turn to look
For him but late estranged in book:　　　　90
Asleep he lay; the face bent down

Viewless between the crossing arms,
One slack hand on the good book thrown
In peace that every care becharms.
Then died the shadow off from Vine:
A spirit seemed he not unblest
As here he made a quiet sign
Unto the monk: Spare to molest;
Let this poor dreamer take his rest,
His fill of rest.
          But now at stand   100
Who there alertly glances up
By grotto of the Bitter Cup—
Spruce, and with volume light in hand
Bound smartly, late in reference scanned?
Inquisitive Philistine: lo,
Tourists replace the pilgrims so.
  At peep of that brisk dapper man
Over Vine's face a ripple ran
Of freakish mockery, elfin light;
Whereby what thing may Clarel see?   110
O angels, rescue from the sight!
Paul Pry? and in Gethsemane?
He shrunk the thought of it to fan;
Nor liked the freak in Vine that threw
Such a suggestion into view;
Nor less it hit that fearful man.

31. ROLFE

The hill above the garden here
They rove; and chance ere long to meet
A second stranger, keeping cheer
Apart. Trapper or pioneer
He looked, astray in Judah's seat—
Or one who might his business ply
On waters under tropic sky.
Perceiving them as they drew near,
He rose, removed his hat to greet,
Disclosing so in shapely sphere   10

A marble brow over face embrowned:
So Sunium by her fane is crowned.
One read his superscription clear—
A genial heart, a brain austere—
And further, deemed that such a man
Though given to study, as might seem,
Was no scholastic partisan
Or euphonist of Academe,
But supplemented Plato's theme
With daedal life in boats and tents,   20
A messmate of the elements;
And yet, more bronzed in face than mind,
Sensitive still and frankly kind—
Too frank, too unreserved, may be,
And indiscreet in honesty.
    But what implies the tinge of soil—
Like tarnish on Pizarro's spoil,
Precious in substance rudely wrought,
Peruvian plate—which here is caught?
What means this touch of the untoward   30
In aspect hinting nothing froward?

    From Baalbec, for a new sojourn,
To Jewry Rolfe had made return;
To Jewry's inexhausted shore
Of barrenness, where evermore
Some lurking thing he hoped to gain—
Slip quite behind the parrot-lore
Conventional, and—what attain?
    Struck by each clear or latent sign
Expressive in the stranger's air,   40
The student glanced from him to Vine:
Peers, peers—yes, needs that these must pair.
Clarel was young. In promise fine,
To him here first were brought together
Exceptional natures, of a weather
Strange as the tropics with strange trees,
Strange birds, strange fishes, skies and seas,
To one who in some meager land
His bread wins by the horny hand.

What now may hap? what outcome new
Elicited by contact true—
Frank, cordial contact of the twain?
Crude wonderment, and proved but vain.
If average mortals social be,
And yet but seldom truly meet,
Closing like halves of apple sweet—
How with the rarer in degree?
   The informal salutation done,
Vine into his dumb castle went—
Not as all parley he would shun,   60
But looking down from battlement,
Ready, if need were, to accord
Reception to the other's word—
Nay, far from wishing to decline,
And neutral not without design,
May be.—
              "Look, by Christ's belfry set,
Appears the Moslem minaret!"
So—to fill trying pause alone—
Cried Rolfe; and o'er the deep defile   70
Of Kedron, pointed toward the Town,
Where, thronged about by many a pile
Monastic, but no vernal bower,
The Saracen shaft and Norman tower
In truce stand guard beside that Dome
Which canopies the Holy's home:
"The tower looks lopped; it shows forlorn
A stunted oak whose crown is shorn;
But see, palmlike the minaret stands
Superior, and the tower commands."   80
   "Yon shaft," said Clarel, "seems ill-placed."
"Ay, *seems*; but 'tis for memory based.
The story's known: how Omar there
After the town's surrender meek—
Hallowed to him, as dear to Greek—
Clad in his clouts of camel's hair,
And with the Patriarch robed and fine
Walking beneath the dome divine,
When came the Islam hour for prayer

Declined to use the carpet good   90
Spread for him in the church, but stood
Without, even yonder where is set
The monumental minaret;
And, earnest in true suppliance cried,
Smiting his chest: 'Me overrule!
Allah, to me be merciful!'
'Twas little shared he victor-pride
Though victor. So the church he saved
Of purpose from that law engraved
Which prompt transferred to Allah sole
Each fane where once his rite might roll.   100
Long afterward, the town being stormed
By Christian knights, how ill conformed
The butchery then to Omar's prayer
And heart magnanimous. But spare."

    Response they looked; and thence he warmed:
"Yon gray Cathedral of the Tomb,
Who reared it first? a woman weak,
A second Mary, first to seek
In pagan darkness which had come,
The place where they had laid the Lord: 110
Queen Helena, she traced the site,
And cleared the ground, and made it bright
With all that zeal could then afford.
But Constantine—there falls the blight!
The mother's warm emotional heart,
Subserved it still the son's cold part?
Even he who, timing well the tide,
Laced not the Cross upon Rome's flag
Supreme, till Jove began to lag
Behind the new religion's stride   120
And Helena—ah, may it be
The saint herself not quite was free
From that which in the years bygone,
Made certain stately dames of France,
Such as the fair De Maintenon,
To string their rosaries of pearl,
And found brave chapels—sweet romance:

Coquetry of the borrowed curl?—
You let me prate."

              "Nay, nay—go on,"
Cried Clarel, yet in such a tone   130
It showed disturbance.—
              "Laud the dame:
Her church, admit, no doom it fears.
Unquelled by force of battering years—
Years, years and sieges, sword and flame;
Fallen—rebuilt, to fall anew;
By armies shaken, earthquake too;
Lo, it abides—if not the same,
In self-same spot. Last time 'twas burnt
The Rationalist a lesson learnt.
But you know all."—
             "Nay, not the end ,"   140
Said Vine. And Clarel, "We attend."
   "Well, on the morrow never shrunk
From wonted rite the steadfast monk,
Though hurt and even maimed were some
By crash of the ignited dome.
Staunch stood the walls. As friars profess
(And not in fraud) the central cell—
Christ's tomb and faith's last citadel—
The flames did tenderly caress,
Nor harm; while smoking, smouldering beams,   150
Fallen across, lent livid gleams
To Golgotha. But none the less
In robed procession of his God
The mitred one the cinders trod;
Before the calcined altar there
The host he raised; and hymn and prayer
Went up from ashes. These, ere chill,
Away were brushed; and trowel shrill
And hod and hammer came in place.
'Tis now some three score years ago.   160
   "In Lima's first convulsion so,
When shock on shock had left slim trace
Of hundred temples; and—in mood
Of malice dwelling on the face

Itself has tortured and subdued
To uncomplaint—the cloud pitch-black
Lowered o'er the rubbish; and the land
Not less than sea, did countermand
Her buried corses—heave them back;
And flocks and men fled on the track   170
Which wins the Andes; then went forth
The prelate with intrepid train
Rolling the anthem 'mid the rain
Of ashes white. In rocking plain
New boundaries staked they, south and north,
For ampler piles. These stand. In cheer
The priest reclaimed the quaking sphere.
Hold it he shall, so long as spins
This star of tragedies, this orb of sins."
  "That," Clarel said, "is not my mind.   180
Rome's priest forever rule the world?"
  "The priest, I said. Though some be hurled
From anchor, nor a haven find;
Not less religion's ancient port,
Till the crack of doom, shall be resort
In stress of weather for mankind.
Yea, long as children feel affright
In darkness, men shall fear a God;
And long as daisies yield delight
Shall see His footprints in the sod.   190
Is't ignorance? This ignorant state
Science doth but elucidate—
Deepen, enlarge. But though 'twere made
Demonstrable that God is not—
What then? it would not change this lot:
The ghost would haunt, nor could be laid."
  Intense he spake, his eyes of blue
Altering, and to eerie hue,
Like Tyrrhene seas when overcast;
The which Vine noted, nor in joy,   200
Inferring thence an ocean-waste
Of earnestness without a buoy:
An inference which afterward
Acquaintance led him to discard

Or modify, or not employ.
   Clarel ill-relished.

              Rolfe, in tone
Half elegiac, thus went on:
"Phylae, upon thy sacred ground
Osiris' broken tomb is found:
A god how good, whose good proved vain—   210
In strife with bullying Python slain.
For long the ritual chant or moan
Of pilgrims by that mystic stone
Went up, even much as now ascend
The liturgies of yearning prayer
To one who met a kindred end—
Christ, tombed in turn, and worshiped *there,*"
And pointed.—"Hint you," here asked Vine,
"In Christ Osiris met decline
Anew?"—"Nay, nay; and yet, past doubt,   220
Strange is that text St. Matthew won
From gray Hosea in sentence: *Out
Of Egypt have I called my son.*"
   Here Clarel spake, and with a stir
Not all assured in eager plight:
"But does not Matthew there refer
Only to the return from flight,
Flight into Egypt?"—"May be so,"
Said Rolfe; "but then Hosea?—Nay,
We'll let it pass."—And fell delay   230
Of talk; they mused.—
             "To Cicero,"
Rolfe sudden said, "is a long way
From Matthew; yet somehow he comes
To mind here—he and his fine tomes,
Which (change the gods) would serve to read
For modern essays. And indeed
His age was much like ours: doubt ran,
Faith flagged; negations which sufficed
Lawyer, priest, statesman, gentleman,
Not yet being popularly prized,   240
The augurs hence retained some state—
Which served for the illiterate.

Still, the decline so swiftly ran
From stage to stage, that *To Believe,*
Except for slave or artisan,
Seemed heresy. Even doubts which met
Horror at first, grew obsolete,
And in a decade. To bereave
Of founded trust in Sire Supreme,
Was a vocation. Sophists throve—   250
Each weaving his thin thread of dream
Into the shroud for Numa's Jove.
Caesar his atheism avowed
Before the Senate. But why crowd
Examples here: the gods were gone.
Tully scarce dreamed they could be won
Back into credence; less that earth
Ever could know yet mightier birth
Of deity. He died. Christ came.
And, in due hour, that impious Rome,   260
Emerging from vast wreck and shame,
Held the fore front of Christendom.
The inference? the lesson?—come:
Let fools count on faith's closing knell—
Time, God, are inexhaustible.—
But what? so earnest? ay, again."

    "Hard for a fountain to refrain,"
Breathed Vine. Was that but irony?
At least no envy in the strain.
Rolfe scarce remarked, or let go by.   270
    For Clarel—when ye, meeting, scan
In waste the Bagdad caravan,
And solitude puts on the stir,
Clamor, dust, din of Nineveh,
As horsemen, camels, footmen all,
Soldier and merchant, free and thrall,
Pour by in tide processional;
So to the novice streamed along
Rolfe's filing thoughts, a wildering throng.
Their sway he owned. And yet how Vine—   280
Who breathed few words, or gave dumb sign—
Him more allured, suggestive more

Of choicer treasure, rarer store
Reserved, like Kidd's doubloons long sought
Without the wand.
                    The ball of thought
And chain yet dragging, on they strained
Oblique along the upland—slow
And mute, until a point they gained
Where devotees will pause, and know
A tenderness, may be. Here then,   290
While tarry now these pilgrim men,
The interval let be assigned
A niche for image of a novel mind.

32. OF RAMA

That Rama whom the Indian sung—
A god he was, but knew it not;
Hence vainly puzzled at the wrong
Misplacing him in human lot.
Curtailment of his right he bare
Rather than wrangle; but no less
Was taunted for his tameness there.
A fugitive without redress,
He never the Holy Spirit grieved,
Nor the divine in him bereaved,   10
Though what that was he might not guess.

    Live they who, like to Rama, led
Unspotted from the world aside,
Like Rama are discredited—
Like him, in outlawry abide?
May life and fable so agree?—
    The innocent if lawless elf,
Etherial in virginity,
Retains the consciousness of self.
Though black frost nip, though white frost chill,   20
Nor white frost nor the black may kill
The patient root, the vernal sense
Surviving hard experience

As grass the winter. Even that curse
Which is the wormwood mixed with gall—
Better dependent on the worse—
Divine upon the animal—
That can not make such natures fall.
    Though yielding easy rein, indeed,
To impulse which the fibers breed,   30
Nor quarreling with indolence;
Shall these the cup of grief dispense
Deliberate to any heart?
Not craft they know, nor envy's smart.
Theirs be the thoughts that dive and skim,
Theirs the spiced tears that overbrim,
And theirs the dimple and the lightsome whim.
    Such natures, and but such, have got
Familiar with strange things that dwell
Repressed in mortals; and they tell   40
Of riddles in the prosiest lot.
    Mince ye some matter for faith's sake
And heaven's good name? 'Tis these shall make
Revolt there, and the gloss disclaim.
    They con the page kept down with those
Which Adam's secret frame disclose,
And Eve's; nor dare dissent from truth
Although disreputable, sooth.
    The riches in them be a store
Unmerchantable in the ore.   50
No matter: "'Tis an open mine:
Dig; find ye gold, why, make it thine.
The shrewder knack hast thou, the gift:
Smelt then, and mold, and good go with thy thrift."

    Was ever earth-born wight like this?
Ay—in the verse, may be, he is.

33. BY THE STONE

Over against the Temple here
A monastery unrestored—

Named from Prediction of Our Lord—
Crumbled long since. Outlying near,
Some stones remain, which seats afford:
And one, the fond traditions state,
Is that whereon the Saviour sate
And prophesied, and sad became
To think, what, under sword and flame,
The proud Jerusalem should be,   10
Then spread before him sunnily—
Pillars and palms—the white, the green—
Marble enfoliaged, a fair scene;
But *now*—a vision here conferred
Pale as Pompeii disinterred.

    Long Rolfe, on knees his elbows resting
And head enlocked in hands upright,
Sat facing it in steadfast plight
And brooded on that town slow wasting.
"And here," he said, "here did He sit—   20
In leafy covert, say—*Beheld*
The city, and wept over it:
Luke's words, and hard to be excelled,
So just the brief expression there:
Truth's rendering."—With earnest air,
More he threw out, in kind the same,
The which did Clarel ponder still;
For though the words might frankness claim,
With reverence for site and name;
No further went they, nor could fill   30
Faith's measure—scarce her dwindled gill
Now standard. On the plain of Troy
(Mused Clarel) as one might look down
From Gargarus with quiet joy
In verifying Homer's sites,
Yet scarce believe in Venus' crown
And rescues in those Trojan fights
Whereby she saved her supple son;
So Rolfe regards from these wan heights
Yon walls and slopes to Christians dear.   40
Much it annoyed him and perplexed:

Than free concession so sincere—
Concession due both site and text—
Dissent itself would less appear
To imply negation.
                    But anon
They mark in groups, hard by the gate
Which overlooks Jehoshaphat,
Some Hebrew people of the town.
"Who marvels that outside they come
Since few within have seemly home,"   50
Said Rolfe; "they chat there on the seats,
But seldom gossip in their streets.
Who here may see a busy one?
Where's naught to do not much is done.
How live they then? what bread can be?
In almost every country known
Rich Israelites these kinsmen own:
The hat goes round the world. But see!"
    Moved by his words, their eyes more reach
Toward that dull group. Dwarfed in the dream   60
Of distance sad, penguins they seem
Drawn up on Patagonian beach.

    "O city," Rolfe cried; "house on moor,
With shutters burst and blackened door—
Like that thou showest; and the gales
Still round thee blow the Banshee-wails:
Well might the priest in temple start,
"Hearing the voice— *'Woe, we depart!'*"

    Clarel gave ear, albeit his glance
Diffident skimmed Vine's countenance,   70
As mainly here he interest took
In all the fervid speaker said,
Reflected in the mute one's look:
A face indeed quite overlaid
With tremulous meanings, which evade
Or shun regard, nay, hardly brook
Fraternal scanning.
                    Rolfe went on:

"The very natives of the town
Methinks would turn from it and flee
But for that curse which is its crown—
That curse which clogs so, poverty.
See them, but see yon cowering men:
The brood—the brood without the hen!"—

"City, that dost the prophets stone,
How oft against the judgment dread,
How often would I fain have spread
My wings to cover thee, mine own;
And ye would not! Had'st thou but known
The things which to thy peace belong!"
        Nehemiah it was, rejoining them—
Gray as the old Jerusalem
Over which how earnestly he hung.
But him the seated audience scan
As he were sole surviving man
Of tribe extinct or world. The ray
Which lit his features, died away;
He flagged; and, as some trouble moved,
Apart and aimlessly he roved.

80

90

Part Two: The Wilderness

29. BY THE MARGE

The legend round a Grecian urn,
The sylvan legend, though decay
Have wormed the garland all away,
And fire have left its Vandal burn;
Yet beauty inextinct may charm
In outline of the vessel's form.
Much so with Sodom, shore and sea.
Fair Como would like Sodom be
Should horror overrun the scene
And calcine all that makes it green,
Yet haply sparing to impeach

10

The contour in its larger reach.
In graceful lines the hills advance,
The valley's sweep repays the glance,
And wavy curves of winding beach;
But all is charred or crunched or riven,
Scarce seems of earth whereon we dwell;
Though framed within the lines of heaven
The picture intimates a hell.

    That marge they win. Bides Mortmain there?   20
No trace of man, not anywhere.
    It was the salt wave's northern brink.
No gravel bright nor shell was seen,
Nor kelpy growth nor coralline,
But dead boughs stranded, which the rout
Of Jordan, in old freshets born
In Libanus, had madly torn
Green from her arbor and thrust out
Into the liquid waste. No sound
Nor motion but of sea. The land   30
Was null: nor bramble, weed, nor trees,
Nor anything that grows on ground,
Flexile to indicate the breeze;
Though hitherward by south winds fanned
From Usdum's brink and Bozrah's site
Of bale, flew gritty atoms light.
Toward Karek's castle lost in blur,
And thence beyond toward Aroer
By Arnon where the robbers keep,
Jackal and vulture, eastward sweep   40
The waters, while their western rim
Stretches by Judah's headlands grim,
Which make in turns a sea-wall steep.
There, by the cliffs or distance hid,
The Fount or Cascade of the Kid
An Eden makes of one high glen,
One vernal and contrasted scene
In jaws of gloomy crags uncouth—
Rosemary in the black boar's mouth.
Alike withheld from present view   50
(And, until late, but hawk and kite

Visited the forgotten site),
The Maccabees' Masada true;
Stronghold which Flavian arms did rend,
The Peak of Eleazer's end,
Where patriot warriors made with brides
A martyrdom of suicides.
There too did Mariamne's hate
The death of John accelerate.
A crag of fairest, foulest weather—   60
Famous, and infamous together.
    Hereof they spake, but never Vine,
Who little knew or seemed to know
Derived from books, but did incline
In docile way to each one's flow
Of knowledge bearing anyhow
In points less noted.
                Southernmost
The sea indefinite was lost
Under a catafalque of cloud.
    Unwelcome impress to disown   70
Or light evade, the priest, aloud
Taking an interested tone
And brisk, "Why, yonder lies Mount Hor,
E'en thereaway—that southward shore."
    "Ay," added Rolfe, "and Aaron's cell
Thereon. A mountain sentinel,
He holds in solitude austere
The outpost of prohibited Seir
In cut-off Edom."
               "God can sever!"
Brake in the saint, who nigh them stood;   80
"The satyr to the dragon's brood
Crieth! God's word abideth ever:
None there pass through—no, never, never!"
    "My friend Max Levi, he passed through."
They turned. It was the hardy Jew.
Absorbed in vision here, the saint
Heard not. The priest in flushed constraint
Showed mixed emotion; part he winced
And part a humor pleased evinced—

Relish that would from qualms be free—   90
Aversion involved with sympathy.
But changing, and in formal way—
"Admitted; nay, 'tis tritely true;
Men pass thro' Edom, through and through.
But surely, few so dull to-day
As not to make allowance meet
For Orientalism's display
In Scripture, where the chapters treat
Of mystic themes."
                    With eye askance,
The apostate fixed no genial glance: 100
"Ay, Keith's grown obsolete. And, pray,
How long will these last glosses stay?
The agitating influence
Of knowledge never will dispense
With teasing faith, do what ye may.
Adjust and readjust, ye deal
With compass in a ship of steel."
    "Such perturbations do but give
Proof that faith's vital: sensitive
Is faith, my friend."
                    "Go to, go to: 110
Your black bat! how she hangs askew,
Torpid, from wall by claws of wings:
Let drop the left—sticks fast the right;
Then this unhook—the other swings;
Leave—she regains her double plight."
    "Ah, look," cried Derwent; "ah, behold!
From the blue battlements of air,
Over saline vapors hovering there,
A flag was flung out—curved in fold—
Fiery, rosy, violet, green—   120
And, lovelier growing, brighter, fairer,
Transfigured all that evil scene;
And Iris was the standard-bearer.
    None spake. As in a world made new,
With upturned faces they review
That oriflamme, the which no man

Would look for in such clime of ban.
'Twas northern; and its home-like look
Touched Nehemiah. He, late with book
Gliding from Margoth's dubious sway,   130
Was standing by the ass apart;
And when he caught that scarf of May
How many a year ran back his heart:
Scythes hang in orchard, hay-cocks loom
After eve-showers, the mossed roofs gloom
Greenly beneath the homestead trees;
He tingles with these memories.
      For Vine, over him suffusive stole
An efflorescence; all the soul
Flowering in flush upon the brow.   140
But 'twas ambiguously replaced
In words addressed to Clarel now—
"Yonder the arch dips in the waste;
Thither! and win the pouch of gold."
      Derwent reproached him: "ah, withhold!
See, even death's pool reflects the dyes—
The rose upon the coffin lies!"
      "Brave words," said Margoth, plodding near;
"Brave words; but yonder bow's forsworn.
The covenant made on Noah's morn,   150
Was that well kept? why, hardly here,
Where whelmed by fire and flood, they say,
The townsfolk sank in after day,
Yon sign in heaven should reappear."
      They heard, but in such torpid gloom
Scarcely they recked, for now the bloom
Vanished from sight, and half the sea
Died down to glazed monotony.
      Craved solace here would Clarel prove,
Recalling Ruth, her glance of love.   160
But nay; those eyes so frequent known
To meet, and mellow on his own—
Now, in his vision of them, swerved;
While in perverse recurrence ran
Dreams of the bier Armenian.

Against their sway his soul he nerved:
"Go, goblins; go, each funeral thought—
Bewitchment from this Dead Sea caught!"

    Westward they move, and turn the shore
Southward, till, where wild rocks are set,   170
Dismounting, they would fain restore
Ease to the limb. But haunts them yet
A dumb dejection lately met.

30. Of Petra

"The City Red in cloud-land lies
Yonder," said Derwent, quick to inter
The ill, or light regard transfer:
"But Petra must we leave unseen—
Tell us"—to Rolfe—"there hast thou been."
    "With dragons guarded roundabout
'Twas a new Jason found her out—
Burckhardt, you know." "But tell." "The flume
Or mountain corridor profound
Whereby ye win the inner ground   10
Petraean; this, from purple gloom
Of cliffs—whose tops the suns illume
Where oleanders wave the flag—
Winds out upon the rosy stain,
Warm color of the natural vein,
Of porch and pediment in crag.
One starts. In Esau's waste are blent
Ionian form, Venetian tint.
Statues salute ye from that fane,
The warders of the Horite lane.   20
They welcome, seem to point ye on
Where sequels which transcend them dwell;
But tarry, for just here is won
Happy suspension of the spell."
"But expectation's raised."
                   "No more!
'Tis then when bluely blurred in shore,

It looms through azure haze at sea—
Then most 'tis Colchis charmeth ye.
So ever, and with all! But, come,
Imagine us now quite at home   30
Taking the prospect from Mount Hor.
Good. Eastward turn thee—skipping o'er
The intervening craggy blight:
Mark'st thou the face of yon slabbed hight
Shouldered about by hights? what Door
Is that, sculptured in elfin freak?
The portal of the Prince o' the Air?
Thence will the god emerge, and speak?
El Deir it is, and Petra's there,
Down in her cleft. Mid such a scene   40
Of Nature's terror, how serene
That ordered form. Nor less 'tis cut
Out of that terror—does abut
Thereon: there's Art."
      "Dare say—no doubt;
But, prithee, turn we now about
And closer get thereto in mind;
That portal lures me."
       "Nay, forbear;
A bootless journey. We should wind
Along ravine by mountain-stair,—
Down which in season torrents sweep—   50
Up, slant by sepulchers in steep,
Grotto and porch, and so get near
Puck's platform, and thereby El Deir.
We'd knock. An echo. Knock again—
Ay, knock forever: none requite:
The live spring filters through cell, fane,
And tomb: a dream the Edomite!"
  "And dreamers all who dream of him—
Though Sinbad's pleasant in the skim.
Paestum and Petra: good to use   60
For sedative when one would muse.
  But look, our Emir.—Ay, Djalea,
We guess why thou com'st mutely here
And hintful stand'st before us so."

"Ay, ay," said Rolfe; "stirrups, and go!"
"But first," the priest said, "let me creep
And rouse our poor friend slumbering low
Under yon rock—queer place to sleep."

"*Queer?*" muttered Rolfe as Derwent went;
"*Queer* is the furthest he will go   70
In phrase of a disparagement.
But—ominous, with haggard rent—
To me yon crag's brow-beating brow
Looks horrible—and I *say* so."

31. THE INSCRIPTION

While yet Rolfe's foot in stirrup stood,
Ere the light vault that wins the seat,
Derwent was heard: "What's this we meet?
A Cross? and—if one could but spell—
Inscription Sinaitic? Well,
Mortmain is nigh—*his* crazy freak;
Whose else? A closer view I'll seek;
I'll climb."
            In moving there aside
The rock's turned brow he had espied;
In rear this rock hung o'er the waste   10
And Nehemiah in sleep embraced
Below. The forepart gloomed Lot's wave
So nigh, the tide the base did lave.
Above, the sea-face smooth was worn
Through long attrition of that grit
Which on the waste of winds is borne.
And on the tablet high of it—
Traced in dull chalk, such as is found
Accessible in upper ground—
Big there between two scrawls, below   20
And over—a cross; three stars in row
Upright, two more for thwarting limb
Which drooped oblique.

The rest drew near; and every eye
Marked the device.—Thy passion's whim,
Wild Swede, mused Vine in silent heart.

"Looks like the *Southern Cross* to me,"
Said Clarel; "so 'tis down in chart."
"And so," said Rolfe, "'tis set in sky—
Though error slight of place prevail   30
In midmost star here chalked. At sea,
Bound for Peru, when south ye sail,
Startling that novel cluster strange
Peers up from low; then as ye range
Cape-ward still further, brightly higher
And higher the stranger doth aspire,
'Till off the Horn, when at full hight
Ye slack your gaze as chilly grows the night.
But Derwent—see!"
                      The priest having gained
Convenient lodge the text below,   40
They called: "What's that in curve contained
Above the stars? Read: we would know."
"Runs thus: *By one who wails the loss,*
This altar to the Slanting Cross."
"Ha! under that?" "Some crow's-foot scrawl."
"Decipher, quick! we're waiting all."
"Patience: for ere one try rehearse,
'Twere well to make it out. 'Tis verse."
"Verse, say you? Read." "'Tis mystical;

"'Emblazoned bleak in austral skies—   50
A heaven remote, whose starry swarm
Like Science lights but cannot warm—
Translated Cross, hast thou withdrawn,
Dim paling too at every dawn,
With symbols vain once counted wise,
And gods declined to heraldries?
Estranged, estranged: can friend prove so?
Aloft, aloof, a frigid sign:
How far removed, thou Tree divine,

Whose tender fruit did reach so low—   60
Love apples of New-Paradise!
About the wide Australian sea
The planted nations yet to be—
When, ages hence, they lift their eyes,
Tell, what shall they retain of thee?
But class thee with Orion's sword?
In constellations unadored,
Christ and the Giant equal prize?
The atheist cycles—*must* they be?
Fomentors as forefathers we?'   70

"Mad, mad enough," the priest here cried,
Down slipping by the shelving brinks;
"But 'tis not Mortmain," and he sighed.
    "Not Mortmain?" Rolfe exclaimed. "Methinks,"
The priest, "'tis hardly in his vein."
"How? fraught with feeling is the strain?
His heart's not ballasted with stone—
He's crank." "Well, well, e'en let us own
That Mortmain, Mortmain is the man.
We've then a pledge here at a glance   80
Our comrade's met with no mischance.
Soon he'll rejoin us." "There, amen!"
"But now to wake Nehemiah in den
Behind here.—But kind Clarel goes.
Strange how he naps nor trouble knows
Under the crag's impending block,
Nor fears its fall, nor recks of shock."

    Anon they mount; and much advance
Upon that chalked significance.
The student harks, and weighs each word,   90
Intent, he being newly stirred.
    But tarries Margoth? Yes, behind
He lingers. He placards his mind:
Scaling the crag he rudely scores
With the same chalk (how here abused!)
Left by the other, after used,
A sledge or hammer huge as Thor's;

A legend lending—this, to wit:
"*I, Science, I whose gain's thy loss,*
I slanted thee, thou Slanting Cross."
    But sun and rain, and wind, with grit
Driving, these haste to cancel it.

100

32. THE ENCAMPMENT

Southward they find a strip at need
Between the mount and marge, and make,
In expectation of the Swede,
Encampment there, nor shun the Lake.
'Twas afternoon. With Arab zest
The Bethlehemites their spears present,
Whereon they lift and spread the tent
And care for all.
                    As Rolfe from rest
Came out, toward early eventide,
His comrades sat the shore beside,   10
In shadow deep, which from the west
The main Judaean mountains flung.
That ridge they faced, and anxious hung
Awaiting Mortmain, some having grown
The more concerned, because from stone
Inscribed, they had indulged a hope:
But now in ill surmise they grope.
Anew they question grave Djalea
But what knows *he*?
                    Their hearts to cheer,
"Trust," Derwent said, "hope's silver bell;   20
Nor dream he'd do his life a wrong—
No, never!"
            "Demons here which dwell,"
Cried Rolfe, "riff-raff of Satan's throng,
May fetch him steel, rope, poison—well,
He'd spurn them, hoot their scurvy hell:
There's nobler.—But what *other* knell
Of hap—" He turned him toward the sea.
    Like leagues of ice which slumberous roll

About the pivot of the pole—
Vitreous—glass it seemed to be.   30
Beyond, removed in air sublime,
As 'twere some more than human clime,
In flanking towers of Etna hue
The Ammonitish mounts they view
Enkindled by the sunset cast
Over Judah's ridgy headlands massed
Which blacken baseward. Ranging higher
Where vague glens pierced the steeps of fire,
Imagination time repealed—
Restored there, and in fear revealed   40
Lot and his daughters twain in flight,
Three shadows flung on reflex light
Of Sodom in her funeral pyre.

    Some fed upon the natural scene,
Deriving many a wandering hint
Such as will ofttimes intervene
When on the slab ye view the print
Of perished species.—Judge Rolfe's start
And quick revulsion, when, apart,
Derwent he saw at ease reclined,   50
With page before him, page refined
And appetizing, which threw ope
New parks, fresh walks for Signor Hope
To saunter in.
        "And read you here?
Scarce suits the ground with bookish cheer.
Escaped from forms, enlarged at last,
Pupils we be of wave and waste—
Not books; nay, nay!"
        "Book-comment, though,"—
Smiled Derwent—"were it ill to know?"
"But how if nature vetoes all   60
Her commentators? Disenthrall
Thy heart. Look round. Are not here met
Books and that truth no type shall set?"—
Then, to himself in refluent flow:
"Earnest again!—well, let it go."
    Derwent quick glanced from face to face,

Lighting upon the student's hue
Of pale perplexity, with trace
Almost of twinge at Rolfe: "Believe,
Though here I random page review,   70
Not books I let exclusive cleave
And sway. Much too there is, I grant,
Which well might Solomon's wisdom daunt—
Much that we mark. Nevertheless,
Were it a paradox to confess
A book's a man? If this be so,
Books be but part of nature. Oh,
'Tis studying nature, reading books:
And 'tis through Nature each heart looks
Up to a God, or whatsoe'er   80
One images beyond our sphere.
Moreover, Siddim's not the world:
There's Naples. Why, yourself well know
What breadths of beauty lie unfurled
All round the bays where sailors go.
So, prithee, do not be severe,
But let me read."
           Rolfe looked esteem:
"You suave St. Francis! Him, I mean,
Of Sales, not that soul whose dream
Founded the bare-foot Order lean.   90
Though wise as serpents, Sales proves
The throbbings sweet of social doves.
I like you."
           Derwent laughed; then, "Ah,
From each Saint Francis am I far!"
And grave he grew.
           It was a scene
Which Clarel in his memory scored:
How reconcile Rolfe's wizard chord
And forks of esoteric fire,
With common-place of laxer mien?
May truth be such a spendthrift lord?   100
Then Derwent: he reviewed in heart
His tone with Margoth; his attire
Of tolerance; the easy part

He played. Could Derwent, having gained
A certain slant in liberal thought,
Think there to bide, like one detained
Half-way adown the slippery glacier caught?
Was honesty his, with lore and art
Not to be fooled?—But if in vain
One tries to comprehend a man,
How think to sound God's deeper heart!

110

33. LOT'S SEA

Roving along the winding verge
Trying these problems as a lock,
Clarel upon the further marge
Caught sight of Vine. Upon a rock
Low couchant there, and dumb as that,
Bent on the wave Vine moveless sat.
The student after pause drew near:
Then, as in presence which though mute
Did not repel, without salute
He joined him.
     Unto these, by chance   10
In ruminating slow advance
Came Rolfe, and lingered.
      At Vine's feet
A branchless tree lay lodged ashore,
One end immersed. Of form complete—
Half fossilized—could this have been,
In ages back, a palm-shaft green?
Yes, long detained in depths which store
A bitter virtue, there it lay,
Washed up to sight—free from decay
But dead.
    And now in slouched return   20
From random prowlings, brief sojourn
As chance might prompt, the Jew they espy
Coasting inquisitive the shore
And frequent stooping. Ranging nigh,
In hirsute hand a flint he bore—

A flint, or stone, of smooth dull gloom:
"A jewel? not asphaltum—no:
Observe it, pray. Methinks in show
'Tis like the flagging round that Tomb
Ye celebrate."

          Rolfe, glancing, said,   30
"I err, or 'twas from Siddim's bed
Or quarry here, those floor-stones came:
'Tis Stone-of-Moses called, they vouch;
The Arabs know it by that name."

   "Moses? who's Moses?" Into pouch
The lump he slipped; while wistful here
Clarel in silence challenged Vine;
But not responsive was Vine's cheer,
Discharged of every meaning sign.

     With motive, Rolfe the talk renewed: 40
"Yes, here it was the cities stood
That sank in reprobation. See,
The scene and record well agree."

   "Tut, tut—tut, tut. Of aqueous force,
Vent igneous, a shake or so,
One here perceives the sign—of course;
All's mere geology, you know."

   "Nay, how should one know that?"

                  "By sight,

Touch, taste—all senses in assent
Of common sense their parliament   50
Judge now; this lake, with outlet none
And into which five streams discharge
From south; which east and west is shown
Walled in by Alps along the marge;
North, in this lake, the waters end
Of Jordan—end here, or dilate
Rather, and so evaporate
From surface. But do you attend?"

   "Most teachably."

             "Well, now: assume
This lake was formed, even as they tell,   60
Then first when the Five Cities fell;

Where, I demand, ere yet that doom,
Where emptied Jordan?"
                              "Who can say?
Not I."
                    "No, none. A point I make:
Coeval are the stream and lake!
I say no more."
                         As came that close
A hideous hee-haw horrible rose,
Rebounded in unearthly sort
From shore to shore, as if retort
From all the damned in Sodom's Sea   70
Out brayed at him. "Just God, what's that?"
"The ass," breathed Vine, with tropic eye
Freakishly impish, nor less shy;
Then, distant as before, he sat.
     Anew Rolfe turned toward Margoth then;
"May not these levels high and low
Have undergone derangement when
The cities met their overthrow?
Or say there was a lake at first—
A supposition not reversed   80
By Writ—a lake enlarged through doom
Which overtook the cities? Come!"—
     The Jew, recovering from decline
Arising from late asinine
Applause, replied hereto in way
Eliciting from Rolfe—"Delay:
What knowest thou? or what know I?
Suspect you may ere yet you die
Or afterward perchance may learn,
That Moses' God is no mere Pam   90
With painted clubs, but true I AM."
     "Hog-Latin," was the quick return;
"Plague on that ass!" for here again
Brake in the pestilent refrain.
Meanwhile, as if in a dissent
Not bordering their element,
Vine kept his place, aloof in air.
They could but part and leave him there;

The Hebrew railing as they went—
"Of all the dolorous dull men!   100
He's like a poor nun's pining hen.
And *me* too: should I let it pass?
Ass? did he say it was the ass?"
Hereat, timed like the clerk's *Amen*
Yet once more did the hee-haw free
Come in with new alacrity.

    Vine tarried; and with fitful hand
Took bits of dead drift from the sand
And flung them to the wave, as one
Whose race of thought long since was run—   110
For whom the spots enlarge that blot the golden sun.

34. MORTMAIN REAPPEARS

While now at poise the wings of shade
Outstretched overhang each ridge and glade,
Mortmain descends from Judah's hight
Through sally-port of minor glens:
Against the background of black dens
Blacker the figure glooms enhanced.
    Relieved from anxious fears, the group
In friendliness would have advanced
To greet, but shrank or fell adroop.
    Like Hecla ice inveined with marl   10
And frozen cinders showed his face
Rigid and darkened. Shunning parle
He seated him aloof in place,
Hands clasped about the knees drawn up
As round the cask the binding hoop—
Condensed in self, or like a seer
Unconscious of each object near,
While yet, informed, the nerve may reach
Like wire under wave to furthest beach.
    By what brook Cherith had he been,   20
Watching it shrivel from the scene—
Or voice aerial had heard,

That now he murmured the wild word;
"But, hectored by the impious years,
What god invoke, for leave to unveil
That gulf whither tend these modern fears,
And deeps over which men crowd the sail?"
        Up, as possessed, he rose anon,
And crying to the beach went down:
"Repent! repent in every land   30
Or hell's hot kingdom is at hand!
                        Yea, yea,
In pause of the artillery's boom,
While now the armed world holds its own,
The comet peers, the star dips down;
Flicker the lamps in Syria's tomb,
While Anti-Christ and Atheist set
On Anarch the red coronet!"

        "Mad John," sighed Rolfe, "dost there betray
The dire *Vox Clamans* of our day?"   40
        "Why heed him?" Derwent breathed: "alas!
Let him alone, and it will pass.—
What would he now?" Before the bay
Low bowed he there, with hand addressed
To scoop. "Unhappy, hadst thou best?"
Djalea it was; then calling low
Unto a Bethlehemite whose brow
Was wrinkled like the bat's shrunk hide—
"Your salt-song, Beltha: warn and chide."

            "Would ye know what bitter drink   50
                They gave to Christ upon the Tree?
            Sip the wave that laps the brink
                Of Siddim: taste, and God keep ye!
            It drains the hills where alum's hid—
            Drains the rock-salt's ancient bed;
                Hither unto basin fall
                The torrents from the steeps of gall—
            Here is Hades' water-shed.
                Sinner, would ye that your soul
                Bitter were and like the pool?   60

Sip the Sodom waters dead;
But never from thy heart shall haste
The Marah—yea, the after-taste."

He closed.—Arrested as he stooped,
Did Mortmain his pale hand recall?
No; undeterred the wave he scooped,
And tried it—madly tried the gall.

35. PRELUSIVE

In Piranesi's rarer prints,
Interiors measurelessly strange,
Where the distrustful thought may range
Misgiving still—what mean the hints?
Stairs upon stairs which dim ascend
In series from plunged Bastiles drear—
Pit under pit; long tier on tier
Of shadowed galleries which impend
Over cloisters, cloisters without end;
The hight, the depth—the far, the near;   10
Ring-bolts to pillars in vaulted lanes,
And dragging Rhadamanthine chains;
These less of wizard influence lend
Than some allusive chambers closed.
    Those wards of hush are not disposed
In gibe of goblin fantasy—
Grimace—unclean diablery:
Thy wings, Imagination, span
Ideal truth in fable's seat:
The thing implied is one with man,   20
His penetralia of retreat—
The heart, with labyrinths replete:
In freaks of intimation see
Paul's "mystery of iniquity:"
Involved indeed, a blur of dream;
As, awed by scruple and restricted
In first design, or interdicted
By fate and warnings as might seem;

The inventor miraged all the maze,
Obscured it with prudential haze;   30
Nor less, if subject unto question,
The egg left, egg of the suggestion.
    Dwell on those etchings in the night,
Those touches bitten in the steel
By aqua-fortis, till ye feel
The Pauline text in gray of light;
Turn hither then and read aright.

    For ye who green or gray retain
Childhood's illusion, or but feign;
As bride and suit let pass a bler—   40
So pass the coming canto here.

Part Four: Bethlehem

10. A MONUMENT

Wise Derwent, that discourse to end,
Pointed athwart the dale divine:
"What's yonder object—fountain? shrine?
Companions, let us thither go
And make inspection."
                        In consent
Silent they follow him in calm.
It proved an ancient monument—
Rude stone; but tablets lent a charm:
Three tablets on three sides. In one
The Tender Shepherd mild looked down   10
Upon the rescued weanling lost,
Snugged now in arms. In emblem crossed
By pastoral crook, Christ's monogram
(Wrought with a medieval grace)
Showed on the square opposed in face.
But chiefly did they feel the claim
Of the main tablet; there a lamb
On passive haunches upright sate

In patience which reproached not fate;
The two fine furry fore-legs drooping   20
Like tassels; while the shearer, stooping,
Embraced it with one arm; and all
The fleece rolled off in seamless shawl
Flecked here and there with hinted blood.
It did not shrink; no cry did come:
In still life of that stone subdued
Shearer and shorn alike were dumb.

    As with a seventy-four, when lull
Lapses upon the storm, the hull
Rights for the instant, while a moan   30
Of winds succeeds the howl; so here
In poise of heart and altered tone
With Ungar. Respite brief though dear
It proved; for he: "This type's assigned
To One who sharing not man's mind
Partook man's frame; whose mystic birth
Wrecked him upon this reef of earth
Inclement and inhuman. Yet,
Through all the trials that beset,
He leaned on an upholding arm—   40
Foreknowing, too, reserves of balm.
But how of them whose souls may claim
Some link with Christ beyond the name,
Which share the fate, but never share
Aid or assurance, and nowhere
Look for requital? Such there be;
In by-lanes o'er the world ye see
The Calvary-faces." All averse
Turned Derwent, murmuring, "Forbear.
Such breakers do the heaven asperse!"   50
    But timely he alert espied,
Upon the mountain humbly kneeling,
Those shepherds twain, while morning-tide
Rolled o'er the hills with golden healing.
It was a rock they kneeled upon,
Convenient for their rite avowed—
Kneeled, and their turbaned foreheads bowed—

Bowed over, till they kissed the stone:
Each shaggy sur-coat heedful spread
For rug, such as in mosque is laid.   60
About the ledge's favored hem
Mild fed their sheep, enringing them;
While, facing as by second-sight,
Toward Mecca they direct the rite.
    "Look; and their backs on Bethlehem turned,"
Cried Rolfe. The priest then, who discerned
The drift, replied, "Yes, for they pray
To Allah. Well, and what of that?
Christ listens, standing in heaven's gate—
Benignant listens, nor doth stay   70
Upon a syllable in creed:
Vowels and consonants indeed!"
    And Rolfe: "But here were Margoth now,
Seeing yon shepherds praying so,
His gibe would run from man to man:
'Which is the humble publican?
Or do they but prostrate them there
To flout you Franks with Islam's prayer?' "
    "Doubtless: some shallow thing he'd say,
Poor fellow," Derwent then; "but, nay,   80
Earnest they are; nor yet they'd part
(if pealed the hour) in street or mart,
From like observance."
                         "If 'tis so"
The refugee, "let all avow
As openly faith's loyal heart.
By Christians too was God confessed
How frankly! in those days that come
No more to misnamed Christendom!
Religion then was the good guest,
First served, and last, in every gate: 90
What mottoes upon wall and plate!
She every human venture shared:
The ship in manifest declared
That not disclaiming heaven she thrust
Her bowsprit into fog and storm:
Some current silver bore the palm

Of Christ, token of saint, or bust;
In line devout the pikemen kneeled—
To battle by the rite were sealed.
Men were not lettered, but had sense   100
Beyond the mean intelligence
That knows to read, and but to read—
Not think. 'Twas harder to mislead
The people then, whose smattering now
Does but the more their ignorance show—
Nay, them to peril more expose—
Is as the ring in the bull's nose
Whereby a pert boy turns and winds
This monster of a million minds.
Men owned true masters; kings owned God—   110
Their master; Louis plied the rod
Upon himself. In high estate,
Not puffed up like a democrat
In office, how with Charlemagne?
Look up he did, look up in reign—
Humbly look up, who might look down:
His meekest thing was still his crown:
How meek on *him*; since, graven there,
Among the Apostles twelve—behold,
Stern Scriptural precepts were enrolled,   120
High admonitions, meet for kings.
The coronation was a prayer,
Which yet in ceremonial clings.
The church was like a bonfire warm:
All ranks were gathered round the charm."
    Derwent, who vainly had essayed
To impede the speaker, or blockade,
Snatched at the bridle here: "Ho, wait;
A word, impetuous laureate!
This *bric-a-brac-ish* style (outgrown   130
Almost, where first it gave the tone)
Of lauding the quaint ages old—
But nay, that's satire; I withhold.
Grant your side of the shield part true:
What then? why, turn the other: view
The buckler in reverse. Don't sages

Denominate those times Dark Ages?
Dark Middle Ages, time's midnight!"
   "If night, it was no starless one;
Art still admires what then was done: 140
A strength they showed which is of light.
Not more the Phidian marbles prove
The graces of the Grecian prime
And indicate what men they were,
Than the grand minsters in remove
Do intimate, if not declare
A magnanimity which our time
Would envy, were it great enough
To comprehend. Your counterbuff,
However, holds. Yes, frankly, yes,   150
Another side there is, admit.
Nor less the very worst of it
Reveals not such a shamelessness
Of evildoer and hypocrite,
And sordid mercenary sin
As these days vaunt and revel in."
   "No use, no use," the priest aside;
"Patience! it is the maddest tide;"
And seated him.
             And Ungar then:
"What's overtaken ye pale men?   160
Shrewd are ye, the main chance ye heed:
Has God quite lost his throne indeed
That lukewarm now ye grow? Wilt own,
Council ye take with fossil-stone?
Your sects do nowadays create
Churches as worldly as the state.
And, for your more established forms—
Ah, once in York I viewed through storms
The Minster's majesty of mien—
Towers, peaks, and pinnacles sublime—   170
Faith's iceberg, stranded on a scene
How alien, and an alien time;
But now"—he checked himself, and stood.

Whence this strange bias of his mood
(Thought they) leaning to things corroded,
By many deemed for aye exploded?
But, truly, knowing not the man,
At fault they in conjecture ran.
But Ungar (as in fitter place
Set down) being sprung from Romish race,   180
Albeit himself had spared to feed
On any one elected creed
Or rite, though much he might recall
In annals bearing upon all;
And, in this land named of Behest,
A wandering Ishmael from the West;
Inherited the Latin mind,
Which late—blown by the adverse wind
Of harder fortunes that molest—
Kindled from ember into coal.   190
    The priest, as one who keeps him whole,
Anew turns toward the kneeling twain:
"Your error's slight, or, if a stain,
'Twill fade. Our Lord enjoins good deeds
Nor catechiseth in the creeds."
    A something in the voice or man,
Or in assumption of the turn
Which prior theme did so adjourn,
Pricked Ungar, and a look he ran
Toward Derwent—an electric light   200
Chastising in its fierce revolt;
Then settled into that still night
Of cloud which has discharged the bolt.

11. DISQUIET

At breakfast in refectory there
The priest—if Clarel not mistook—
The good priest wore the troubled air
Of honest heart striving to brook
Injury, which from words abstained,
And, hence, not readily arraigned;

Which to requite in its own sort
Is not allowed in heaven's high court,
Or self-respect's. Such would forget,
But for the teasing doubt or fret   10
Lest unto worldly witness mere
The injury none the less appear
To challenge notice at the least.

　　Ungar withdrew, leaving the priest
Less ill at ease; who now a thought
Threw out, as 'twere in sad concern
For one whose nature, sour or stern,
Still dealt in all unhandsome flings
At happy times and happy things:
"'*The bramble sayeth it is naught:*'   20
Poor man!" But that; and quite forbore
To vent his grievance. Nor less sore
He felt it—Clarel so inferred,
Recalling here too Mortmain's word
Of cutting censorship. How then?
While most who met him frank averred
That Derwent ranked with best of men,
The Swede and refugee unite
In one repugnance, yea, and slight.
How take, construe their ill-content?   30
A thing of vein and temperament?
Rolfe liked him; and if Vine said naught,
Yet even Vine seemed not uncheered
By fair address. Then stole the thought
Of how the priest had late appeared
In that one confidential hour,
Ambiguous on Saba's tower.
There he dismissed it, let it fall:
To probe overmuch seems finical.
Nor less (for still the point did tease,   40
Nor would away and leave at ease),
Nor less, I wonder, if ere long
He'll turn this off, not worth a song,
As lightly as of late he turned
Poor Mortmain's sally when he burned?

Marking the priest not all sedate,
Rolfe, that a friend might fret discard,
Turned his attention to debate
Between two strangers at the board.
In furtherance of his point or plea
One said:
        "Late it was told to me,
And by the man himself concerned,
A merchant Frank on Syria's coast,
That in a fire which traveled post,
His books and records being burned,   10
His Christian debtors held their peace;
The Islam ones disclaimed release,
And came with purses and accounts."
   "And duly rendered their amounts?
'Twas very kind. But oh, the greed,
Rapacity, and crime at need
In satraps which oppress the throng."
"True. But with these 'tis, after all,
Wrong-doing purely personal—
Not legislated–not a wrong   20
Law-sanctioned. No: the Turk, admit,
In scheme of state, the scheme of it,
Upon the civil arm confers
A sway above the scimeter's—
The civil power itself subjects
Unto that Koran which respects
Nor place nor person. Nay, adjourn
The jeer; for now aside we'll turn.
Dismembered Poland and her throe
In Ninety-Five, all unredressed: 30
Did France, did England then protest?"
   "England? I'm sure I do not know.
Come, I distrust your shifting so.
Pray, to what end now is this pressed?"
   "Why, here armed Christendom looking on,
In protest the Sultan stood alone."
   "Indeed? But all this, seems to me,

Savors of Urquhart's vanity."
    "The commentator on the East?"
    "The same: that very inexact   40
Eccentric ideologist
Now obsolete."
        "And that's your view?
He stands for God."
         "I stand by fact."
    "Well then, another fact or two;
When Poland's place in Thirty-One
Was blotted out, the Turk again
Protested, with one other man,
The Pope; these, and but these alone;
And in the protest both avowed
'Twas made for justice's sake and God.—   50
You smile."
        "Oh no: but very clear
The protest prompted was by fear
In Turk and Pope, that time might come
When spoliation should drive home
Upon themselves. Besides, you know
The Polish church was Catholic:
The Czar would wrest it to the Greek:
'Twas *that* touched Rome. But let it go.—
In pith, what is it you would show?
Are Turks our betters? Very strange   60
Heaven's favor does not choicely range
Upon these Islam people good:
Bed-rid they are, behindhand all,
While Europe flowers in plenitude
Of wealth and commerce."
           "I recall
Nothing in Testament which saith
That worldliness shall not succeed
In that wherein it laboreth.
Howbeit, the Sultan's coming on:
Fine lesson from ye has he won   70
Of late; apt pupil he indeed:
Ormus, that riches did confer,
Ormus is made a borrower:

Selim, who grandly turbaned sat,
Verges on bankruptcy and—hat.
But this don't touch the rank and file;
At least, as yet. But preach and work:
You'll civilize the barbarous Turk—
Nay, all the East may reconcile:
That done, let Mammon take the wings of even,   80
And mount and civilize the saints in heaven."
    "I laugh—I like a brave caprice!
And, sir—"
                But here did Rolfe release
His ear, and Derwent too. A stir
In court was heard of man and steed—
Neighings and mountings, din indeed;
And Rolfe: "Come, come; our traveler."

13. THE CHURCH OF THE STAR

They rise, and for a little space
In farewell Agath they detain,
Transferred here to a timelier train
Than theirs. A work-day, passive face
He turns to Derwent's *Luck to thee!*
No slight he means—'tis far from that;
But, schooled by the inhuman sea,
He feels 'tis vain to wave the hat
In God-speed on this mortal strand,
Recalling all the sailing crews   10
Destined to sleep in ocean sand,
Cheered from the wharf with blithe adieus.
Nor less the heart's farewell they say,
And bless the old man on his way.

    Led by a slender monk and young,
With curls that ringed the shaven crown,
Courts now and shrines they trace. That thong
Ascetic which can life chastise
Down to her bleak necessities,
They mark in coarse serge of his gown,   20

And girdling rope, with cross of wood
For tag at end; and hut-like hood
Superfluous now behind him thrown;
And sandals which expose the skin
Transparent, and the blue vein thin
Meandering there: the feet, the face
Alike in lucid marble grace.
His simple manners self-possessed
Both saint and noble-born suggest;
Yet under quietude they mark   30
The slumbering of a vivid spark—
Excitable, if brought to test.
A Tuscan, he exchanged the charm
Val d'Arno yields, for this dull calm
Of desert. Was his youth self-given
In frank oblation unto heaven?
Or what inducement might disarm
This Isaac when too young to know?

   Hereon they, pacing, muse—till, lo,
The temple opens in dusk glades   40
Of long-drawn double colonnades:
Monoliths two-score and eight.
Rolfe looked about him, pleased in state:
"But this is goodly! Here we rove
As down the deep Dodona grove:
Years, years and years these boles have stood!—
Late by the spring in idle mood
My will I made (if ye recall),
Providing for the Inn of Trees:
But ah, to set out trunks like these   50
In harbor open unto all
For generations!" So in vein
Rolfe free descanted as through fane
They passed. But noting now the guide
In acquiescence by their side,
He checked himself. "Why prate I here?
This brother—I usurp his sphere."

They came unto a silver star
In pavement set which none do mar
By treading. Here at pause remained   60
The monk; till, seeing Rolfe refrained,
And all, from words, he said: "The place,
Signori, where that shining grace
Which led the Magi, stood; below,
The Manger is." They comment none;
Not voicing everything they know,
In cirque about that silver star
They quietly gaze thereupon.
But, turning now, one glanced afar
Along the columned aisles, and thought   70
Of Baldwin whom the mailed knights brought,
While Godfrey's requiem did ring,
Hither to Bethlehem, and crowned
His temples helmet-worn, with round
Of gold and velvet—crowned him king—
King of Jerusalem, on floor
Of this same nave august, above
The Manger in its low remove
Where lay, a thousand years before,
The Child of awful worshiping,   80
Destined to prove all slights and scorns,
And a God's coronation—thorns.

    Not Derwent's was that revery;
Another thing his heart possessed,
The clashing of the East and West,
Odd sense of incongruity;
He felt a secret impulse move
To start a humorous comment slant
Upon the monk, and sly reprove.
But no: I'll curb the Protestant   90
And modern in me—at least here
For time I'll curb it. Perish truth
If it but act the boor, in sooth,
Requiting courtesy with jeer;
For courteous is our guide, with grace
Of a pure heart.

Some little trace,
May be, of Derwent's passing thought
The Tuscan from his aspect caught;
And turned him: "Pardon! but the crypt:
This way, signori—follow me."
Down by a rock-hewn stair they slipped,
Turning by steps which winding be,
Winning a sparry chamber brave
Unsearched by that prose critic keen,
The daylight. Archimago's cave
Was here? or that more sorcerous scene
The Persian Sibyl kept within
For turbaned musings? Bowing o'er,
Crossing himself, and on the knee,
Straight did the guide that grot adore;   110
Then, rising, and as one set free:
"The place of the Nativity."

    Dim pendent lamps, in cluster small
Were Plelads of the mystic hall;
Fair lamps of silver, lamps of gold—
Rich gifts devout of monarchs old,
Kings catholic. Rare objects beamed
All round, recalling things but dreamed:
Solomon's talismans garnered up,
His sword, his signet-ring and cup.   120
In further caverns, part revealed,
What silent shapes like statues kneeled;
What brown monks moved by twinkling shrines
Like Aztecs down in silver mines.

    This, this the Stable mean and poor?
Noting their looks, to ward surprise,
The Italian: " 'Tis incrusted o'er
With marbles, so that now one's eyes
Meet not the natural wall. This floor—"

    "But how? within a cave we stand!"   130
"Yes, caves of old to use were put
For cattle, and with gates were shut.
One meets them still—with arms at hand,
The keepers nigh. Sure it need be

That if in Gihon ye have been,
Or hereabouts, yourselves have seen
The grots in question."

They agree;
And silent in their hearts confess
The strangeness, but the truth no less.
    Anew the guide: "Ere now we get   140
Further herein, indulge me yet;"
But paused awhile: "Though o'er this cave,
Where Christ" (and crossed himself) "had birth,
Constantine's mother reared the Nave
Whose Greek mosaics fade in bloom,
No older church in Christendom;
And generations, with the girth
Of domes and walls, have still enlarged
And built about; yet convents, shrines,
Cloisters and towers, take not for signs,   150
Entreat ye, of meek faith submerged
Under proud masses. Be it urged
As all began from these small bounds,
So, by all avenues and gates,
All here returns, hereto redounds:
In this one Cave all terminates:
In honor of the Manger sole
Saints, kings, knights, prelates reared the whole."
    He warmed. Ah, fervor bought too dear:
The fingers clutching rope and cross;   160
Life too intense; the cheek austere
Deepening in hollow, waste and loss.
They marked him; and at heart some knew
Inklings they loved not to pursue.
But Rolfe recalled in fleeting gleam
The first Franciscan, richly born—
The youthful one who, night and morn,
In Umbria ranged the hills in dream,
And first devised the girdling cord
In type that rebel senses so   170
Should led be—led like beast abroad
By halter. Tuscan! in the glow
And white light of thy faith's illumings,

In vigils, fervent prayers and trances,
Agonies and self-consumings—
Renewest thou the young Saint Francis?
    So inly Rolfe; when, in low tone
Considerate Derwent whispered near:
"'Tis doubtless the poor boy's first year
In Bethlehem; time will abate   180
This novice-ardor; yes, sedate
He'll grow, adapt him to the sphere."

Close to the *Sanctum* now they drew,
A semicircular recess;
And there, in marble floor, they view
A silver sun which (friars profess)
Is set in plummet-line exact
Beneath the star in pavement-tract
Above; and raying from this sun
Shoot jasper-spikes, which so point out   190
Argent inscription roundabout
In Latin text; which thus may run:
THE VIRGIN HERE BROUGHT FORTH THE SON.
    The Tuscan bowed him; then with air
Friendly he turned; but something there
In Derwent's look—no matter what—
An open levity 'twas not—
Disturbed him; and in accents clear,
As challenged in his faith sincere:
"I trust tradition! Here He lay   200
Who shed on Mary's breasts the ray:
Salvator Mundi!"
                Turning now,
He noted, and he bade them see
Where, with a timid piety
A band of rustics bent them low
In worship mute: "Shepherds these are,
And come from pastoral hills not far
Whereon they keep the night-watch wild:
These, like their sires, adore the CHILD,
And in same spot. But, mixed with these,   210
Mark ye yon poor swart images

In other garb? But late they fled
From over Jordan hither; yes,
Escaping so the heinousness
Of one with price upon his head.
But look, and yet seem not to peer,
Lest pain ye give: an eye, an ear,
A hand, is mutilate or gone:
The mangler marked them for his own;
But Christ redeems them." Derwent here   220
His eyes withdrew, but Ungar not,
While visibly the red blood shot
Into his thin-skinned scar, and sent,
As seemed, a pulse of argument
Confirming so some angry sense
Of evil, and malevolence
In man toward man.
                              Now, lower down
The cave, the Manger they descry,
With marble lined; and, o'er it thrown,
A lustrous saint-cloth meets the eye.   230
And suits of saint-cloths here they have
Wherewith to deck the Manger brave:
Gifts of the Latin princes, these—
Fair Christmas gifts, these draperies.
A damask one of gold and white
Rich flowered with pinks embroidered bright,
Was for the present week in turn
The adornment of the sacred Urn.
Impressive was it here to note
Those herdsmen in the shaggy coat: 240
Impressive, yet partook of dream;
It touched the pilgrims, as might seem;
Which pleased the monk; but in disguise
Modest he dropped his damsel-eyes.
    Thought Derwent then: Demure in sooth!
'Tis like a maid in lily of youth
Who grieves not in her core of glee,
By spells of grave virginity
To cozen men to foolish looks;
While she—who reads such hearts' hid nooks?—   250

What now? "Signori, here, believe,
Where night and day, while ages run,
Faith in these lamps burns on and on,
'Tis good to spend one's Christmas Eve;
Yea, better rather than in land
Which may your holly tree command,
And greens profuse which ye inweave."

14. SOLDIER AND MONK

Fervid he spake. And Ungar there
Appeared (if looks allow surmise)
In latent way to sympathize,
Yet wonder at the votary's air;
And frequent too he turned his face
To note the grotto, and compare
These haunted precincts with the guide,
As so to realize the place,
Or fact from fable to divide;
At times his changeful aspect wore   10
Touch of the look the simple shepherds bore.
    The Tuscan marked; he pierced him through,
Yet gently, gifted with the clew—
Ascetic insight; and he caught
The lapse within the soldier's thought,
The favorable frame, nor missed
Appealing to it, to enlist
Or influence, or drop a seed
Which might some latter harvest breed.
Gently approaching him, he said: 20
"True sign you bear: your sword's a cross."
Ungar but started, as at loss
To take the meaning, and yet led
To marvel how that mannered word
Did somehow slip into accord
With visitings that scarce might cleave—
Shadows, but shadows fugitive.
He lifted up the steel: the blade
Was straight; the hilt, a bar: "'Tis true;

A cross, it is a cross," he said; 30

And touched seemed, though 'twas hardly new.

    Then glowed the other; and, again:
"Ignatius was a soldier too,
And Martin. 'Tis the pure disdain
Of life, or, holding life the real,
Still subject to a brave ideal—
'Tis this that makes the tent a porch
Whereby the warrior wins the church:
The habit of renouncing, yes,
'Tis good, a good preparedness.— 40
Our founder"—here he raised his eyes
As unto all the sanctities—
"Footing it near Rieti town
Met a young knight on horseback, one
Named Angelo Tancredi: 'Lo,'
He said, 'Thy belt thou'lt change for cord,
Thy spurs for mire, good Angelo,
And be a true knight of the Lord.'
And he, the cavalier—" Aside
A brother of the cowl here drew 50
This ardent proselyting guide,
Detaining him in interview
About some matter. Ungar stood
Lost in his thoughts.

                In neighborhood
Derwent by Rolfe here chanced to bide;
And said. "It just occurs to me
As interesting in its way,
That these Franciscans steadily
Have been custodians of the Tomb
And Manger, ever since the day 60
Of rescue under Godfrey's plume
Long centuries ago." Rolfe said:
"Ay; and appropriate seems it too
For the Franciscan retinue
To keep these places, since their head,
St. Francis, spite his scouted hood,
May claim more of similitude
To Christ, than any man we know.

Through clouds of myth investing him—
Obscuring, yet attesting him,   70
He burns with the seraphic glow
And perfume of a holy flower.
Sweetness, simplicity, with power!
By love's true miracle of charm
He instituted a reform
(Not insurrection) which restored
For time the spirit of his Lord
On earth. If sad perversion came
Unto his order—what of that?
All Christianity shares the same: 80
Pure things men need adulterate
And so adapt them to the kind."

    "Oh, oh! But I have grown resigned
To these vagaries.—And for him,
Assisi's saint—a good young man,
No doubt, and beautiful to limn;
Yes, something soft, Elysian;
Nay, rather, the transparent hue
Unearthly of a maiden tranced
In sleep somnambulic; no true   90
Color of health; beauty enhanced
To enervation. In a word,
For all his charity divine,
Love, self-devotion, ardor fine—
Unmanly seems he!"

                  "Of our Lord
The same was said by Machiavel,
Or hinted, rather. Prithee, tell,
What is it to be *manly?*"

                    "Why,   100
To be man-like"—and here the chest
Bold out he threw—"man at his best!"
But even at best, one might reply,
Man is that thing of sad renown
Which moved a deity to come down
And save him. Lay not too much stress
Upon the carnal manliness:
The Christliness is better—higher;

And Francis owned it, the first friar.
Too orthodox is that?" 110
                    "See, see,"
Said Derwent, with kind air of one
Who would a brother's weak spot shun:
"Mark this most delicate drapery;
If woven by some royal dame—
God bless her and her tambour frame!"

15. SYMPHONIES

Meanwhile with Vine there, Clarel stood
Aside in friendly neighborhood,
And felt a flattering pleasure stir
At words—nor in equivocal tone
Freakish, or leaving to infer,
Such as beforetime he had known—
Breathed now by that exceptional one
In unconstraint:
                    "Tis very much
The cold fastidious heart to touch
This way; nor is it mere address   10
That so could move one's silver chord.
How he transfigured Ungar's sword!
Delusive is this earnestness
Which holds him in its passion pale—
Tenant of melancholy's dale
Of mirage? To interpret him,
Perhaps it needs a swallow-skim
Over distant time. Migrate with me
Across the years, across the sea.—
How like a Poor Clare in her cheer   20
(Grave Sister of his order sad)
Showed nature to that Cordelier
Who, roving in the Mexic glade,
Saw in a bud of happy dower
Whose stalk entwined the tropic tree,
Emblems of Christ's last agony:
In anthers, style, and fibers torn,

The five wounds, nails, and crown of thorn;
And named it so the passion-flower.
What beauty in that sad conceit!   30
Such charm, the title still we meet.
Our guide, methinks, where'er he turns
For him this passion-flower burns;
And all the world is elegy.
A green knoll is to you and me
But pastoral, and little more:
To him 'tis even Calvary
Where feeds the Lamb. This passion-flower—
But list!"

        Hid organ-pipes unclose
A timid rill of slender sound,   40
Which gains in volume—grows, and flows
Gladsome in amplitude of bound.
Low murmurs creep. From either side
Tenor and treble interpose,
And talk across the expanding tide:
Debate, which in confusion merges—
Din and clamor, discord's hight:
Countering surges—paeans—dirges—
Mocks, and laughter light.
    But rolled in long ground-swell persistent,   50
A tone, an under-tone assails
And overpowers all near and distant;
Earnest and sternest, it prevails.
    Then terror, horror—wind and rain—
Accents of undetermined fear,
And voices as in shipwreck drear:
A sea, a sea of spirits in pain!
    The suppliant cries decrease—
The voices in their ferment cease:
One wave rolls over all and whelms to peace.   60

    But hark—oh, hark!
Whence, whence this stir, this whirr of wings?
Numbers numberless convening—
    Harps and child-like carolings
In happy holiday of meaning:

To God be glory in the hight,
    For tidings glad we bring;
Good will to men, and peace on earth
    We children-cherubs sing!

To God be glory in the depth,
    As in the hight be praise;   70
He who shall break the gates of death
    A babe in manger rays.

Ye people all in every land,
    Embrace, embrace, be kin:
Immanuel's born in Bethlehem,
    And gracious years begin!

   It dies; and, half around the heavenly sphere,
Like silvery lances lightly touched aloft—
Like Northern Lights appealing to the ear,   80
An elfin melody chimes low and soft.
That also dies, that last strange fairy-thrill:
Slowly it dies away, and all is sweetly still.

16. THE CONVENT ROOF

To branching grottoes next they fare,
Old caves of penitence and prayer,
Where Paula kneeled—her urn is there—
Paula the Widow, Scipio's heir
But Christ's adopted. Well her tomb
Adjoins her friend's, renowned Jerome.
   Never the attending Druze resigned
His temperate poise, his moderate mind;
While Belex, in punctilious guard,
Relinquished not the martial ward: 10
"If by His tomb hot strife may be,
Trust ye His cradle shall be free?
Heed one experienced, sirs." His sword,
Held cavalier by jingling chain,
Dropping at whiles, would clank amain

Upon the pave.
                    "I pray ye now,"
To him said Rolfe in accents low,
"Have care; for see ye not ye jar
These devotees? they turn—they cease
(Hearing your clanging scimeter)   20
Their suppliance to the Prince of Peace."

    Like miners from the shaft, or tars
From forth the hold, up from those spars
And grottoes, by the stony stair
They climb, emerge, and seek the air
In open space.
                    "Save me, what now?"
Cried Derwent, foremost of the group—
"The holy water!"
                    Hanging low
Outside, was fixed a scalloped stoup
Or marble shell, to hold the wave   30
Of Jordan, for true ones to lave
The finger, and so make the sign,
The Cross's sign, ere in they slip
And bend the knee. In this divine
Recess, deliberately a lip
Was lapping slow, with long-drawn pains,
The liquid globules, last remains
Of the full stone. Astray, alas,
Athirst and lazed, it was—the ass;
The friars, withdrawn for time, having left   40
That court untended and bereft.
"Was ever Saracen so bold!"
    "Well, things have come to pretty pass—
The mysteries slobbered by an ass!"
    "Mere Nature do we here behold?"
So they. But he, the earnest guide,
Turning the truant there aside,
Said, and in unaffected tone:
"What should it know, this foolish one?
It is an infidel we see: 50
Ah, the poor brute's stupidity!"

"I hardly think so," Derwent said;
"For, look, it hangs the conscious head."
The friar no relish had for wit,
No sense, perhaps, too rapt for it,
Pre-occupied. So, having seen
The ass led back, he bade adieu;
But first, and with the kindliest mien:
"Signori, would ye have fair view
Of Bethlehem of Judaea, pray   60
Ascend to roof. ye take yon stair.
And now, heaven have ye in its care—
Me save from sin, and all from error!
Farewell."—But Derwent: "Yet delay:
Fain would we cherish when away:
Thy name, then?" "Brother Salvaterra."
"'Tis a fair name. And, brother, we
Are not insensible, conceive,
To thy most Christian courtesy.—
He goes. Sweet echo does he leave   70
In *Salvaterra*: may it dwell!
Silver in every syllable!"
"And import too," said Rolfe.
                                    They fare
And win the designated stair,
And climb; and, as they climb, in bell
Of Derwent's repetition, fell:
Me save from sin, and all from error!
So prays good brother Salvaterra."

In paved flat roof, how ample there,
They tread a goodly St. Mark's Square   80
Aloft. An elder brother lorn
They meet, with shrunken cheek, and worn
Like to a slab whereon may weep
The unceasing water-drops. And deep
Within his hollow gown-sleeves old
His viewless hands he did enfold.
He never spake, but moved away
With shuffling pace of dragged infirm delay.
"Seaward he gazed," said Rolfe, "toward home:

An empty longing!"

              "Cruel Rome!"   90

Sighed Derwent; "See, though, good to greet

The vale of eclogue, Boaz' seat.

Trips Ruth there, yonder?" thitherward

Down pointing where the vineyards meet.

At that dear name in Bethlehem heard,

How Clarel starts. Not Agar's child—

Naomi's! Then, unreconciled,

And in reaction falling low,

He saw the files Armenian go,

The tapers round the virgin's bier,   100

And heard the boys' light strophe free

Overborne by the men's antistrophe.

Illusion! yet he knew a fear:

"Fixed that this second night we bide

In Bethlehem?" he asked aside.

Yes, so 'twas planned. For moment there

He thought to leave them and repair

Alone forthwith to Salem. Nay,

Doubt had unhinged so, that her sway,

In minor things even, could retard   110

The will and purpose. And, beyond,

Prevailed the tacit pilgrim-bond—

Of no slight force in his regard;

Besides, a diffidence was sown:

None knew his heart, nor might he own;

And, last, feared he to prove the fear?

With outward things he sought to clear

His mind; and turned to list the tone

Of Derwent, who to Rolfe: "Here now

One stands emancipated."

              "How?"   120

"The air—the air, the liberal air!

Those witcheries of the cave ill fare

Reviewed aloft. Ah, Salvaterra,

So winning in thy dulcet error—

How fervid thou! Nor less thy tone,

So heartfelt in sincere effusion,

Is hardly that more chastened one

We Protestants feel. But the illusion!
Those grottoes: yes, void now they seem
As phantoms which accost in dream—   130
Accost and fade. Hold you with me?"
    "Yes, partly: I in part agree.
In Kedron too, thou mayst recall,
The monkish night of festival,
And masque enacted—how it shrank
When, afterward, in nature frank,
Upon the terrace thrown at ease,
Like magi of the old Chaldaea,
Viewing Rigel and Betelguese,
We breathed the balm-wind from Sabaea.   140
All shows and forms in Kedron had—
Nor hymn nor banner made them glad
To me. And yet—why, who may know!
These things come down from long ago.
While so much else partakes decay,
While states, tongues, manners pass away,
How wonderful the Latin rite
Surviving still like oak austere
Over crops rotated year by year,
Or Caesar's tower on London's site.   150
But, tell me: stands it true in fact
That robe and ritual—every kind
By Rome employed in ways exact—
However strange to modern mind,
Or even absurd (like cards Chinese
In ceremonial usages),
Not less of faith or need were born—
Survive untampered with, unshorn;
Date far back to a primal day,
Obscure and hard to trace indeed—   160
The springing of the planted seed
In the church's first organic sway?
Still for a type, a type or use,
Each decoration so profuse
Budding and flowering? Tell me here."
    "If but one could! To be sincere,
Rome's wide campania of old lore

Ecclesiastic—that waste shore
I've shunned: an instinct makes one fear
Malarial places. But I'll tell   170
That at the mass this very morn
I marked the broidered maniple
Which by the ministrant was worn:
How like a napkin does it show,
Thought I, a napkin on the arm
Of servitor. And hence we know
Its origin. In the first days
(And who denies their simple charm!)
When the church's were like household ways,
Some served the flock in humble state—   180
At Eucharist, passed cup or plate.
The thing of simple use, you see,
Tricked out—embellished—has become
Theatric and a form. There's Rome!
Yet what of this, since happily
Each superflux men now disown."

   "Perchance!—" 'Tis an ambiguous time;
And periods unforecast come on.
Recurs to me a Persian rhyme:
In Pera late an Asian man,   190
With stately cap of Astracan,
I knew in arbored coffee-house
On bluff above the Bosphorus.
Strange lore was his, and Saadi's wit:
Over pipe and Mocha long we'd sit
Discussing themes which thrive in shade.
In pause of talk a way he had
Of humming a low air of his:
I asked him once, What trills your bird?
And he recited it in word,   200
To pleasure me, and this it is:

     "Flamen, flamen, put away
    Robe and mitre glorious:
       Doubt undeifies the day!
    Look, in vapors odorous
       As the spice-king's funeral-pyre,

Dies the Zoroastrian fire
   On your altars in decay:
The rule, the Magian rule is run,
And Mythra abdicates the sun!"   210

255

Excerpts from

Clarel

EDITOR'S NOTES

Walter Bezanson's edition of *Clarel* contains an "Introduction," "The Characters: A Critical Index," and "Explanatory Notes," all of which are of the greatest value to any student of the poem. The Northwestern/Newberry edition of *Clarel* (1991) reprints this material with supplements updating it and a textual history and some related documents. Book-length studies of the poem include Vincent Kenny, *Herman Melville's Clarel: A Spiritual Autobiography*, and Stan Goldman, *Melville's Protest Theism: The Hidden and Silent God in Clarel*. Articles by Hershel Parker and Bryan Short offer valuable insights. Larry Edward Wegener's *Concordance to Herman Melville's* Clarel: A Poem and Pilgrimage in the Holy Land is a valuable resource for study of the details in the poem.

Part One

CANTOS 29 – 33. Clarel, a young student, has arrived in Jerusalem on a pilgrimage. He rambles around the city and meets a number of interesting companions, including Nehemiah, an old man "touched by the chastenings of Eld" who carries the Bible with him and offers himself as a guide. The two men, young and old, proceed to see all that Jerusalem has to offer. In their rambles they encounter Celio, a young hunchback who enunciates his defiance of Christian beliefs. At the Wailing Wall, Clarel first sees Ruth and is struck by her beauty. Clarel falls in love with Ruth and she with him, but they are restricted in the time they can spend together. In further ramblings, he encounters Vine, whose appearance makes a deep impression upon him: A low wind waves his "Lydian" hair; "A funeral man, yet richly fair— / Fair as the sabled violets be" (I.18.41 – 43).

CANTO 29. This tells more of Vine and speculates on his richly ambiguous character; he possesses a "charm of subtle virtue" but is not saintly. Instead, a "ripe flush, Venetian mould / Evinced no nature saintly fine, / But blood like swart Vesuvian wine." He is associated in the poet's mind with myth as he "gleamed the richer for the shade / About him, as in somber glade / Of Virgil's wood the Sibyl's Golden Bough." Vine has been identified as Hawthorne, but, in Melville's poetic version, he has become something more than a character based on a friend. Like others in the poem, he is very much a representative man, standing for certain views and attitudes.

CANTOS 30–31. Visiting the Garden of Gethsemane, the new friends encounter Rolfe, a remarkable person who will come to dominate much of the poem. He is a sort of ideal figure for Clarel and becomes a leader for the other pilgrims and guides by virtue of his knowledge and outspoken views about the world. His is a rich personality. The young man sees Rolfe and Vine as "peers" from whom he can learn much.

CANTO 32. Rama is the name given to any of three heroic incarnations of Vishnu: Balarama, Parashurama, and Ramachandra, the last of whom, often called "Rama," is the hero of the Hindu epic poem *Ramayana*. As eldest son, Rama was to succeed as king, but palace intrigues caused his exile, the "curtailment of his right." He consented to go into exile without a struggle, a "fugitive without redress." Interrupting his narrative for a canto of meditation, the poet enumerates some of the virtues of such a person, who must not suffer from "craft" or "envy's smart" but must be one whose thoughts "dive and skim." Such a combination of virtues Clarel believes he has found in Rolfe, since Vine will eventually prove unfit for the role.

CANTO 33. The narrative continues with a visit to the ruins of a monastery. Rolfe comments on Christ's seeing the city from this vantage point and weeping over it (The source is a passage in Luke 19:41ff.) Enemies invading the city "shall not leave in thee one stone upon another." In a passage of counterpoint, Clarel muses over the Trojan war and the destruction of that city.

When Ruth's father, Nathan, is killed, she is not allowed to see Clarel until the period of mourning has concluded. He decides to go on a tour with Rolfe, Vine, Nehemiah, and others. The account of this pilgrimage will take up most of the poem.

Part Two, "The Wilderness"

CANTOS 29–35. Those making the pilgrimage include Derwent, an Anglican priest; an elder of the Presbyterian church; and an unnamed banker, who is an epicurean, accompanied by his future son-in-law, Glaucon. These are carefully chosen by the poet to be representative of a variety of opinions, which they, for the most part, express very articulately. Mortmain, another member of the group, is introduced through his conversation and invective in Canto 3. An exile and a wanderer, he has a dark vision of mankind. "Man's vicious," he asserts, "snaffle him with kings; / Or, if kings cease to curb, devise / Severer bit" (2.3.189–91). In the fourth canto, "Of Mortmain," more is told about his background. Having failed in idealistic revolutionary movements, he has come to believe in the dominance of fate, "some power / Unknowable, thou'lt yet adore. / *That* steers the world, not man" (2.4.106–8). The term *mortmain*, meaning "dead hand," is one used in law to indicate permanent possession of properties by some institution, frequently the church. Margoth, a geologist the pilgrims meet on their way, represents the scientific view and the materialism of the time; nothing exists that the sciences—especially his geology—cannot explain. With argumentation and discussion, the group proceeds east from the city to the Dead Sea.

CANTO 29. "By the Marge" describes the Dead Sea and its ugly shoreline, and the poet offers a conjecture about it: "Though framed within the lines of heaven / The picture intimates a hell" (19–20). Each member of the party responds in his own way to the sight, until a rainbow appears above the sea and excites new thoughts.

CANTO 30. Because this group is proceeding north along the shore of the Dead Sea, they will not see the fabulous city of Petra, to the south. Rolfe, who has visited the ruins, gives an account of its beauties. "Lost" for centuries, the city was discovered in 1812 and then visited by travelers who wrote about it. Melville owned Arthur Penrhyn Stanley's *Sinai and Palestine in Connection with Their History* (1865), his chief source in describing Petra. He may have read Harriet Martineau's account of the city in her *Eastern Life, Present and Past* (1848).

CANTO 31–33. The narrative recommences with the discovery of the incised rock and inscription. The pilgrims set up a camp, awaiting the return of Mortmain, who had left the group, briefly. At the edge of the Dead Sea, Clarel encounters Vine, Rolfe, and Margoth for a discussion of the history of the region.

CANTOS 34–35. When Mortmain returns, he inspires some fear by his appearance, "his face / Rigid and darkened," and tastes the water of the sea. Canto 35 is another section of meditation, this time on the labyrinthine human spirit, as complex as the etchings of Piranesi. Giovanni Battista Piranesi (1720–1778) composed complex pictures of prisons with arches, passages, and instruments of torture. "Paul's 'mystery of iniquity'" (Thessalonians 2:7) is a phrase Melville will use again to describe the labyrinthine plots of Claggart in *Billy Budd*. The canto is "prelusive" to Mortmain's declaration of human criminality and sin, which includes a number of "sins there be inscrutable, / Unutterable" (2.36.84–85).

In the remainder of Part 2, Nehemiah is drowned in the Dead Sea. His body, discovered by Vine, is buried at the sea shore: "Inside a hollow free from stone / With Camel-ribs they scooped a trench" (2.39.94–95). As they complete the obsequies, there is an avalanche of rock, which harms no one, and then a rainbow above the sea.

Part Three, "Mar Saba"

During this part of the poem (no excerpts given here), the pilgrims proceed north to the monastery of Mar Saba. Welcomed by the monks, they visit various sites within the complex and take part in some of the ceremonies. Clarel is impressed by the religious atmosphere, as are most of the others. He contemplates the idea of a monkish life rather than marriage with Ruth. Toward the end of their stay, Mortmain is missed; he has died on one of the ledges of the monastery. Since he cannot be part of the religious brotherhood, he is buried outside the walls. The death of Mortmain, following that of Nehemiah, sets a tone that will be evident in the concluding portions of the poem, preparing the reader for other deaths.

Part Four, "Bethlehem"

CANTOS 10 – 16. As the pilgrims turn back toward Jerusalem, they are joined by Ungar, a Civil War veteran, who, with his skepticism and bitterness, more than adequately fills the role of the dead Mortmain. He denounces the materialism of the present, and, as Bezanson puts it (633), he emphasizes the evil within man and the need man has for religion. The group stops at Bethlehem, an important site in any pilgrimage to the Holy Land.

CANTOS 10 – 13. The pilgrims find an ancient monument showing Christ as shepherd, with a lamb being sheared (4.x.8 – 28). They visit the Church of the Star, guided by a monk, and come to the site of the Nativity (Canto 13). A debate between Derwent and Ungar follows (Canto 14), while Clarel, with Vine, listens to organ music (Canto 15).

The rest of the story is soon told. Returning to Jerusalem, Clarel learns that both Ruth and her mother have died. His reaction during the next few days is described: "bound he sate / In film of sorrow without moan" (4.32.2 – 3). The others must go on their way, but he remains in Jerusalem until the Easter celebrations and then joins another group of pilgrims. In the final canto, the poet meditates upon the inability of science to solve the theological problems and holds out some hope: "Even death may prove unreal at the last, / And stoics be astounded into heaven." The poem has a peroration addressed to the young pilgrim who has decided nothing about his own destiny:

> Then keep thy heart, though yet but ill-resigned—
> Clarel, thy heart, the issues there but mind;
> That like the crocus budding through the snow—
> That like a swimmer rising from the deep—
> That like a burning secret which doth go
> Even from the bosom that would hoard and keep;
> Emerge thou mayst from the last whelming sea,
> And prove that death but routs life into victory. (4.35.25 – 34)

It should be noted that the bulk of the poem is composed in tetrameter couplets, with occasional changes in the rhyme scheme. But the epilogue is cast into iambic pentameter. Melville had adequate sanction for using the tetrameter form in his long narrative. It was the form adopted for many narrative poems, including Sir Walter Scott's *The Lady of the Lake*, Lord Byron's *The Giaour*, *The Bride of Abydos*, *The Siege of Corinth*, and *The Prisoner of Chillon*. Among American poets who used the form are John Greenleaf Whittier in *Snow-Bound: A Winter Idyl* (1866) and Henry Wadsworth Longfellow in *The Song of Hiawatha* (1855). The public success of these poems may have convinced Melville that he, too, could write a best-seller.

John Marr and Other Sailors —
with *Some Sea Pieces*

John Marr, toward the close of the last century born in America of a mother unknown, and from boyhood up to maturity a sailor under divers flags, disabled at last from further maritime life by a crippling wound received at close quarters with pirates of the Keys, eventually betakes himself for a livelihood to less active employment ashore. There, too, he transfers his rambling disposition acquired as a sea-farer.

After a variety of removals, at first as a sail-maker from sea-port to sea-port, then adventurously inland as a rough bench-carpenter, he, finally, in the last-named capacity, settles down about the year 1838 upon what was then a frontier-prairie, sparsely sprinkled with small oak-groves and yet fewer log-houses of a little colony but recently from one of our elder inland States. Here, putting a period to his rovings, he marries.

Ere long a fever, the bane of new settlements on teeming loam, and whose sallow livery was certain to show itself, after an interval, in the complexions of too many of these people, carries off his young wife and infant child. In one coffin, put together by his own hands, they are committed with meager rites to the earth—another mound, though a small one, in the wide prairie, not far from where the mound-builders of a race only conjecturable had left their pottery and bones, one common clay, under a strange terrace serpentine in form.

With an honest stillness in his general mien—swarthy and black-browed, with eyes that could soften or flash, but never harden, yet disclosing at times a melancholy depth this kinless man had affections which, once placed, not readily could be dislodged or resigned to a substituted object. Being now arrived at middle-life, he resolves never to quit the soil that holds the only beings ever connected with him by love in the family tie. His log-house he lets to a new-comer, one glad enough to get it, and dwells with the household.

While the acuter sense of his bereavement becomes mollified by time, the void at heart abides. Fain, if possible, would he fill that void by cultivating social relations yet nearer than before with a people whose lot he purposes sharing to the end—relations superadded to that mere work-a-day bond arising from participation in the same outward hardships, making reciprocal helpfulness a matter of course. But here, and nobody to blame, he is obstructed.

More familiarly to consort, men of a practical turn must sympathetically converse, and upon topics of real life. But, whether as to persons or events, one cannot always be talking about the present, much less speculating about the future; one must needs recur to the past, which, with the mass of men, where the past is in any personal way a common inheritance, supplies to most practical natures the basis of sympathetic communion.

But the past of John Marr was not the past of these pioneers. Their hands had rested on the plow-tail, his upon the ship's helm. They knew but their own kind and their own usages; to him had been revealed something of the checkered globe. So limited unavoidably was the mental reach, and by consequence the range of sympathy, in this particular hand of domestic emigrants, hereditary tillers of the soil, that the ocean, but a hearsay to their fathers, had now through yet deeper inland removal become to themselves little more than a rumor traditional and vague.

They were a staid people; staid through habituation to monotonous hardship; ascetics by necessity not less than through moral bias; nearly all of them sincerely, however narrowly, religious. They were kindly at need, after their fashion; but to a man wonted—as John Marr in his previous homeless sojournings could not but have been—to the free-and-easy tavern-clubs affording cheap recreation of an evening in certain old and comfortable sea-port towns of that time, and yet more familiar with the companionship afloat of the sailors of the same period, something was lacking. That something was geniality, the flower of life springing from some sense of joy in it, more or less. This their lot could not give to these hard-working endurers of the dispiriting malaria,—men to whom a holiday never came,—and they had too much of uprightness and no art at all or desire to affect what they did not really feel. At a corn-husking, their least grave of gatherings, did the lone-hearted mariner seek to divert his own thoughts from sadness, and in some degree interest theirs, by adverting to aught removed from the crosses and trials of their personal surroundings, naturally enough he would slide into some marine story or picture, but would soon recoil upon himself and be silent, finding no encouragement to proceed. Upon one such occasion an elderly man—a blacksmith, and at Sunday gatherings an earnest exhorter—honestly said to him, "Friend, we know nothing of that here."

Such unresponsiveness in one's fellow-creatures set apart from factitious life, and by their vocation—in those days little helped by machinery—standing, as it were, next of kin to Nature; this, to John Marr, seemed of a piece with the apathy of Nature herself as envisaged to him here on a prairie where none but the perished mound-builders had as yet left a durable mark.

The remnant of Indian thereabout—all but exterminated in their recent and final war with regular white troops, a war waged by the Red Men for their native soil and natural rights—had been coerced into the occupancy of wilds not very far beyond the Mississippi—wilds *then,* but now the seats of municipalities and States. Prior to that, the bisons, once streaming countless in processional herds, or browsing as in an endless battle-line over these vast aboriginal pastures, had retreated, dwindled in number, before the hunters, in main a race distinct from the agricultural pioneers, though generally their advance-guard. Such a double exodus of man and beast left the plain a desert, green or blossoming indeed, but almost as forsaken as the Siberian Obi. Save the prairie-hen, sometimes startled from its lurking-place in the rank grass; and, in their migratory season, pigeons, high overhead on the wing, in dense multitudes eclipsing the day like a passing storm-cloud; save these—there being no wide woods with their underwood—birds were strangely few.

Blank stillness would for hours reign unbroken on this prairie. "It is the bed of a dried-up sea," said the companionless sailor— no geologist—to himself, musing at twilight upon the fixed undulations of that immense alluvial expanse bounded only by the horizon, and missing there the stir that, to alert eyes and ears, animates at all times the apparent solitudes of the deep.

But a scene quite at variance with one's antecedents may yet prove suggestive of them. Hooped round by a level rim, the prairie was to John Marr a reminder of ocean.

With some of his former shipmates, *chums* on certain cruises, he had contrived, prior to this last and more remote removal, to keep up a little correspondence at odd intervals. But from tidings of anybody or any sort he, in common with the other settlers, was now cut off; quite cut off, except from such news as might be conveyed over the grassy billows by the last-arrived prairie-schooner—the vernacular term, in those parts and times, for the emi-grant-wagon arched high over with sail-cloth, and voyaging across the vast champaign. There was no reachable post-office as yet; not even the rude little receptive box with lid and leather hinges, set up at convenient intervals on a stout stake along some solitary green way, affording a perch for birds, and which, later in the unintermitting advance of the frontier, would perhaps decay into a mossy monument, attesting yet another successive overleaped limit of civilized life; a life which in America can to-day hardly be said to have any western bound but the ocean that washes Asia. Throughout these plains, now in places overpopulous with towns over-opulent; sweeping plains, elsewhere fenced off in every di-rection into flourishing farms—pale townsmen and hale farmers alike, in part, the descendants of the first sallow settlers; a region that half a century ago produced little for the sustenance of man, but to-day launching its superabundant wheat-harvest on the world;—of this prairie, now everywhere intersected with wire and rail, hardly can it be said that at the period here written of there was so much as a traceable road. To the long-distance trav-eller the oak-groves, wide apart, and varying in compass and form; these, with recent settlements, yet more widely separate, offered some landmarks; but otherwise he steered by the sun. In early midsummer, even going but from one log-encampment to the next, a journey it might be of hours or good part of a day, travel was much like navigation. In some more enriched depres-sions between the long, green, graduated swells, smooth as those of ocean becalmed receiving and subduing to its own tranquillity the voluminous surge raised by some far-off hurricane of days previous, here one would catch the first indication of advancing strangers either in the distance, as a far sail at sea, by the glistening white canvas of the wagon, the wagon itself wading through the rank vegetation and hidden by it, or, failing that, when near to, in the ears of the team, peeking, if not above the tall tiger-lilies, yet above the yet taller grass.

Luxuriant, this wilderness; but, to its denizen, a friend left behind anywhere in the world seemed not alone absent to sight, but an absentee from existence.

Though John Marr's shipmates could not all have departed life, yet as subjects of meditation they were like phantoms of the dead. As the growing sense of his environment threw him more and more upon retrospective musings, these phantoms, next to those of his wife and child, became spiritual companions, losing something of their first indistinctness and putting on it last a dim semblance of mute life; and they were lit by that aureola circling over any object of the affections of the past for reunion with which an imaginative heart passionately yearns.

He invokes these visionary ones,—striving, as it were, to get into verbal communion with them, or, under yet stronger illusion, reproaching them for their silence:—

Since as in night's deck-watch ye show,
Why, lads, so silent here to me,
Your watchmate of times long ago?

Once, for all the darkling sea,
You your voices raised how clearly,
Striking in when tempest sung;
Hoisting up the storm-sail cheerly,
Life is storm—let storm! you rung.
Taking things as fated merely,
Child-like though the world ye spanned;
Nor holding unto life too dearly,
Ye who held your lives in hand—
Skimmers, who on oceans four
Petrels were, and larks ashore.

O, not from memory lightly flung,
Forgot, like strains no more availing,
The heart to music haughtier strung;
Nay, frequent near me, never staleing,
Whose good feeling kept ye young.
Like tides that enter creek or stream,
Ye come, ye visit me, or seem
Swimming out from seas of faces,
Alien myriads memory traces,
To enfold me in a dream!

I yearn as ye. But rafts that strain,
Parted, shall they lock again?

Twined we were, entwined, then riven,
Ever to new embracements driven,
Shifting gulf-weed of the main!
And how if one here shift no more,
Lodged by the flinging surge ashore?
Nor less, as now, in eve's decline,
Your shadowy fellowship is mine.
Ye float around me, form and feature:—
Tattooings, ear-rings, love-locks curled;
Barbarians of man's simpler nature,
Unworldly servers of the world.
Yea, present all, and dear to me,
Though shades, or scouring China's sea.

Whither, whither, merchant-sailors,
Whitherward now in roaring gales?
Competing still, ye huntsman-whalers,
In leviathan's wake what boat prevails?
And man-of-war's men, whereaway?
If now no dinned drum beat to quarters
On the wilds of midnight waters—
Foemen looming through the spray;
Do yet your gangway lanterns, streaming,
Vainly strive to pierce below,
When, tilted from the slant plank gleaming,
A brother you see to darkness go?

But, gunmates lashed in shotted canvas,
If where long watch-below ye keep,
Never the shrill *"All hands up hammocks!"*
Breaks the spell that charms your sleep,
And summoning trumps might vainly call,
And booming guns implore—
A beat, a heart-beat musters all,
One heart-beat at heart-core.
It musters. But to clasp, retain;
To see you at the halyards main—
To hear your chorus once again!

BRIDEGROOM DICK
(1876)

269

John Marr
and
Other Sailors

Sunning ourselves in October on a day
Balmy as spring, though the year was in decay,
I lading my pipe, she stirring her tea,
My old woman she says to me,
"Feel ye, old man, how the season mellows?"
And why should I not, blessed heart alive,
Here mellowing myself, past sixty-five,
To think o', the May-time o' pennoned young fellows
This stripped old hulk here for years may survive.

Ere yet, long ago, we were spliced, Bonny Blue,
(Silvery it gleams down the moon-glade o' time,
Ah, sugar in the bowl and berries in the prime!)
Coxswain I o' the Commodore's crew,—
Under me the fellows that manned his fine gig,
Spinning him ashore, a king in full fig.
Chirrupy even when crosses rubbed me,
Bridegroom Dick lieutenants dubbed me.
Pleasant at a yarn, Bob O'Linkum in a song,
Diligent in duty and nattily arrayed,
Favored I was, wife, and *fleeted* right along;
And though but a tot for such a tall grade,
A high quartermaster at last I was made.

All this, old lassie, you have heard before,
But you listen again for the sake e'en o' me;
No babble stales o' the good time o' yore
To Joan, if Darby the babbler be.

Babbler?—O' what? Addled brains, they forget!
O—quartermaster I; yes, the signals set,
Hoisted the ensign, mended it when frayed,
Polished up the binnacle, minded the helm,
And prompt every order blithely obeyed.
To me would the officers say a word cheery—
Break through the starch o' the quarter-deck realm;
His coxswain late, so the Commodore's pet.

Ay, and in night-watches long and weary,
Bored nigh to death with the naval etiquette,
Yearning, too, for full, some younker, a cadet,
Dropping for time each vain bumptious trick,
Boy-like would unbend to Bridegroom Dick.
But a limit there was—check, d'ye see:
Those fine young aristocrats knew their degree.

Well, stationed aft where their lordships keep,—
Seldom going forward excepting to sleep,—
I, boozing now on by-gone years,
My betters recall along with my peers.
Recall them? Wife, but I see them plain:
Alive, alert, every man stirs again.
Ay, and again on the lee-side pacing,
My spy-glass carrying, a truncheon in show,
Turning at the taffrail, my footsteps retracing,
Proud in my duty, again methinks I go.
And Dave, Dainty Dave, I mark where he stands,
Our trim sailing-master, to time the high-noon,
That thingumbob sextant perplexing eyes and hands,
Squinting at the sun, or twigging o' the moon;
Then, touching his cap to Old Chock-a-Block
Commanding the quarter-deck,—"Sir, twelve o'clock."

Where sails he now, that trim sailing-master,
Slender, yes, as the ship's sky-s'l pole?
Dimly I mind me of some sad disaster—
Dainty Dave was dropped from the navy-roll!
And ah, for old Lieutenant Chock-a-Block—
Fast, wife, chock-fast to death's black dock!
Buffeted about the obstreperous ocean,
Fleeted his life, if lagged his promotion.
Little girl, they are all, all gone, I think,
Leaving Bridegroom Dick here with lids that wink.

Where is Ap Catesby? The fights fought of yore
Famed him, and laced him with epaulets, and more.
But fame is a wake that after-wakes cross,

And the waters wallow all, and laugh *Where's the loss?*
But John Bull's bullet in his shoulder bearing
Ballasted Ap in his long sea-faring.
The middies they ducked to the man who had messed
With Decatur in the gun-room, or forward pressed
Fighting beside Perry, Hull, Porter, and the rest.

Humped veteran o' the Heart-o'-Oak war,
Moored long in haven where the old heroes are,
Never on *you* did the iron-clads jar!
Your open deck when the boarder assailed,
The frank old heroic hand-to-hand then availed.

But where's Guert Gan? Still heads he the van?
As before Vera-Cruz, when he dashed splashing through
The blue rollers sunned, in his brave gold-and-blue,
And, ere his cutter in keel took the strand,
Aloft waved his sword on the hostile land!
Went up the cheering, the quick chanticleering;
All hands vying—all colors flying:
"Cock-a-doodle-doo!" and "Row, boys, row!"
"Hey, Starry Banner!" "Hi, Santa Anna!"—
Old Scott's young dash at Mexico.
Fine forces o' the land, fine forces o' the sea,
Fleet, army, and flotilla—tell, heart o' me,
Tell, if you can, whereaway now they be!

But ah, how to speak of the hurricane unchained
The Union's strands parted in the hawser over-strained;
Our flag blown to shreds, anchors gone altogether—
The dashed fleet o' States in Secession's foul weather.

Lost in the smother o' that wide public stress,
In hearts, private hearts, what ties there were snapped!
Tell, Hal——vouch, Will, o' the ward-room mess,
On you how the riving thunder-bolt clapped.
With a bead in your eye and beads in your glass,
And a grip o' the flipper, it was part and pass:
"Hal, must it be; Well, if come indeed the shock,

To North or to South, let the victory cleave,
Vaunt it he may on his dung-hill the cock,
But *Uncle Sam's* eagle never crow will, believe."

Sentiment: ay, while suspended hung all,
Ere the guns against Sumter opened there the ball,
And partners were taken, and the red dance began,
War's red dance o' death!—Well, we, to a man,
We sailors o' the North, wife, how could we lag?—
Strike with your kin, and you stick to the flag!
But to sailors o' the South that easy way was barred.
To some, dame, believe (and I speak o' what I know),
Wormwood the trial and the Uzzite's black shard;
And the faithfuller the heart, the crueller the throe.
Duty? It pulled with more than one string,
This way and that, and anyhow a sting.
The flag and your kin, how be true unto both?
If one plight ye keep, then ye break the other troth.
But elect here they must, though the casuists were out;
Decide—hurry up—and throttle every doubt.

Of all these thrills thrilled at keelson, and throes,
Little felt the shoddyites a-toasting o' their toes;
In mart and bazar Lucre chuckled the huzza,
Coining the dollars in the bloody mint of war,
But in men, gray knights o' the Order o' Scars,
And brave boys bound by vows unto Mars,
Nature grappled honor, intertwisting in the strife:—
But some cut the knot with a thoroughgoing knife.
For how when the drums beat? How in the fray
In Hampton Roads on the fine balmy day?

There a lull, wife, befell—drop o' silence in the din.
Let us enter that silence ere the belchings re-begin.—
Through a ragged rift aslant in the cannonade's smoke
An iron-clad reveals her repellent broadside
Bodily intact. But a frigate, all oak,
Shows honeycombed by shot, and her deck crimson-dyed.
And a trumpet from port of the iron-clad hails,
Summoning the other, whose flag never trails:

"Surrender that frigate, Will! Surrender,
Or I will sink her—*ram,* and end her!"
'Twas Hal. And Will, from the naked heart-o'-oak,
Will, the old messmate, minus trumpet, spoke,
Informally intrepid,—"Sink her, and be damned!"
Enough. Gathering way, the iron-clad *rammed.*
The frigate, heeling over, on the wave threw a dusk.
Not sharing in the slant, the clapper of her bell
The fixed metal struck—uninvoked struck the knell
Of the *Cumberland* stilettoed by the *Merrimac's* tusk;
While, broken in the wound underneath the gun-deck,
Like a sword-fish's blade in leviathan waylaid,
The tusk was left infixed in the fast-foundering wreck.
There, dungeoned in the cockpit, the wounded go down,
And the chaplain with them. But the surges uplift
The prone dead from deck, and for moment they drift
Washed with the swimmers, and the spent swimmers drown.
Nine fathom did she sink,—erect, though hid from light
Save her colors unsurrendered and spars that kept the height.

Nay, pardon, old aunty! Wife, never let it fall,
That big started tear that hovers on the brim;
I forgot about your nephew and the *Merrimac's* ball;
No more then of her, since it summons up him.

But talk o' fellows' hearts in the wine's genial cup:—
Trap them in the fate, jamb them in the strait,
Guns speak their hearts then, and speak right up.

The troublous colic o' intestine war
Its sets the bowels o' affection ajar.
But, lord, old dame, so spins the whizzing world,
A humming-top, ay, for the little boy-gods
Flogging it well with their smart little rods,
Tittering at time and the coil uncurled.

Now, now, sweetheart, you sidle away,
No, never you like *that* kind o' *gay;*
But sour if I get, giving truth her due,
Honey-sweet forever, wife, will Dick be to *you!*

But avast with the War! Why recall racking days
Since set up anew are the ship's started stays?
Nor less, though the gale we have left behind,
Well may the heave o' the sea remind.
It irks me now, as it troubled me then,
To think o' the fate in the madness o' men.
If Dick was with Farragut on the night-river,
When the boom-chain we burst in the fire-raft's glare,
That blood-dyed the visage as red as the liver;
In the *Battle for the Bay* too if Dick had a share,
And saw one aloft a-piloting the war—
Trumpet in the whirlwind, a Providence in place—
Our Admiral old whom the captains huzza,
Dick joys in the man nor brags about the race.

But better, wife, I like to booze on the days
Ere the Old Order foundered in these very frays,
And tradition was lost and we learned strange ways.
Often I think on the brave cruises then;
Re-sailing them in memory, I hail the press o'men
On the gunned promenade where rolling they go,
Ere the dog-watch expire and break up the show.
The Laced Caps I see between forward guns;
Away from the powder-room they puff the cigar;
"Three days more, hey, the donnas and the dons!"
"Your Xeres widow, will you hunt her up, Starr?"
The Laced Caps laugh, and the bright waves too;
Very jolly, very wicked, both sea and crew,
Nor heaven looks sour on either, I guess,
Nor Pecksniff he bosses the gods' high mess.

Wistful ye peer, wife, concerned for my head,
And how best go get me betimes to my bed.

But king o' the club, the gayest golden spark,
Sailor o' sailors, what sailor do I mark?
Tom Tight, Tom Tight, no fine fellow finer,
A cutwater-nose, ay, a spirited soul;
But, boozing away at the well-brewed bowl,
He never bowled back from that voyage to China.

Tom was lieutenant in the brig-o'-war famed
When an officer was hung for an arch-mutineer,
But a mystery cleaved, and the captain was blamed,
And a rumpus too raised, though his honor it was clear.
And Tom he would say, when the mousers would try him,
And with cup after cup o' Burgundy ply him:
"Gentlemen, in vain with your wassail you beset,
For the more I tipple, the tighter do I get."
No blabber, no, not even with the can—
True to himself and loyal to his clan.

Tom blessed us starboard and d——d us larboard,
Right down from rail to the streak o' the garboard.
Nor less, wife, we liked him.—Tom was a man
In contrast queer with Chaplain Le Fan,
Who blessed us at morn, and at night yet again,
D——ning us only in decorous strain;
Preaching 'tween the guns—each cutlass in its place—
From text that averred old Adam a hard case.
I see him—Tom—on *horse-block* standing,
Trumpet at mouth, thrown up all amain,
An elephant's bugle, vociferous demanding
Of topmen aloft in the hurricane of rain,
"Letting that sail there your faces flog?
Manhandle it, men, and you'll get the good grog!"
O Tom, but he knew a blue-jacket's ways,
And how a lieutenant may genially haze;
Only a sailor sailors heartily praise.

Wife, where be all these chaps, I wonder?
Trumpets in the tempest, terrors in the fray,
Boomed their commands along the deck like thunder;
But silent is the sod, and thunder dies away.

But Captain Turret, *"Old Hemlock"* tall,
(A leaning tower when his tank brimmed all,)
Manoeuvre out alive from the war did he?
Or, too old for that, drift under the lee?
Kentuckian colossal, who, touching at Madeira,
The huge puncheon shipped o' prime *Santa-Clara;*

Then rocked along the deck so solemnly!
No wit the less though judicious was enough
In dealing with the Finn who made the great huff;
Our three-decker's giant, a grand boatswain's mate,
Manliest of men in his own natural senses;
But driven stark mad by the devil's drugged stuff,
Storming all aboard from his run-ashore late,
Challenging to battle, vouchsafing no pretenses,
A reeling King Ogg, delirious in power,
The quarter-deck carronades he seemed to make cower.
"Put him in *brig* there!" said Lieutenant Marrot.
"Put him in *brig!*" back he mocked like a parrot;
"Try it, then!" swaying a fist like Thor's sledge,
And making the pigmy constables hedge—
Ship's corporals and the master-at-arms.
"In *brig* there, I say!"—They dally no more;
Like hounds let slip on a desperate boar,
Together they pounce on the formidable Finn,
Pinion and cripple and hustle him in.
Anon, under sentry, between twin guns,
He slides off in drowse, and the long night runs.

Morning brings a summons. Whistling it calls,
Shrilled through the pipes of the boatswain's four aids;
Trilled down the hatchways along the dusk halls:
Muster to the Scourge!—Dawn of doom and its blast!
As from cemeteries raised, sailors swarm before the mast,
Tumbling up the ladders from the ship's nether shades.

Keeping in the background and taking small part,
Lounging at their ease, indifferent in face,
Behold the trim marines uncompromised in heart;
Their Major, buttoned up, near the staff finds room—
The staff o' lieutenants standing grouped in their place.
All the Laced Caps o' the ward-room come,
The Chaplain among them, disciplined and dumb.
The blue-nosed boatswain, complexioned like slag,
Like a blue Monday shows—his implements in bag.
Executioners, his aids, a couple by him stand,
At a nod there the thongs to receive from his hand.
Never venturing a caveat whatever may betide,

Though functionally here on humanity's side,
The grave Surgeon shows, like the formal physician
Attending the rack o' the Spanish Inquisition.

The angel o' the "brig" brings his prisoner up;
Then, steadied by his old *Santa-Clara,* a sup,
Heading all erect, the ranged assizes there,
Lo, Captain Turret, and under starred bunting,
(A florid full face and fine silvered hair,)
Gigantic the yet greater giant confronting.

Now the Culprit he liked, as a tall captain can
A Titan subordinate and true *sailor-man;*
And frequent he'd shown it—no worded advance,
But flattering the Finn with a well-timed glance.
But what of that now? In the martinet-mien
Read the *Articles of War,* heed the naval routine;
While, cut to the heart a dishonor there to win,
Restored to his senses, stood the Anak Finn;
In racked self-control the squeezed tears peeping,
Scalding the eye with repressed inkeeping,
Discipline must be; the scourge is deemed due.
But ah for the sickening and strange heart-benumbing,
Compassionate abasement in shipmates that view;
Such a grand champion shamed there succumbing!

"Brown, tie him up."—The cord he brooked:
How else?—His arms spread apart—never threaping;
No, never he flinched, never sideways he looked,
Peeled to the waistband, the marble flesh creeping,
Lashed by the sleet the officious winds urge.
In function his fellows their fellowship merge—
The twain standing high—the two boatswain's mates,
Sailors of his grade, ay, and brothers of his mess.
With sharp thongs adroop the junior one awaits
The word to uplift.

                    "Untie him—so!
Submission is enough, Man, you may go."
Then, promenading aft, brushing fat Purser Smart,
"Flog? Never meant it—hadn't any heart.

Degrade that tall fellow?"—Such, wife, was he,
Old Captain Turret, who the brave wine could stow.
Magnanimous, you think?—but what does Dick see?
Apron to your eye! Why, never fell a blow,
Cheer up, old wifie, 't was a long time ago.

But where's that sore one, crabbed and severe,
Lieutenant Long Lumbago, an arch scrutineer?
Call the roll to-day, would he answer—*Here!*
When the *Blixum's* fellows to quarters mustered
How he'd lurch along the lane of gun-crews clustered,
Testy as touchwood, to pry and to peer.
Jerking his sword underneath larboard arm,
He ground his worn grinders to keep himself calm.
Composed in his nerves, from the fidgets set free,
Tell, Sweet Wrinkles, alive now is he,
In Paradise a parlor where the even tempers be?

Where's Commander All-a-Tanto?
Where's Orlop Bob singing up from below?
Where's Rhyming Ned? has he spun his last canto?
Where's Jewsharp Jim? Where's Rigadoon Joe?
Ah, for the music over and done,
The band all dismissed save the droned trombone!
Where's Glen o' the gun-room, who loved Hot-Scotch—
Glen, prompt and cool in a perilous watch?
Where's flaxen-haired Phil? a gray lieutenant?
Or rubicund, flying a dignified pennant?
But where sleeps his brother?—the cruise it was o'er,
But ah, for death's grip that welcomed him ashore!
Where's Sid, the cadet, so frank in his brag,
Whose toast was audacious—*"Here's Sid, and Sid's flag!"*
Like holiday-craft that have sunk unknown,
May a lark of a lad go lonely down?
Who takes the census under the sea?
Carl others like old ensigns be,
Bunting I hoisted to flutter at the gaff—
Rags in end that once were flags
Gallant streaming from the staff?
Such scurvy doom could the chances deal

To Top—Gallant Harry and Jack Genteel?
Lo, Genteel Jack in hurricane weather,
Shagged like a bear, like a red lion roaring;
But O, so fine in his chapeau and feather,
In port to the ladies never once *jawing;*
All bland *politesse,* how urbane was he—
"*Oui, mademoiselle*"—"*Ma chère amie!*"

'T was Jack got up the ball at Naples,
Gay in the old *Ohio* glorious;
His hair was curled by the berth-deck barber,
Never you'd deemed him a cub of rude Boreas.
In tight little pumps, with the grand dames in rout,
A-flinging his shapely foot all about;
His watch-chain with love's jeweled tokens abounding,
Curls ambrosial shaking out odors,
Waltzing along the batteries, astounding
The gunner glum and the grim-visaged loaders.

Wife, where be all these blades, I wonder,
Pennoned fine fellows, so strong, so gay?
Never their colors with a dip dived under;
Have they hauled them down in a lack-lustre day,
Or beached their boats in the Far, Far Away?

Hither and thither, blown wide asunder,
Where's this fleet, I wonder and wonder.
Slipt their cables, rattled their adieu,
(Whereaway painting? to what rendezvous?)
Out of sight, out of mind, like the crack *Constitution,*
And many a keel time never shall renew—
Bon Homme Dick o' the buff Revolution,
The Black Cockade and the staunch *True-Blue.*

Doff hats to Decatur! But where is his blazon?
Must merited fame endure time's wrong—
Glory's ripe grape wizen up to a raisin?
Yes! for Nature teems, and the years are strong,
And who can keep the tally o' the names that fleet along!

But his frigate, wife, his bride? Would blacksmiths brown
Into smithereens smite the solid old renown?

Rivetting the bolts in the iron-clad's shell,
Hark to the hammers with a rat-tat-tat;
"Handier a *derby* than a laced cocked hat!
The *Monitor* was ugly, but she served us right well,
Better than the *Cumberland,* a beauty and the belle."

Better than the Cumberland!—Heart alive in me!
That battlemented hull, Tantallon o' the sea,
Kicked in, as at Boston the taxed chests o' tea!
Ay, spurned by the *ram,* once a tall, shapely craft,
But lopped by the *Rebs* to an iron-beaked raft—
A blacksmith's unicorn armed *cap-a-pie.*

Under the water-line a *ram's* blow is dealt:
And foul fall the knuckles that strike below the belt.
Nor brave the inventions that serve to replace
The openness of valor while dismantling the grace.

Aloof from all this and the never-ending game,
Tantamount to teetering, plot and counterplot;
Impenetrable armor—all-perforating shot;
Aloof, bless God, ride the war-ships of old,
A grand fleet moored in the roadstead of fame;
Not submarine sneaks with *them* are enrolled;
Their long shadows dwarf us, their flags are as flame.

Don't fidget so, wife; an old man's passion
Amounts to no more than this smoke that I puff;
There, there now, buss me in good old fashion;
A died-down candle will flicker in the snuff.

But one last thing let your old babbler say,
What Decatur's coxswain said who was long ago hearsed,
"Take in your flying-kites, for there comes a lubber's day
When gallant things will go, and the three-deckers first."

My pipe is smoked out, and the grog runs slack;
But bowse away, wife, at your blessed Bohea;
This empty can here must needs solace me—
Nay, sweetheart, nay; I take that back;
Dick drinks from your eyes and he finds no lack!

TOM DEADLIGHT
(1810)

During a tempest encountered homeward-bound from the Mediterranean, a grizzled petty-officer, one of the two captains of the
forecastle, dying at night in his hammock, swung in the *sick-bay*
under the tiered gun-decks of the British *Dreadnought*, 98, wandering in his mind, though with glimpses of sanity, and starting
up at whiles, sings by snatches his good-bye and last injunctions
to two messmates, his watchers, one of whom fans the fevered tar
with the flap of his old sou'-wester. Some names and phrases,
with here and there a line, or part of one; these, in his aberration,
wrested into incoherency from their original connection and
import, he involuntarily derives, as he does the measure, from a
famous old sea-ditty, whose cadences, long rife, and now humming in the collapsing brain, attune the last flutterings of distempered thought.

Farewell and adieu to you noble hearties,—
    Farewell and adieu to you ladies of Spain,
For I've received orders for to sail for the Deadman,
    But hope with the grand fleet to see you again.

I have hove my ship to, with main-top-sail aback, boys;
    I have hove my ship to, for to strike soundings clear—
The black scud a'flying; but, by God's blessing, dam' me,
    Right up the Channel for the Deadman I'll steer.

I have worried through the waters that are called the Doldrums,
    And growled at Sargasso that clogs while ye grope—
Blast my eyes, but the light-ship is hid by the mist, lads:—
    Flying Dutchman—odds bobbs—off the Cape of Good Hope!

But what's this I feel that is fanning my cheek, Matt?
   The white goney's wing?—How she rolls!—'t is the Cape!
Give my kit to the mess, Jock, for kin none is mine, none;
   And tell *Holy Joe* to avast with the crape.

Dead reckoning, says *Joe*, it won't do to go by;
   But they doused all the glims, Matt, in sky t' other night.
Dead reckoning is good for to sail for the Deadman;
   And Tom Deadlight he thinks it may reckon near right.

The signal!—it streams for the grand fleet to anchor.
   The captains—the trumpets—the hullabaloo!
Stand by for blue-blazes, and mind your shank-painters,
   For the Lord High Admiral, he's squinting at you!

But give me my *tot,* Matt, before I roll over;
   Jock, let's have your flipper, it's good for to feel;
And don't sew me up without *baccy* in mouth, boys,
   And don't blubber like lubbers when I turn up my keel.

JACK ROY

Kept up by relays of generations young
Never dies at halyards the blithe chorus sung;
While in sands, sounds, and seas where the storm-petrels cry,
Dropped mute around the globe, these halyard singers lie.
Short-lived the clippers for racing-cups that run,
And speeds in life's career many a lavish mother's-son.

But thou, manly king o' the old *Splendid's* crew,
The ribbons o' thy hat still a-fluttering, should fly—
A challenge, and forever, nor the bravery should rue.
Only in a tussle for the starry flag high,
When 't is piety to do, and privilege to die.
Then, only then, would heaven think to lop
Such a cedar as the captain o' the *Splendid's* main-top:
A belted sea-gentleman; a gallant, off-hand
Mercutio indifferent in life's gay command.

Magnanimous in humor; when the splintering shot fell,
"Tooth-picks a-plenty, lads; thank 'em with a shell!"

Sang Larry o' the Cannakin, smuggler o' the wine,
At mess between guns, lad in jovial recline:
"In Limbo our Jack he would chirrup up a cheer,
The martinet there find a chaffing mutineer;
From a thousand fathoms down under hatches o' your Hades,
He'd ascend in love-ditty, kissing fingers to your ladies!"

Never relishing the knave, though allowing for the menial,
Nor overmuch the king, Jack, nor prodigally genial.
Ashore on liberty he flashed in escapade,
Vaulting over life in its levelness of grade,
Like the dolphin off Africa in rainbow a-sweeping—
Arch iridescent shot from seas languid sleeping.

Larking with thy life, if a joy but a toy,
Heroic in thy levity wert thou, Jack Roy.

Sea Pieces

THE HAGLETS

By chapel bare, with walls sea-beat
The lichened urns in wilds are lost
About a carved memorial stone
That shows, decayed and coral-mossed,
A form recumbent, swords at feet,
Trophies at head, and kelp for a winding-sheet.

I invoke thy ghost, neglected fane,
Washed by the waters' long lament;
I adjure the recumbent effigy
To tell the cenotaph's intent—
Reveal why fagotted swords are at feet,
Why trophies appear and weeds are the winding-sheet.

By open ports the Admiral sits,
And shares repose with gains that tell
Of power that smote the arm'd Plate Fleet
Whose sinking flag-ship's colors fell;
But over the Admiral floats in light
His squadron's flag, the red-cross Flag of the White.
    The eddying waters whirl astern,
The prow, a seedsman, sows the spray;
With bellying sails and buckling spars
The black hull leaves a Milky Way;
Her timbers thrill, her batteries roll,
She revelling speeds exulting with pennon at pole,
    But ah, for standards captive trailed
For all their scutcheoned castles' pride—
Castilian towers that dominate Spain,
Naples, and either Ind beside;
Those haughty towers, armorial ones,
Rue the salute from the Admiral's dens of guns.

Ensigns and arms in trophy brave,
Braver for many a rent and scar,
The captor's naval hall bedeck,
Spoil that insures an earldom's star—
Toledoes great, grand draperies too,
Spain's steel and silk, and splendors from Peru.
    But crippled part in splintering fight,
The vanquished flying the victor's flags,
With prize-crews, under convoy-guns,
Heavy the fleet from Opher drags—
The Admiral crowding sail ahead,
Foremost with news who foremost in conflict sped.
    But out from cloistral gallery dim,
In early night his glance is thrown;
He marks the vague reserve of heaven,
He feels the touch of ocean lone;
Then turns, in frame part undermined,
Nor notes the shadowing wings that fan behind.

There, peaked and gray, three haglets fly,
And follow, follow fast in wake

Where slides the cabin-lustre shy,
And sharks from man a glamour take,
Seething along the line of light
In lane that endless rules the war-ship's flight.
      The sea-fowl here, whose hearts none know,
They followed late the flag-ship quelled,
(As now the victor one) and long
Above her gurgling grave, shrill held
With screams their wheeling rites—then sped
Direct in silence where the victor led.
      Now winds less fleet, but fairer, blow,
A ripple laps the coppered side,
While phosphor sparks make ocean gleam,
Like camps lit tip in triumph wide;
With lights and tinkling cymbals meet
Acclaiming seas the advancing conqueror greet.

But who a flattering tide may trust,
Or favoring breeze, or aught in end?—
Careening under startling blasts
The sheeted towers of sails impend;
While, gathering bale, behind is bred
A livid storm-bow, like a rainbow dead.
      At trumpet-call the topmen spring;
And, urged by after-call in stress,
Yet other tribes of tars ascend
The rigging's howling wilderness;
But ere yard-ends alert they win,
Hell rules in heaven with hurricane-fire and din.
      The spars, athwart as spiry height,
Like quaking Lima's crosses rock;
Like bees the clustering sailors cling
Against the shrouds, or take the shock
Flat on the swept yard-arms aslant,
Dipped like the wheeling condor's pinions gaunt.

A lull! and tongues of languid flame
Lick every boom, and lambent show
Electric 'gainst each face aloft;
The herds of clouds with bellowings go:

The black ship rears—beset—harassed,
Then plunges far with luminous antlers vast.
     In trim betimes they turn from land,
Some shivered sails and spars they stow;
One watch, dismissed, they troll the can,
While loud the billow thumps the bow—
Vies with the fist that smites the board,
Obstreperous at each reveller's jovial words.
     Of royal oak by storms confirmed,
The tested bull her lineage shows:
Vainly the plungings whelm her prow—
She rallies, rears, she sturdier grows;
Each shot-hole plugged, each storm-sail home,
With batteries housed she rams the watery dome.

Dim seen adrift through driving scud,
The wan moon shows in plight forlorn;
Then, pinched in visage, fades and fades
Like to the faces drowned at morn,
When deeps engulfed the flag-ship's crew,
And, shrilling round, the inscrutable haglets flew.
     And still they fly, nor now they cry,
But constant fan a second wake,
Unflagging pinions ply and ply,
Abreast their course intent they take;
Their silence marks a stable mood,
They patient keep their eager neighborhood.
     Plumed with a smoke, a confluent sea,
Heaved in a combing pyramid full,
Spent at its climax, in collapse
Down headlong thundering stuns the hull:
The trophy drops; but, reared again,
Shows Mars' high-altar and contemns the main.

Rebuilt it stands, the brag of arms,
Transferred in site—no thought of where
The sensitive needle keeps its place,
And starts, disturbed, a quiverer there;
The helmsman rubs the clouded glass—
Peers in, but lets the trembling portent pass.

Let pass as well his shipmates do
(Whose dream of power no tremors jar)
Fears for the fleet convoyed astern:
"Our flag they fly, they share our star;
Spain's galleons great in hull are stout:
Manned by our men—like us they'll ride it out."
     Tonight's the night that ends the week—
Ends day and week and month and year:
A fourfold imminent flickering time,
For now the midnight draws anear:
Eight bells! and passing-bells they be—
The Old year fades, the Old year dies at sea.

He launched them well. But shall the New
Redeem the pledge the Old Year made,
Or prove a self-asserting heir?
But healthy hearts few qualms invade:
By shot-chests grouped in bays 'tween guns
The gossips chat, the grizzled, sea-beat ones.
     And boyish dreams some graybeards blab:
"To sea, my lads, we go no more
Who share the Acapulco prize;
We'll all night in, and bang the door;
Our ingots red shall yield us bliss:
Lads, golden years begin to-night with this!"
     Released from deck, yet waiting call,
Glazed caps and coats baptized in storm,
A watch of Laced Sleeves round the board
Draw near in heart to keep them warm:
"Sweethearts and wives!" clink, clink, they meet,
And, quaffing, dip in wine their beards of sleet.

"Ay, let the star-light stay withdrawn,
So here her hearth-light memory fling,
So in this wine-light cheer be born,
And honor's fellowship weld our ring—
Honor! our Admiral's aim foretold:
A tomb or a trophy, and lo, 't is a trophy and gold!"
     But he, a unit, sole in rank,
Apart needs keep his lonely state,

The sentry at his guarded door
Mute as by vault the sculptured Fate;
Belted he sits in drowsy light,
And, hatted, nods—the Admiral of the White.
      He dozes, aged with watches passed—
Years, years of pacing to and fro;
He dozes, nor attends the stir
In bullioned standards rustling low,
Nor minds the blades whose secret thrill
Perverts overhead the magnet's Polar will;—

Less heeds the shadowing three that ply
And follow, follow fast in wake,
Untiring wing and lidless eye—
Abreast their course intent they take;
Or sigh or sing, they hold for good
The unvarying flight and fixed inveterate mood.
      In dream at last his dozings merge,
In dream he reaps his victory's fruit:
The Flags-o'-the-Blue, the Flags-o'-the-Red,
Dipped flags of his country's fleets salute
His Flag-o'-the-White in harbor proud—
But why should it blench? Why turn to a painted shroud?
      The hungry seas they hound the hull,
The sharks they dog the haglets' flight;
With one consent the winds, the waves
In hunt with fins and wings unite,
While drear the harps in cordage sound
Remindful wails for old Armadas drowned.

Ha—yonder! are they Northern Lights?
Or signals flashed to warn or ward?
Yea, signals lanced in breakers high;
But doom on warning follows hard:
While yet they veer in hope to shun,
They strike! and thumps of hull and heart are one.
      But beating hearts a drum-beat calls
And prompt the men to quarters go;
Discipline, curbing nature, rules—
Heroic makes who duty know:

They execute the trump's command,
Or in peremptory places wait and stand.
      Yet cast about in blind amaze—
As through their watery shroud they peer:
"We tacked from land: then how betrayed?
Have currents swerved us—snared us here?"
None heed the blades that clash in place
Under lamps dashed down that lit the magnet's case.

Ah, what may live, who mighty swim,
Or boat-crew reach that shore forbid,
Or cable span? Must victors drown—
Perish, even as the vanquished did?
Man keeps from man the stifled moan,
They shouldering stand, yet each in heart how lone.
      Some heaven invoke; but rings of reefs
Prayer and despair alike deride
In dance of breakers forked or peaked,
Pale maniacs of the maddened tide;
While, strenuous yet some end to earn.
The haglets spin, though now no more astern.
      Like shuttles hurrying in the looms
Aloft through rigging frayed they ply—
Cross and recross—weave and inweave,
Then lock the web with clinching cry
Over the seas on seas that clasp
The weltering wreck where gurgling ends the gasp.

Ah for the Plate-Fleet trophy now
The victor's voucher, flags and arms;
Never they'll hang in Abbey old
And take Time's dust with holier palms;
Nor less content, in liquid night,
Their captor sleeps—the Admiral of the White.

     Imbedded deep with shells
     And drifted treasure deep,
     Forever he sinks deeper in
     Unfathomable sleep—
     His cannon round him thrown,

His sailors at his feet,
  The wizard sea enchanting them
  Where never haglets beat.

On nights when meteors play
And light the breakers dance,
The Oreads from the caves
With silvery elves advance;
And up from ocean stream,
And down from heaven far,
The rays that blend in dream
The abysm and the star.

THE AEOLIAN HARP
at the Surf Inn

List the harp in window wailing
  Stirred by fitful gales from sea:
Shrieking tip in mad crescendo—
  Dying down in plaintive key!

Listen: less a strain ideal
  Than Ariel's rendering of the Real.
What that Real is, let hint
  A picture stamped in memory's mint.

Braced well up, with beams aslant,
Betwixt the continents sails the *Phocion,*
To Baltimore bound from Alicant.
Blue breezy skies white fleeces fleck
Over the chill blue white-capped ocean:
From yard-arm comes—"Wreck ho, a wreck!"

Dismasted and adrift,
Long time a thing forsaken;
Overwashed by every wave
Like the slumbering kraken;
Heedless if the billow roar,
Oblivious of the lull,

Leagues and leagues from shoal or shore,
It swims—a levelled hull:
Bulwarks gone—a shaven wreck,
Nameless, and a grass-green deck.
A lumberman: perchance, in hold
Prostrate pines with hemlocks rolled.

It has drifted, waterlogged,
Till by trailing weeds beclogged:
    Drifted, drifted, day by day,
    Pilotless on pathless way.
It has drifted till each plank
Is oozy as the oyster-bank:
    Drifted, drifted, night by night,
    Craft that never shows a light;
Nor ever, to prevent worse knell,
Tolls in fog the warning bell.

From collision never shrinking,
Drive what may through darksome smother;
Saturate, but never sinking,
Fatal only to the *other!*
    Deadlier than the sunken reef
Since still the snare it shifteth,
    Torpid in dumb ambuscade
Waylayingly it drifteth.

O, the sailors–O, the sails!
O, the lost crews never heard of!
Well the harp of Ariel wails
Thoughts that tongue can tell no word of!

Minor Sea Pieces

TO THE MASTER OF THE "METEOR"

Lonesome on earth's loneliest deep,
Sailor! who dost thy vigil keep—

Off the Cape of Storms dost musing sweep
Over monstrous waves that curl and comb;
Of thee we think when here from brink
We blow the mead in bubbling foam.

Of thee we think, in a ring we link;
To the shearer of ocean's fleece we drink,
And the *Meteor* rolling home.

FAR OFF-SHORE

Look, the raft, a signal flying,
   Thin—a shred;
None upon the lashed spars lying,
   Quick or dead.

Cries the sea-fowl, hovering over,
   "Crew, the crew?"
And the billow, reckless, rover,
   Sweeps anew!

THE MAN-OF-WAR HAWK

Yon black man-of-war-hawk that wheels in the light
O'er the black ship's white sky-s'l, sunned cloud to the sight,
Have we low-flyers wings to ascend to his height?

No arrow can reach him; nor thought can attain
To the placid supreme in the sweep of his reign.

THE FIGURE-HEAD

The *Charles-and-Emma* seaward sped,
(Named from the carven pair at prow)
He so smart, and a curly head,
She tricked forth as a bride knows how:
   Pretty stem for the port, I trow!

But iron-rust and alum-spray
And chafing gear, and sun and dew
Vexed this lad and lassie gay,
Tears in their eyes, salt tears nor few;
    And the hug relaxed with the failing glue.

But came in end a dismal night,
With creaking beams and ribs that groan,
A black lee-shore and waters white:
Dropped on the reef, the pair lie prone:
    O, the breakers dance, but the winds they moan!

THE GOOD CRAFT "SNOW-BIRD"

Strenuous need that head-wind be
    From purposed voyage that drives at last
The ship, sharp-braced and dogged still,
    Beating up against the blast.

Brigs that figs for market gather,
    Homeward-bound upon the stretch,
Encounter oft this uglier weather,
    Yet in end their port they fetch.

Mark yon craft from sunny Smyrna
    Glazed with ice in Boston Bay,
Out they toss the fig-drums cheerly,
    Livelier for the frosty ray.

What if sleet off-shore assailed her.
    What though ice yet plate her yards;
In wintry port not less she renders
    Summer's gift with warm regards!

And, look, the underwriters' man,
    Timely, when the stevedore's done,
Puts on his *specs* to pry and scan,
    And sets her down—*A, No. 1.*

Bravo, master! Brava, brig!
    For slanting snows out of the West
Never the *Snow-Bird* cares one fig;
    And foul winds steady her, though a pest.

Old Counsel
of the young master of a wrecked California clipper

Come out of the Golden Gate,
Go round the Horn with streamers,
Carry royals early and late;
But, brother, be not over-elate—
All hands save ship! has startled dreamers.

The Tuft of Kelp

All dripping in tangles green,
    Cast up by a lonely sea
If purer for that, O Weed,
    Bitterer, too, are ye?

The Maldive Shark

About the Shark, phlegmatical one,
Pale sot of the Maldive sea,
The sleek little pilot-fish, azure and slim,
How alert in attendance be.
From his saw-pit of mouth, from his charnel of maw
They have nothing of harm to dread,
But liquidly glide on his ghastly flank
Or before his Gorgonian head;
Or lurk in the port of serrated teeth
In white triple tiers of glittering gates,
And there find a leaven when peril's abroad,
An asylum in jaws of the Fates!
They are friends; and friendly they guide him to prey,
Yet never partake of the treat—

Eyes and brains to the dotard lethargic and dull,
Pale ravener of horrible meat.

To Ned

Where is the world we roved, Ned Bunn?
    Hollows thereof lay rich in shade
By voyagers old inviolate thrown
    Ere Paul Pry cruised with Pelf and Trade.
To us old lads some thoughts come home
Who roamed a world young lads no more shall roam.

Nor less the satiate year impends
    When, wearying of routine-resorts,
The pleasure-hunter shall break loose,
    Ned, for our Pantheistic ports:—
Marquesas and glenned isles that be
Authentic Edens in a Pagan sea.

The charm of scenes untried shall lure,
    And, Ned, a legend urge the flight—
The Typee-truants tinder stars
    Unknown to Shakespere's *Midsummer-Night;*
And man, if lost to Saturn's Age,
Yet feeling life no Syrian pilgrimage.

But, tell, shall he, the tourist, find
    Our isles the same in violet-glow
Enamoring us what years and years—
    Ah, Ned, what years and years ago!
Well, Adam advances, smart in pace,
But scarce by violets that advance you trace.

But we, in anchor-watches calm,
    The Indian Psyche's languor won,
And, musing, breathed primeval balm
    From Edens ere yet overrun;
Marvelling mild if mortal twice,
Here and hereafter, touch a Paradise.

CROSSING THE TROPICS
(from "The Saya-Y-Manto")

While now the Pole Star sinks from sight
    The Southern Cross it climbs the sky;
But losing thee, my love, my light,
O bride but for one bridal night,
    The loss no rising joys supply.

Love, love, the Trade Winds urge abaft,
And thee, from thee, they steadfast waft.

By day the blue and silver sea
    And chime of waters blandly fanned—
Nor these, nor Gama's stars to me
May yield delight since still for thee
    I long as Gama longed for land.

I yearn, I yearn, reverting turn,
My heart it streams in wake astern.
When, cut by slanting sleet, we swoop
    Where raves the world's inverted year,
If roses all your porch shall loop,
Not less your heart for me will droop
    Doubling the world's last outpost drear.

O love, O love, these oceans vast:
Love, love, it is as death were past!

THE BERG
(a dream)

I saw a ship of martial build
(Her standards set, her brave apparel on)
Directed as by madness mere
Against a stolid iceberg steer,
Nor budge it, though the infatuate ship went down.
The impact made huge ice-cubes fall

Sullen, in tons that crashed the deck;
But that one avalanche was all—
No other movement save the foundering wreck.

Along the spurs of ridges pale,
Not any slenderest shaft and frail,
A prism over glass-green gorges lone,
Toppled; or lace of traceries fine,
Nor pendant drops in grot or mine
Were jarred, when the stunned ship went down.
Nor sole the gulls in cloud that wheeled
Circling one snow-flanked peak afar,
But nearer fowl the floes that skimmed
And crystal beaches, felt no jar.
No thrill transmitted stirred the lock
Of jack-straw needle-ice at base;
Towers undermined by waves—the block
Atilt impending—kept their place.
Seals, dozing sleek on sliddery ledges
Slipt never, when by loftier edges
Through very inertia overthrown,
The impetuous ship in bafflement went down.

Hard Berg (methought), so cold, so vast,
With mortal damps self-overcast;
Exhaling still thy dankish breath—
Adrift dissolving, bound for death;
Though lumpish thou, a lumbering one—
A lumbering lubbard loitering slow,
Impingers rue thee and go down,
Sounding thy precipice below,
Nor stir the slimy slug that sprawls
Along thy dead indifference of walls.

THE ENVIABLE ISLES
(from "Rammon.")

Through storms you reach them and from storms are free.
    Afar descried, the foremost drear in hue,
But, nearer, green; and, on the marge, the sea
    Makes thunder low and mist of rainbowed dew.

But, inland, where the sleep that folds the hills
A dreamier sleep, the trance of God, instills—
On uplands hazed, in wandering airs aswoon,
    Slow-swaying palms salute love's cypress tree
Adown in vale where pebbly runlets croon
    A song to lull all sorrow and all glee.

Sweet-fern and moss in many a glade are here,
    Where, strown in flocks, what cheek-flushed myriads lie
Dimpling in dream—unconscious slumberers mere,
    While billows endless round the beaches die.

PEBBLES

I
Though the Clerk of the Weather insist,
    And lay down the weather-law,
Pintado and gannet they wist
That the winds blow whither they list
    In tempest or flaw.

II
Old are the creeds, but stale the schools,
    Revamped as the mode may veer,
But Orm from the schools to the beaches strays,
And, finding a Conch hoar with time, he delays
    And reverent lifts it to ear.
That Voice, pitched in far monotone,
Shall it swerve? Shall it deviate ever?
The Seas have inspired it, and Truth—
    Truth, varying from sameness never.

III

In hollows of the liquid hills
   Where the long Blue Ridges run,
The flattery of no echo thrills,
   For echo the seas have none;
Nor aught that gives man back man's strain—
The hope of his heart, the dream in his brain.

IV

On ocean where the embattled fleets repair,
Man, suffering inflictor, sails on sufferance there.

V

Implacable I, the old implacable Sea:
   Implacable most when most I smile serene—
Pleased, not appeased, by myriad wrecks in me.

VI

Curled in the comb of yon billow Andean,
   Is it the Dragon's heaven-challenging crest?
Elemental mad ramping of ravening waters—
   Yet Christ on the Mount, and the dove in her nest!

VII

Healed of my hurt, I laud the inhuman Sea—
Yea, bless the Angels Four that there convene;
For healed I am even by their pitiless breath
Distilled in wholesome dew named rosmarine.

END

EDITOR'S NOTES

The best studies of these poems are in the books by William H. Shurr, William
Bysshe Stein, and Clark Davis. Articles by Bryan Short, Edgar Dryden, and
Juana Celia Djelal treat the volume or individual poems within it.

"JOHN MARR." This combination of prose and poetry is especially interesting
for its experimentation. Melville was using such combinations a number of

times in his late writings, among which the unpublished works "Rammon" and "RipVan Winkle's Lilac" are examples, as is the original poem "Billy in the Darbies" and its headnote, which grew into the narrative of *Billy Budd*. The prose scenario is sometimes read for its autobiographical suggestions, but these apart, the prose sketch presents a clearly limned character who effects his release from the psychological trauma of exile and loneliness by remembering and meditating on all he had learned of life at sea.

"BRIDEGROOM DICK." Robert Penn Warren's notes for this piece (411–22) identify Melville's allusion and indicates revisions he made to the poem after its publication. Stein (25–33) offers a lengthy, interesting interpretation of the poem, concentrating on Melville's sexual imagery, bawdry, and blasphemy.

"THE HAGLETS." Melville apparently arrived at a final version of this poem after at least two earlier versions. The first, which remained in manuscript, under the title "The Admiral of the White" and was probably written at some time before 1885, perhaps as early as 1860, as Leon Howard conjectures, tells a simple story in which captured French swords and armaments affect the ship's compass and cause the destruction of the British ship. The last two stanzas read as follows:

> O jagged the rocks, repeated she knocks,
>   Splits the hull like a cracked filbert there,
> Her boats are torn, and ground-up are thrown,
>   Float the small chips like filbert-bits there.
>
> Pale, pale, but proud, 'neath the billows loud,
> The Admiral sleeps tonight;
>   Pale, pale, but proud, in his sea-weed shroud,—
> The Admiral of the White,
>   And by their guns the dutiful ones,
> Who had fought, bravely fought, the good fight.

The complete poem can be found in Robert Penn Warren's edition of *Selected Poems* (425–27); a later version, still with the title "The Admiral of the White," was published in newspapers in 1885.

"THE MALDIVE SHARK." Part of the Indian Ocean, the Maldive Sea provides the name that Melville wants for specifying his particular shark. Melville had written of the shovel-nosed shark, "a clumsy, lethargic monster," in chapter 18 of *Mardi*. Here, his description dwells on the hideous monstrosity: the shark is "phlegmatical," has a "saw-pit of mouth" and a "charnel of maw" and is a "pale sot" with a "Gorgonian head." He is a "dotard" and a "pale ravener." Against this picture of a horrifying but clumsy creature, the pilot-fish are quick and sleek and find safety within his jaws. Stein incorrectly attaches the next poem, "To Ned," to "The Maldive Shark" and thus misreads the meaning of the piece (54–56).

"CROSSING THE TROPICS." The piece is ostensibly a love poem, but Melville seemingly undercuts its tone with his epigraph. The words *saya* and *manto* had a special meaning for Melville. Both refer to the dress of women of Lima; the saya is a shawl that women used to cover their faces when engaging in extra-marital affairs. In *Benito Cereno*, the strange ship that Captain Amasa Delano sees is limned against a background of sun and clouds "not unlike a Lima *intriguante's* one sinister eye peering across the Plaza from the Indian loop-hole of her dusk *saya-y-manta.*" In the light of this knowledge, can the poem be read merely as a sailor's love song addressed to "my love, my light"?

"THE BERG." Melville returns again and again to the inhuman and powerful side of Nature—neither friend nor enemy to mankind but capable of wield-ing destructive forces. Like the Maldive shark, the berg is a manifestation of the "stolidity" of Nature. It is a "lumbering lubbard," unmoved by the collision that destroys the ship but continuing in "dead indifference." In copies of *John Marr*, Melville, dissatisfied with what he had allowed in publication, revised the last line of the poem to change "dead indifference" to "dense stolidity."

"PEBBLES." The seven numbered epigrams that conclude the volume dwell on the harsh power of the "old implacable Sea," where man sails only "on suffer-ance." The sixth epigram signals a meliorating view in which the "ravening waters" also offer a place for Christ and the dove. At the poem's conclusion, John Marr is finally able to assert that he has been healed by his cathartic imaginings of the sea and lauds it for its inhumanity.

Timoleon, Etc. ➷

I

If more than once, as annals tell,
   Through blood without compunction spilt,
An egotist arch rule has snatched
And stamped the seizure with his sabre's hilt,
   And, legalized by lawyers, stood;
Shall the good heart whose patriot fire
Leaps to a deed of startling note,
Do it, then flinch? Shall good in weak expire?
   Needs goodness lack the evil grit
That stares down censorship and ban,
And dumfounds saintlier ones with this—
God's will avouched in each successful man?
   Or, put it, where dread stress inspires
A virtue beyond man's standard rate,
Seems virtue there a strain forbid—
Transcendence such as shares transgression's fate?
   If so, and wan eclipse ensue,
Yet glory await emergence won,
Is that high Providence, or Chance?
And proved it which with thee, Timoleon?
   O, crowned with laurel twined with thorn,
Not rash thy life's cross-tide I stem,
But reck the problem rolled in pang
And reach and dare to touch thy garment's hem.

II

   When Argos and Cleone strove
Against free Corinth's claim or right,
Two brothers battled for her well:
A footman one, and one a mounted knight.
   Apart in place, each braved the brunt
Till the rash cavalryman, alone,
Was wrecked against the enemy's files,
His bayard crippled and he maimed and thrown.
   Timoleon, at Timophanes' need,
Makes for the rescue through the fray,

Covers him with his shield, and takes
The darts and furious odds and fights at bay;
    Till, wrought to pallor of passion dumb,
Stark terrors of death around he throws,
Warding his brother from the field
Spite failing friends dispersed and rallying foes.
    Here might he rest, in claim rest here,
Rest, and a Phidian form remain;
But life halts never, life must on,
And take with term prolonged some scar or stain.
    Yes, life must on. And latent germs
Time's seasons wake in mead and man;
And brothers, playfellows in youth,
Develop into variance wide in span.

III
    Timophanes was his mother's pride—
Her pride, her pet, even all to her
Who slackly on Timoleon looked:
Scarce he (she mused) may proud affection stir.
    He saved my darling, gossips tell:
If so, 'twas service, yea, and fair;
But instinct ruled and duty bade,
In service such, a henchman e'en might share.
    When boys they were I helped the bent;
I made the junior feel his place,
Subserve the senior, love him, too;
And sooth he does, and that's his saving grace.
    But me the meek one never can serve,
Not he, he lacks the quality keen
To make the mother through the son
An envied dame of power, a social queen.
    But thou, my first-born, thou art I
In sex translated; joyed, I scan
My features, mine, expressed in thee;
Thou art what I would be were I a man.
    My brave Timophanes, 'tis thou
Who yet the world's fore-front shalt win,
For thine the urgent resolute way,
Self pushing panoplied self through thick and thin.

Nor here maternal insight erred:
Foresworn, with heart that did not wince
At slaying men who kept their vows,
Her darling strides to power, and reigns—a Prince.

IV

Because of just heart and humane,
Profound the hate Timoleon knew
For crimes of pride and men-of-prey
And impious deeds that perjurous upstarts do;
    And Corinth loved he, and in way
Old Scotia's clansman loved his clan,
Devotion one with ties how dear
And passion that late to make the rescue ran.
    But crime and kin—the terrorized town,
The silent, acquiescent mother—
Revulsion racks the filial heart,
The loyal son, the patriot true, the brother.
    In evil visions of the night
He sees the lictors of the gods,
Giant ministers of righteousness,
Their *fasces* threatened by the Furies' rods.
    But undeterred he wills to act,
Resolved thereon though Ate rise;
He heeds the voice whose mandate calls,
Or seems to call, peremptory from the skies.

V

Nor less but by approaches mild,
And trying each prudential art,
The just one first advances him
In parley with a flushed intemperate heart.
    The brother first he seeks—alone,
And pleads; but is with laughter met;
Then comes he, in accord with two,
And these adjure the tyrant and beset;
    Whose merriment gives place to rage:
"Go," stamping, "what to me is Right?
I am the Wrong, and lo, I reign,
And testily intolerant too in might:"

And glooms on his mute brother pale,
Who goes aside; with muffled face
He sobs the predetermined word,
And Right in Corinth reassumes its place.

VI

But on his robe, ah, whose the blood?
And craven ones their eyes avert,
And heavy is a mother's ban,
And dismal faces of the fools can hurt.

The whispering-gallery of the world,
Where each breathed slur runs wheeling wide
Eddies a false perverted truth,
Inveterate turning still on fratricide.

The time was Plato's. Wandering lights
Confirmed the atheist's standing star;
As now, no sanction Virtue knew
For deeds that on prescriptive morals jar.

Reaction took misgiving's tone,
Infecting conscience, till betrayed
To doubt the irrevocable doom
Herself had authorized when undismayed.

Within perturbed Timoleon here
Such deeps were bared as when the sea
Convulsed, vacates its shoreward bed,
And Nature's last reserves show nakedly.

He falters, and from Hades' glens
By night insidious tones implore—
Why suffer? hither come and be
What Phocion is who feeleth man no more.

But, won from that, his mood elects
To live—to live in wilding place;
For years self-outcast, he but meets
In shades his playfellow's reproachful face.

Estranged through one transcendent deed
From common membership in mart,
In severance he is like a head
Pale after battle trunkless found apart.

But flood-tide comes though long the ebb,
Nor patience bides with passion long;
Like sightless orbs his thoughts are rolled
Arraigning heaven as compromised in wrong:
  To second causes why appeal?
Vain parleying here with fellow clods.
To you, Arch Principals, I rear
My quarrel, for this quarrel is with gods.
  Shall just men long to quit your world?
It is aspersion of your reign;
Your marbles in the temple stand—
Yourselves as stony and invoked in vain?
  Ah, bear with one quite overborne,
Olympians, if he chide ye now;
Magnanimous be even though he rail
And hard against ye set the bleaching brow.
  If conscience doubt, she'll next recant.
What basis then? O, tell at last,
Are earnest natures staggering here
But fatherless shadows from no substance cast?
  Yea, *are* ye, gods? Then ye, 'tis ye
Should show what touch of tie ye may,
Since ye, too, if not wrung are wronged
By grievous misconceptions of your sway.
  But deign, some little sign be given—
Low thunder in your tranquil skies;
Me reassure, nor let me be
Like a lone dog that for a master cries.

VIII

  Men's moods, as frames, must yield to years,
And turns the world in fickle ways;
Corinth recalls Timoleon—ay,
And plumes him forth, but yet with schooling phrase.
  On Sicily's fields, through arduous wars,
A peace he won whose rainbow spanned
The isle redeemed; and he was hailed
Deliverer of that fair colonial land.
  And Corinth clapt: Absolved, and more!

Justice in long arrears is thine:
Not slayer of thy brother, no,
But savior of the state, Jove's soldier, man divine.
    Eager for thee thy City waits:
Return! with bays we dress your door.
But he, the Isle's loved guest, reposed,
And never for Corinth left the adopted shore.

AFTER THE PLEASURE PARTY
lines traced under an image of amor theatening

    *Fear me, virgin whosoever
Taking pride from love exempt,
    Fear me, slighted. Never, never
Brave me, nor my fury tempt:
Downy wings, but wroth they beat
Tempest even in reason's seat.*

Behind the house the upland falls
With many an odorous tree—
White marbles gleaming through green halls,
Terrace by terrace, down and down,
And meets the starlit Mediterranean Sea.

    'Tis Paradise. In such an hour
Some pangs that rend might take release.
Nor less perturbed who keeps this bower
Of balm, nor finds balsamic peace?
From whom the passionate words in vent
After long revery's discontent?

    Tired of the homeless deep,
Look how their flight yon hurrying billows urge,
Hitherward but to reap
Passive repulse from the iron-bound verge!
Insensate, can they never know
'Tis mad to wreck the impulsion so?

An art of memory is, they tell:
But to forget! forget the glade
Wherein Fate sprung Love's ambuscade,
To flout pale years of cloistral life
And flush me in this sensuous strife.
'Tis Vesta struck with Sappho's smart.
No fable her delirious leap:
With more of cause in desperate heart,
Myself could take it—but to sleep!

Now first I feel, what all may ween,
That soon or late, if faded e'en,
One's sex asserts itself. Desire,
The dear desire through love to sway,
Is like the Geysers that aspire—
Through cold obstruction win their fervid way.
But baffled here—to take disdain,
To feel rule's instinct, yet not reign;
To dote, to come to this drear shame—
Hence the winged blaze that sweeps my soul
Like prairie fires that spurn control,
Where withering weeds incense the flame.

And kept I long heaven's watch for this,
Contemning love, for this, even this?
O terrace chill in Northern air,
O reaching ranging tube I placed
Against yon skies, and fable chased
Till, fool, I hailed for sister there
Starred Cassiopea in Golden Chair.
In dream I throned me, nor I saw
In cell the idiot crowned with straw.

And yet, ah yet scarce ill I reigned,
Through self-illusion self-sustained,
When now—enlightened, undeceived—
What gain I barrenly bereaved!
Than this can be yet lower decline—
Envy and spleen, can these be mine?

The peasant girl demure that trod
Beside our wheels that climbed the way,
And bore along a blossoming rod
That looked the sceptre of May-day—
On her—to fire this petty hell,
His softened glance how moistly fell!
The cheat! on briars her buds were strung;
And wiles peeped forth from mien how meek.
The innocent bare-foot! young, so young!
To girls, strong man's a novice weak.
To tell such beads! And more remain,
Sad rosary of belittling pain.

When after lunch and sallies gay,
Like the Decameron folk we lay
In sylvan groups; and I—let be!
O, dreams he, can he dream that one
Because not roseate feels no sun?
The plain lone bramble thrills with Spring
As much as vines that grapes shall bring.

Me now fair studies charm no more.
Shall great thoughts writ, or high themes sung
Damask wan cheeks—unlock his arm
About some radiant ninny flung?
How glad with all my starry lore,
I'd buy the veriest wanton's rose
Would but my bee therein repose.

Could I remake me! or set free
This sexless bound in sex, then plunge
Deeper than Sappho, in a lunge
Piercing Pan's paramount mystery!
For, Nature, in no shallow surge
Against thee either sex may urge,
Why hast thou made us but in halves—
Co-relatives? This makes us slaves.
If these co-relatives never meet
Self-hood itself seems incomplete.
And such the dicing of blind fate

Few matching halves here meet and mate.
What Cosmic jest or Anarch blunder
The human integral clove asunder
And shied the fractions through life's gate?

Ye stars that long your votary knew
Rapt in her vigil, see me here!
Whither is gone the spell ye threw
When rose before me Cassiopea?
Usurped on by love's stronger reign—
But lo, your very selves do wane:
Light breaks—truth breaks! Silvered no more,
But chilled by dawn that brings the gale
Shivers yon bramble above the vale,
And disillusion opens all the shore.

One knows not if Urania yet
The pleasure-party may forget;
Or whether she lived down the strain
Of turbulent heart and rebel brain;
For Amor so resents a slight,
And hers had been such haught disdain,
He long may wreak his boyish spite,
And boy-like, little reck the pain.

One knows not, no. But late in Rome
(For queens discrowned a congruous home)
Entering Albani's porch she stood
Fixed by an antique pagan stone
Colossal carved. No anchorite seer,
Not Thomas a Kempis, monk austere,
Religious more are in their tone;
Yet far, how far from Christian heart
That form august of heathen Art.
Swayed by its influence, long she stood,
Till surged emotion seething down,
She rallied and this mood she won:

Languid in frame for me,
To-day by Mary's convent shrine,

Touched by her picture's moving plea
In that poor nerveless hour of mine,
I mused—A wanderer still must grieve.
Half I resolved to kneel and believe,
Believe and submit, the veil take on.
But thee, armed Virgin! less benign,
Thee now I invoke, thou mightier one.
Helmeted woman—if such term
Befit thee, far from strife
Of that which makes the sexual feud
And clogs the aspirant life—
O self-reliant, strong and free,
Thou in whom power and peace unite,
Transcender! raise me up to thee,
Raise me and arm me!

         Fond appeal.
For never passion peace shall bring,
Nor Art inanimate for long
Inspire. Nothing may help or heal
While Amor incensed remembers wrong.
Vindictive, not himself he'll spare;
For scope to give his vengeance play
Himself he'll blaspheme and betray.

   Then for Urania, virgins everywhere,
O pray! Example take too, and have care.

The Night-March

With banners furled, and clarions mute,
   An army passes in the night;
And beaming spears and helms salute
   The dark with bright.

In silence deep the legions stream,
   With open ranks, in order true,
Over boundless plains they stream and gleam—
   No chief in view!

Afar, in twinkling distance lost,
    (So legends tell) he lonely wends
And back through all that shining host
    His mandate sends.

THE RAVAGED VILLA

In shards the sylvan vases lie,
    Their links of dance undone,
And brambles wither by thy brim,
    Choked fountain of the sun!
The spider in the laurel spins,
    The weed exiles the flower:
And, flung to kiln, Apollo's bust
    Makes lime for Mammon's tower.

THE MARGRAVE'S BIRTHNIGHT

Up from many a sheeted valley,
From white woods as well,
Down too from each fleecy upland
Jingles many a bell

Jovial on the work-sad horses
Hitched to runners old
Of the toil-worn peasants sledging
Under sheepskins in the cold;

Till from every quarter gathered
Meet they on one ledge,
There from hoods they brush the snow off
Lighting from each sledge

Full before the Margrave's castle,
Summoned there to cheer
On his birth-night, in mid-winter,
Kept year after year.

O the hall, and O the holly!
Tables line each wall;
Guests as holly-berries plenty,
But—no host withal!

May his people feast contented
While at head of board
Empty throne and vacant cover
Speak the absent lord?

Minstrels enter. And the stewards
Serve the guests; and when,
Passing there the vacant cover,
Functionally then

Old observance grave they offer;
But no Margrave fair,
In his living aspect gracious,
Sits responsive there;

No, and never guest once marvels,
None the good lord name,
Scarce they mark void throne and cover—
Dust upon the same.

Mindless as to what importeth
Absence such in hall;
Tacit as the plough-horse feeding
In the palfrey's stall.

Ah, enough for toil and travail,
If but for a night
Into wine is turned the water,
Black bread into white.

MAGIAN WINE

Amulets gemmed, to Miriam dear,
　　Adown in liquid mirage gleam;

Solomon's Syrian charms appear,
    Opal and ring supreme.
The rays that light this Magian Wine
Thrill up from semblances divine.

And, seething through the rapturous wave,
What low Elysian anthems rise:
Sibylline inklings blending rave,
    Then lap the verge with sighs.
Delirious here the oracles swim
Ambiguous in the beading hymn.

THE GARDEN OF METRODORUS

The Athenians mark the moss-grown gate
And hedge untrimmed that hides the haven green:
    And who keeps here his quiet state?
    And shares he sad or happy fate
Where never foot-path to the gate is seen?

Here none come forth, here none go in,
Here silence strange, and dumb seclusion dwell:
    Content from loneness who may win?
    And is this stillness peace or sin
Which noteless thus apart can keep its dell?

THE NEW ZEALOT TO THE SUN

    Persian, you rise
Aflame front climes of sacrifice
    Where adulators sue,
And prostrate man, with brow abased,
Adheres to rites whose tenor traced
    All worship hitherto.

    Arch type of sway,
Meetly your over-ruling ray
    You fling from Asia's plain,

Whence flashed the javelins abroad
Of many a wild incursive horde
   Led by some shepherd Cain.

   Mid terrors dinned
Gods too came conquerors from your Ind,
   The brood of Brahma throve;
They came like to the scythed car,
Westward they rolled their empire far,
   Of night their purple wove.

   Chemist, you breed
In orient climes each sorcerous weed
   That energizes dream-
Transmitted, spread in myths and creeds,
Houris and hells, delirious screeds
   And Calvin's last extreme.

   What though your light
In time's first dawn compelled the flight
   Of Chaos' startled clan,
Shall never all your darted spears
Disperse worse Anarchs, frauds and fears,
   Sprung from these weeds to man?

   But Science yet
An effluence ampler shall beget,
   And power beyond your play—
Shall quell the shades you fail to rout,
Yea, searching every secret out
   Elucidate your ray.

THE WEAVER

For years within a mud-built room
For Arva's shrine he weaves the shawl,
Lone wight, and at a lonely loom,
His busy shadow on the wall.

The face is pinched, the form is bent,
No pastime knows he nor the wine,
Recluse he lives and abstinent
Who weaves for Arva's shrine.

Lamia's Song

Descend, descend!
                Pleasant the downward way—
From your lonely Alp
With the wintry scalp
To our myrtles in valleys of May.
                Wend then, wend:
Mountaineer, descend!
And more than a wreath shall repay.
                Come, ah come!
With the cataracts come,
That hymn as they roam
How pleasant the downward way!

In a Garret

Gems and jewels let them heap—
Wax sumptuous as the Sophi:
For me, to grapple from Art's deep
One dripping trophy!

Monody

To have known him, to have loved him
        After loneness long;
And then to be estranged in life,
        And neither in the wrong;
And now for death to set his seal—
        Ease me, a little ease, my song!

By wintry hills his hermit-mound
    The sheeted snow-drifts drape,
And houseless there the snow-bird flits
    Beneath the fir-trees' crape:
Glazed now with ice the cloistral vine
    That hid the shyest grape.

LONE FOUNTS

Though fast youth's glorious fable flies,
View not the world with worldling's eyes;
Nor turn with weather of the time.
Foreclose the coming of surprise:
Stand where Posterity shall stand;
Stand where the Ancients stood before,
And, dipping in lone founts thy hand,
Drink of the never-varying lore:
Wise once, and wise thence evermore.

THE BENCH OF BOORS

In bed I muse on Tenier's boors,
Embrowned and beery losels all:
    A wakeful brain
    Elaborates pain:
Within low doors the slugs of boors
Laze and yawn and doze again.

In dreams they doze, the drowsy boors,
Their hazy hovel warm and small:
    Thought's ampler bound
    But chill is found:
Within low doors the basking boors
Snugly hug the ember-mound.

Sleepless, I see the slumberous boors
Their blurred eyes blink, their eyelids fall:
      Thought's eager sight
      Aches—overbright!
Within low doors the boozy boors
Cat-naps take in pipe-bowl light.

THE ENTHUSIAST
"Though he slay me yet will I trust in him"

Shall hearts that beat no base retreat
    In youth's magnanimous years—
Ignoble hold it, if discreet
    When interest tames to fears;
Shall spirits that worship light
    Perfidious deem its sacred glow,
    Recant, and trudge where worldlings go,
Conform and own them right?

Shall Time with creeping influence cold
    Unnerve and cow? the heart
Pine for the heartless ones enrolled
    With palterers of the mart?
Shall faith abjure her skies,
    Or pale probation blench her down
    To shrink from Truth so still, so lone
Mid loud gregarious lies?

Each burning boat in Caesar's rear,
    Flames—No return through me!
So put the torch to ties though dear,
    If ties but tempters be.
Nor cringe if come the night:
    Walk through the cloud to meet the pall,
    Though light forsake thee, never fall
From fealty to light.

In placid hours well-pleased we dream
Of many a brave unbodied scheme.
But form to lend, pulsed life create,
What unlike things must meet and mate:
A flame to melt—a wind to freeze;
Sad patience—joyous energies;
Humility—yet pride and scorn;
Instinct and study; love and hate;
Audacity—reverence. These must mate,
And fuse with Jacob's mystic heart,
To wrestle with the angel—Art.

BUDDHA

"For what is your life? It is even a vapor that appeareth for a little time and then vanisheth away."

Swooning swim to less and less,
     Aspirant to nothingness!
Sobs of the worlds, and dole of kinds
     That dumb endurers be—
Nirvana! absorb us in your skies,
     Annul us into thee.

C——'S LAMENT

     How lovely was the light of heaven,
What angels leaned from out the sky
In years when youth was more than wine
And man and nature seemed divine
Ere yet I felt that youth must die.

     Ere yet I felt that youth must die
How insubstantial looked the earth,
Alladin-land! in each advance,
     Or here or there, a new romance;
I never dreamed would come a dearth.

And nothing then but had its worth,
Even pain. Yes, pleasure still and pain
In quick reaction made of life
A lovers' quarrel, happy strife
In youth that never comes again.

But will youth never come again?
Even to his grave-bed has he gone,
And left me lone to wake by night
With heavy heart that erst was light?
O, lay it at his head—a stone!

SHELLEY'S VISION

Wandering late by morning seas
When my heart with pain was low—
Hate the censor pelted me—
Deject I saw my shadow go.

In elf-caprice of bitter tone
I too would pelt the pelted one:
At my shadow I cast a stone,

When lo, upon that sun-lit ground
I saw the quivering phantom take
The likeness of St. Stephen crowned:
Then did self-reverence awake.

FRAGMENTS OF A LOST GNOSTIC POEM
OF THE 12TH CENTURY

★ ★ ★

Found a family, build a state,
The pledged event is still the same:
Matter in end will never abate
His ancient brutal claim.

★ ★ ★

Indolence is heaven's ally here,
And energy the child of hell:
The Good Man pouring from his pitcher clear,
But brims the poisoned well.

THE MARCHIONESS OF BRINVILLIERS

He toned the sprightly beam of morning
    With twilight meek of tender eve,
Brightness interfused with softness,
    Light and shade did weave:
And gave to candor equal place
With mystery starred in open skies;
And, floating all in sweetness, made
    Her fathomless mild eyes.

THE AGE OF THE ANTONINES

While faith forecasts millennial years
    Spite Europe's embattled lines,
Back to the Past one glance be cast—
    The Age of the Antonines!
O summit of fate, O zenith of time
When a pagan gentleman reigned,
And the olive was nailed to the inn of the world
Nor the peace of the just was feigned.
    A halcyon Age, afar it shines,
Solstice of Man and the Antonines.

Hymns to the nations' friendly gods
Went up from the fellowly shrines,
No demagogue beat the pulpit-drum
    In the Age of the Antonines!
The sting was not dreamed to be taken from death,
No Paradise pledged or sought,
But they reasoned of fate at the flowing feast,
    Nor stifled the fluent thought.

We sham, we shuffle while faith declines—
They were frank in the Age of the Antonines.

Orders and ranks they kept degree,
Few felt how the parvenu pines,
No law-maker took the lawless one's fee
    In the Age of the Antonines!
Under law made will the world reposed
And the ruler's right confessed,
For the heavens elected the Emperor then,
The foremost of men the best.
    Ah, might we read in America's signs
The Age restored of the Antonines.

HERBA SANTA

    I
After long wars when comes release
Not olive wands proclaiming peace
    An import dearer share
Than stems of Herba Santa hazed
    In autumn's Indian air.
Of moods they breathe that care disarm,
They pledge us lenitive and calm.

    II
Shall code or creed a lure afford
To win all selves to Love's accord?
When Love ordained a supper divine
    For the wide world of man,
What bickerings o'er his gracious wine!
Then strange new feuds began.

Effectual more in lowlier way,
    Pacific Herb, thy sensuous plea
The bristling clans of Adam sway
    At least to fellowship in thee!
Before thine altar tribal flags are furled,
Fain woulds't thou make one hearthstone of the world.

III

To scythe, to sceptre, pen and hod—
  Yea, sodden laborers dumb;
To brains overplied, to feet that plod,
In solace of the *Truce of God*
  The Calumet has come!

IV

Ah for the world ere Raleigh's find
  Never that knew this suasive balm
That helps when Gilead's fails to heal,
  Helps by an interserted charm.

Insinuous thou that through the nerve
  Windest the soul, and so canst win
Some from repinings, some from sin,
  The Church's aim thou dost subserve.

The ruffled fag fordone with care
  And brooding, Gold would ease this pain:
Him soothest thou and smoothest down
  Till some content return again.

Even ruffians feel thy influence breed
  Saint Martin's summer in the mind,
They feel this last evangel plead,
As did the first, apart from creed,
  Be peaceful, man—be kind!

V

Rejected once on higher plain,
O Love supreme, to come again
  Can this be thine?
Again to come, and win us too
  In likeness of a weed
That as a god didst vainly woo,
  As man more vainly bleed?

Forbear, my soul! and in thine Eastern chamber
 Rehearse the dream that brings the long release:
Through jasmine sweet and talismanic amber
 Inhaling Herba Santa in the passive Pipe of Peace.

Fruit of Travel Long Ago

Venice

With Pantheist energy of will
The little craftsman of the Coral Sea
Strenuous in the blue abyss,
Up-builds his marvelous gallery
 And long arcade,
Erections freaked with many a fringe
 Of marble garlandry,
Envincing what a worm can do.

Laborious in a shallower wave,
 Advanced in kindred art,
A prouder agent proved Pan's might
When Venice rose in reefs of palaces.

In a Bye-Canal

A swoon of noon, a trance of tide,
The hushed siesta brooding wide
 Like calms far off Peru;
No floating wayfarer in sight,
Dumb noon, and haunted like the night
 When Jael the wiled one slew.
A languid impulse from the oar
Plied by my indolent gondolier
Tinkles against a palace hoar,
 And, hark, response I hear!
A lattice clicks; and lo, I see
Between the slats, mute summoning me,

What loveliest eyes of scintillation,
What basilisk glance of conjuration!

    Fronted I have, part taken the span
Of portents in nature and peril in man.
I have swum—I have been
Twixt the whale's black flukes and the white shark's fin;
The enemy's desert have wandered in,
And there have turned, have turned and scanned,
Following me how noiselessly,
Envy and Slander, lepers hand in hand.
All this. But at the latticed eye—
"Hey! Gondolier, you sleep, my man;
Wake up!" And, shooting by, we ran;
The while I mused, This, surely now,
Confutes the Naturalists, allow!
Sirens, true sirens verily be,
Sirens, waylayers in the sea.

    Well, wooed by these same deadly misses,
Is it shame to run?
No! flee them did divine Ulysses,
    Brave, wise, and Venus' son.

PISA'S LEANING TOWER

The Tower in tiers of architraves,
Fair circle over cirque,
A trunk of rounded colonades,
The maker's master-work,
Impends with all its pillared tribes,
And, poising them, debates:
It thinks to plunge—but hesitates;
Shrinks back—yet fain would slide;
Withholds itself—itself would urge;
Hovering, shivering on the verge,
    A would-be suicide!

In vaulted place where shadows flit,
An upright sombre box you see:
A door, but fast, and lattice none,
But punctured holes minutely small
In lateral silver panel square
Above a kneeling-board without,
Suggest an aim if not declare.

 Who bendeth here the tremulous knee
No glimpse may get of him within,
And he immured may hardly see
The soul confessing there the sin;
Nor yields the low-sieved voice a tone
Whereby the murmurer may be known.

 Dread diving-bell! In thee inurned
What hollows the priest must sound,
Descending into consciences
 Where more is hid than found.

MILAN CATHEDRAL

Through light green haze, a rolling sea
 Over gardens where redundance flows,
  The fat old plain of Lombardy,
The White Cathedral shows.

 Of Art the miracles
  Its tribes of pinnacles
Gleam like to ice-peaks snowed; and higher,
Erect upon each airy spire
 In concourse without end,
Statues of saints over saints ascend
Like multitudinous forks of fire.

What motive was the master-builder's here?
Why these synodic hierarchies given,

Sublimely ranked in marble sessions clear,
Except to signify the host of heaven.

PAUSILIPPO
(In the time of Bomba)

A hill there is that laves its feet
In Naples' bay and lifts its head
In jovial season, curled with vines.
Its name, in pristine years conferred
By settling Greeks, imports that none
Who take the prospect thence can pine,
For such the charm of beauty shown
Even sorrow's self they cheerful weened
Surcease might find and thank good Pan.

Toward that hill my landau drew;
And there, hard by the verge, was seen
Two faces with such meaning fraught
One scarce could mark and straight pass on.

A man it was less hoar with time
Than bleached through strange immurement long,
Retaining still, by doom depressed,
Dim trace of some aspiring prime.
Seated he tuned a homely harp
Watched by a girl, whose filial mien
Toward one almost a child again,
Took on a staid maternal tone.
Nor might one question that the locks
Which in smoothed natural silvery curls
Fell on the bowed one's thread-bare coat
Betrayed her ministering hand.

Anon, among some ramblers drawn,
A murmur rose "Tis Silvio, Silvio!"
With inklings more in tone suppressed
Touching his story, part recalled:
Clandestine arrest abrupt by night;

The sole conjecturable cause
The yearning in a patriot ode
Construed as treason; trial none;
Prolonged captivity profound;
Vain liberation late. All this,
With pity for impoverishment
And blight forestalling age's wane.

    Hillward the quelled enthusiast turned,
Unmanned, made meek through strenuous wrong,
Preluding, faltering; then began,
But only thrilled the wire—no more,
The constant maid supplying voice,
flinting by no ineloquent sign
That she was but his mouth-piece mere,
Himself too spiritless and spent.

    Pausilippo, Pausilippo,
Pledging easement unto pain,
    Shall your beauty even solace
If one's sense of beauty wane?

Could light airs that round ye play
Waft heart-heaviness away
Or memory lull to sleep,
    Then, then indeed your balm
    Might Silvio becharm,
And life in fount would leap,
    Pausilippo!

Did not your spell invite,
    In moods that slip between,
    A dream of years serene,
And wake, to dash, delight—
    Evoking here in vision
    Fulfilment and fruition—
Nor mine, nor meant for man!
    Did hope not frequent share
    The mirage when despair
Overtakes the caravan,

Me then your scene might move
    To break from sorrow's snare,
And apt your name would prove,
      Pausilippo!

But I've looked upon your revel—
    It unravels not the pain:
Pausilippo, Pausilippo,
    Named benignly if in vain!

    It ceased. In low and languid tone
The tideless ripple lapped the passive shore;
As listlessly the bland untroubled heaven
Looked down as silver doled was silent given
In pity—futile as the ore!

THE ATTIC LANDSCAPE

Tourist, spare the avid glance
    That greedy roves the sight to see:
Little here of "Old Romance,"
    Or Picturesque of Tivoli.

No flushful tint the sense to warm—
Pure outline pale, a linear charm.
The clear-cut hills carved temples face,
Respond, and share their sculptural grace.

'Tis Art and Nature lodged together,
    Sister by sister, cheek to cheek;
Such Art, such Nature, and such weather
    The All-in-All seems here a Greek.

THE SAME

A circumambient spell it is,
Pellucid on these scenes that waits,
Repose that does of Plato tell—
Charm that his style authenticates.

I

Seen Aloft from Afar
Estranged in site,
Aerial gleaming, warmly white,
You look a suncloud motionless
In noon of day divine;
Your beauty charmed enhancement takes
In Art's long after-shine.

II

Nearer Viewed
Like Lais, fairest of her kind,
In subtlety your form's defined—
The cornice curved, each shaft inclined,
While yet, to eyes that do but revel
    And take the sweeping view,
Erect this seems, and that a level,
    To line and plummet true.

Spinoza gazes; and in mind
Dreams that one architect designed
    Lais—and you!

III

The Frieze
What happy musings genial went
With airiest touch the chisel lent
    To frisk and curvet light
Of horses gay—their riders grave—
Contrasting so in action brave
    With virgins meekly bright,
Clear filing on in even tone
With pitcher each, one after one
    Like water-fowl in flight.

IV

The Last Tile
    When the last marble tile was laid
The winds died down on all the seas;

Hushed were the birds, and swooned the glade;
   Ictinus sat; Aspasia said
"Hist!—Art's meridian, Pericles!"

GREEK MASONRY

Joints were none that mortar sealed:
Together, scarce with line revealed,
The blocks in symmetry congealed.

GREEK ARCHITECTURE

Not magnitude, not lavishness,
But Form—the Site;
Not innovating wilfulness,
But reverence for the Archetype.

OFF CAPE COLONNA

Aloof they crown the foreland lone,
   From aloft they loftier rise—
Fair columns, in the aureola rolled
   From sunned Greek seas and skies.
They wax, sublimed to fancy's view,
A god-like group against the blue.

Over much like gods! Serene they saw
   The wolf-waves board the deck,
And headlong hull of Falconer,
   And many a deadlier wreck.

THE ARCHIPELAGO

Sail before the morning breeze
The Sporads through and Cyclades

They look like isles of absentees—
        Gone whither?

You bless Apollo's cheering ray,
But Delos, his own isle, today
Not e'en a Selkirk there to pray
        God friend me!

Scarce lone these groups, scarce lone and bare
When Theseus roved a Raleigh there,
Each isle a small Virginia fair—
        Unravished.

Nor less through havoc fell they rue,
They still retain in outline true
Their grace of form when earth was new
        And primal.

But beauty clear, the frame's as yet,
Never shall make one quite forget
Thy picture, Pan, therein once set—
        Life's revel!

'Tis Polynesia reft of palms,
Seaward no valley breathes her balms—
Not such as musk thy rings of calms,
        Marquesas!

SYRA
(A transmitted reminiscence.)

Fleeing from Scio's smouldering vines
(Where when the sword its work had done
The Turk applied the torch) the Greek
Came here, a fugitive stript of goods,
Here to an all but tenantless isle,
Nor here in footing gained at first,
Felt safe. Still from the turbaned foe

Dreading the doom of shipwrecked men
Whom feline seas permit to land
Then pounce upon and drag them back,
For height they made, and prudent won
A cone-shaped fastness on whose flanks
With pains they pitched their eyrie camp,
Stone huts, whereto they wary clung;
But, reassured in end, come down—
Multiplied through compatriots now,
Refugees like themselves forlorn—
And building along the water's verge
Begin to thrive; and thriving more
When Greece at last flung off the Turk,
Make of the haven mere a mart.

    I saw it in its earlier day—
Primitive, such an isled resort
As hearthless Homer might have known
Wandering about the Ægean here.
Sheds ribbed with wreck-stuff faced the sea
Where goods in transit shelter found;
And here and there a shanty-shop
Where Fez-caps, swords, tobacco, shawls
Pistols, and orient finery, Eve's—
(The spangles dimmed by hands profane)
Like plunder on a pirate's deck
Lay orderless in such loose way
As to suggest things ravished or gone astray.

    Above a tented inn with fluttering flag
A sunburnt board announced Greek wine
In self-same text Anacreon knew,
Dispensed by one named "Pericles."
Got up as for the opera's scene,
Armed strangers, various, lounged or lazed,
Lithe fellows tall, with gold-shot eyes.
Sunning themselves as leopards may.

    Off-shore lay xebecs trim and light,
And some but dubious in repute.

But on the strand, for docks were none,
What busy bees! no testy fry;
Frolickers, picturesquely odd,
With bales and oil-jars lading boats,
Lighters that served an anchored craft,
Each in his tasseled Phrygian cap,
Blue Eastern drawers and braided vest;
And some with features cleanly cut
As Proserpine's upon the coin.
Such chatterers all! like children gay
Who make believe to work, but play.

I saw, and how help musing too.
Here traffic's immature as yet:
Forever this juvenile fun hold out
And these light hearts? Their garb, their glee,
Alike profuse in flowing measure,
Alike inapt for serious work,
Blab of grandfather Saturn's prime
When trade was not, nor toil, nor stress,
But life was leisure, merriment, peace,
And lucre none and love was righteousness.

Disinterment of the Hermes

What forms divine in adamant fair—
Carven demigod and god,
And hero-marbles rivalling these,
Bide under Latium's sod,
Or lost in sediment and drift
Alluvial which the Grecian rivers sift.

To dig for these, O better far
Than raking arid sands
For gold more barren meetly theirs
Sterile, with brimming hands.

THE APPARITION

*(The Parthenon uplifted on its rock first challenging the view on the
approach to Athens)*

Abrupt the supernatural Cross,
    Vivid in startled air,
Smote the Emperor Constantine
And turned his soul's allegiance there.

With other power appealing down,
    Trophy of Adam's best!
If cynic minds you scarce convert,
You try them, shake them, or molest.

Diogenes, that honest heart,
    Lived ere your date began;
Thee had he seen, he might have swerved
In mood nor barked so much at Man.

IN THE DESERT

Never Pharoah's Night,
Whereof the Hebrew wizards croon,
Did so the Theban flamens try
As me this veritable Noon.

Like blank ocean in blue calm
Undulates the ethereal frame;
In one flowing oriflamme
God flings his fiery standard out.

Battling with the Emirs fierce
Napoleon a great victory won,
Through and through his sword did pierce;
But, bayonetted by this sun
His gunners drop beneath the gun.

Holy, holy, holy Light!
Immaterial incandescence,
Of God the effluence of the essence,
Shekinah intolerably bright!

THE GREAT PYRAMID

Your masonry—and is it man's?
More like some Cosmic artisan's.
Your courses as in strata rise,
Beget you do a blind surmise
           Like Grampians.

Far slanting up your sweeping flank
Arabs with Alpine goats may rank,
And there they find a choice of passes
Even like to dwarfs that climb the masses
           Of glaciers blank.

Shall lichen in your crevice fit?
Nay, sterile all and granite-knit:
Weather nor weather-strain ye rue,
But aridly you cleave the blue
           As lording it.

Morn's vapor floats beneath your peak,
Kites skim your side with pinion weak;
To sand-storms battering, blow on blow,
Raging to work your overthrow,
           You—turn the cheek.

All elements unmoved you stem,
Foursquare you stand and suffer them:
Time's future infinite you dare,
While, for the past, 'tis you that wear
           Eld's diadem.

Slant from your inmost lead the caves
And labyrinths rumored. These who braves
And penetrates (old palmers said)
Comes out afar on deserts dead
    And, dying, raves.

Craftsmen, in dateless quarries dim,
Stones formless into form did trim,
Usurped on Nature's self with Art,
And bade this dumb I AM to start,
    Imposing him.

L'ENVOI
The return of the Sire De Nesle A.D. 16——

My towers at last! These rovings end,
Their thirst is slaked in larger dearth:
The yearning infinite recoils,
  For terrible is earth!

Kaf thrusts his snouted crags through fog:
Araxes swells beyond his span,
And knowledge poured by pilgrimage
  Overflows the banks of man.

But thou, my stay, thy lasting love
One lonely good, let this but be!
Weary to view the wide world's swarm,
  But blest to fold but thee.

EDITOR'S NOTES

The copyright date of May 15, 1891, indicates that publication of the book
came shortly before Melville's death on September 28, 1891. The Houghton
Library at Harvard University possesses two manuscripts of the book, each in
the form of printer's copy. Melville's extensive revisions offer a unique opportunity for the reader to enter the poet's workshop and observe his thinking
about poems and the form they should finally achieve. Jarrard's dissertation

records the various revisions. The studies by Shurr, Stein, Dillingham, and Davis offer excellent readings of the book and its individual poems.

"TIMOLEON." Melville knew the account of Timoleon's life given by Plutarch. The Greek general (411–337 B.C.) was lauded in Pierre Bayle's *Historical and Critical Dictionary* (another of Melville's sources) as one willing to sacrifice his brother for the good of the state. His deeds as soldier and statesman raised him high in his countrymen's eyes, but suspicions arising from the fratricide caused him to retire for many years from useful activity (See Shurr 153–55).

"AFTER THE PLEASURE PARTY." Rightly regarded as one of Melville's most successful poems, this piece stands as a warning to those who refuse to give love its proper place in the human spectrum. The astronomer who sacrifices so much for her studies has been identified as Maria Mitchell (1818–1889), an astronomer and scientific writer whom Melville met as early as 1852 (Philbrick 291–308). The poem has been read as a statement of Melville's own situation, of his giving up much in the obsessive pursuit of his art and its catastrophic results.

"THE RAVAGED VILLA." During Melville's travels in Italy, he observed the "Villa of Hadrian—Solemn scene & solemn guide—Extent of ruin,—fine site" (*Journals,* March 20, 1857). Much of the villa's art treasures were pillaged, some broken and some of the marble statues turned into lime. The poet's meditation on the loss of the beautiful past, ravaged by a commercial and hungry present, represented by "Mammon's tower," is resonant throughout the poems in *Timoleon*.

"MONODY." The poem has been read as Melville's song of grief at the death of Hawthorne, but this reading has certain difficulties. There is no evidence of any estrangement between the two men. Also, the poem was not necessarily written just after Hawthorne's death in 1864; we have no sure date for composition. Because Vine, a character in *Clarel*, has been identified as sharing some characteristics of Hawthorne, the use of "the cloistral vine" in the poem has been taken to be a reference to Hawthorne; but the assumed relationship is far from convincing. It would be as valid to assume that Melville was writing of Malcolm, his eldest son (1849–1867), who, it is assumed, committed suicide.

"LONE FOUNTS." Melville's revisions show that he had considered "Giordano Bruno" as a possible title for the poem. Bruno (1548–1600) was a philosopher who found his beliefs in opposition to the Catholic church and was burned at the stake as a heretic. Perhaps Melville found much to admire in Bruno's concept of the art of memory as magic and its association with hermeticism and Hermes Trismegistus. The poem belongs with others that examine philosophical and religious beliefs, including "Fragments of a Lost Gnostic Poem of the 12th Century," "Buddha," "The New Zealot to the Sun," "C——'s Lament," and "Shelley's Vision."

"THE BENCH OF BOORS." Melville's poem is a description of and meditation on one of the paintings of one of his favorite painters, David Teniers (1610–1690). On April 10, 1857, Melville's journal recording his seeing "charming, Teniers tavern scenes. The remarkable Teniers effect is produced by first dwarfing, then deforming humanity" (112). His manuscript indicates a canceled title, "Suggested by a Flemish Picture." Always fond of ekphrasis, Melville lets the speaker's comments on the painting reflect his contrasting of the pain brought on by "Thought's eager sight" with the comfort of the lazy "slugs of boors" who smoke, drink, and have no recourse to thought.

"THE MARCHIONESS OF BRINVILLIERS." Cohen cites the letters of Madame de Sévigné as a source for this poem. However, an article on the Marchioness appeared in the magazine *The Green Bag* ([January 1890]: 36–41), a good account of the infamous poisoner, and may have served as a source for the poem

"THE AGE OF THE ANTONINES." In a letter to his brother-in-law, John C. Hoadley, dated "Saturday in Easter Week 1877," Melville enclosed a version of this poem. He cited his source as Edward Gibbon's *Decline and Fall of the Roman Empire*. The first volume of Gibbon's history (1776) opens with three chapters dealing with the military forces, the internal prosperity, and the constitution of the Roman Empire during what the author characterizes as "the age of the Antonines," a period from A.D. 96 to 180. The two Antonine emperors were Antoninus Pius (ruled 138–61) and Marcus Aurelius Antoninus (ruled 161–80), but Gibbon includes two previous emperors, Trajan (98–117) and Hadrian (117–38), all of whom contributed to make the second century a "golden age" of the empire. Like the Periclean age of Greece, this is, for Melville, a great historical period, to be contrasted to the mean life of his own time. The poem was further revised in later manuscripts before publication.

"VENICE." This is the first of the poems in the section of the book entitled "Fruit of Travel Long Ago." The heading has often been interpreted to mean that the poems were written early in Melville's time as a poet, possibly as early as the 1850s, and that some of the poems which follow may have made up the content of the 1860 volume, assembled but never published. Melville loved Venice; while visiting the city, he wrote that he would "rather be in Venice on rainy day, than in other capital on fine one" (*Journals* 120). Nature as the great artist is a persistent Melvillean theme, and the coral building creatures construct galleries "freaked with many a fringe / Of marble garlandry," while, in contrast, human artists built up the city "in reefs of palaces." Wallace's "Melville's 'Venice'" indicates some sources that the poet may have considered in his composition of the poem, including Turner's pictures and Charles Darwin's writings.

"PISA'S LEANING TOWER." Upon seeing the tower, Melville wrote "Campanile like pine poised just ere snapping. You wait to hear crash" (*Journals* 114). This

vivid impression takes on a more serious implication in the poem, where the
tower is envisioned as a would-be suicide, hesitant before jumping.

"MILAN CATHEDRAL." The elaborate embellishment of the cathedral makes it
an artwork worthy of ekphrasis. After describing the "miracles" of its pinnacles and statues, the poet questions the motive for the construction of the huge
edifice and finds it in the religious feeling of the builders. On April 7, 1857,
Melville recorded his response to seeing the cathedral: "More satisfactory to
me than St. Peters. A wonderful grandure [sic]. Effect of burning window at
end of aisle . . . . groups of angels on points of pinnacles & everywhere"
(Journals 121).

"THE ATTIC LANDSCAPE." Here, the poet sees the miracle in the way that Art
and Nature are "lodged together." The "carved temples" share the "sculptural
grace" of the hills. Thus, Greek art and architecture meld the natural and the
created in a way, Melville implies, that the modern builders cannot. In his brief
visit to the Greek world, he found that sailing among the islands gave the
impression of "sailing upon gigantic outline engravings" (Journals 99).

"THE PARTHENON." In his visit, Melville noticed especially the pavement, with
its "blocks of ice. (frozen together)—no morter [sic]:—Delicacy of of frost-
work" (Journals 99). Ictinus was the architect who designed the Parthenon.
Pericles (499–429 B.C.), one of the most remarkable of Greek statesmen, gave
his name, "Periclean," to the golden age of Greek life that was ended by the
heavy destruction wrought by the Peloponnesian War (431–404 B.C.) between
Athens and Sparta. Aspasia (ca.470–410 B.C.), mistress of Pericles, was important for her influence upon his thought and famous for conducting a literary
and philosophical salon, a center of intellectual life in Athens. See Madeleine
M. Henry, Prisoner of History: Aspasia of Miletus and Her Biographical Tradition
(New York: Oxford UP, 1995).

"OFF CAPE COLONNA." From the sea, the poet sees the temple of Athena on
a headland and conjectures that in their ages-long serenity they had often
witnesses shipwrecks, including the one described by William Falconer (1732–
1769) in his poem "The Shipwreck" (1762). Melville knew the poem and used
it in his "Extracts" to Moby-Dick.

"DISINTERMENT OF THE HERMES." The marble statue of Hermes was discovered on May 8, 1877, at Olympia and was identified, from the writings of
Pausanias, as a work of Praxiteles. See A. H. Smith, "On the Hermes of Praxiteles," The Journal of Hellenic Studies 3 (1882): 81–95. A lengthy account of the
discovery is in "Praxiteles and the Hermes with the Infant Dionysos," in
Charles Waldstein, ed., Essays on the Art of Pheidias (New York: Cambridge UP,
1885), 373–93. Melville probably read stories of the discovery in newspapers
but may have read Waldstein as well. The poet uses the occasion of the "disinterment" to contrast archeological digs with the commercial activity of

digging for gold during the nineteenth century, another manifestation of the dominance of Mammon in modern times.

"In the Desert." Melville's revisions reveal an interesting idea, removed in the final draft. Line 3 reads, at one point, "Did so the weak-eyed Horace affright," a reference, probably, to the Roman poet Horace (Quintus Horatius Flaccus, 65–8 B.C.). Hennig Cohen calls attention to the Miltonic echoes in the poem and to the use of words like "flamen" and "oriflamme" to suggest the increasing radiance of the sun (*Selected Poems* 250).

"The Great Pyramid." Visiting the pyramids in January 1857, Melville recorded his sense of them as "something vast, indefinite, incomprehensible, and awful" (*Journals* 76). Both Shurr (177–79) and Stein (133–36) provide elaborate readings of the poem. In Wyn Kelley, *Melville's City*, the pyramids are characterized as seeming to be supranatural creations, ignoring the elements; they are the constructions of humans who operate as a divine will (255–56). As the next to last poem in the volume, "The Great Pyramid" is strategically placed to indicate that it is a kind of resolution of the poet's search for religious and philosophical meanings. After it, there can only be a conclusion, and this is given in "L'Envoi," the last poem in *Timoleon*. The speaker of this last poem is clearly not Melville himself but the Sire de Nesle, coming home at some time in the seventeenth century and expressing relief at his return. What he has learned at last is that "terrible is earth." The "dearth" he speaks of is an absence, a lack not to be supplied by search, for the knowledge gained by such a search simply "overflows the banks of man"; we are inundated by the knowledge that cannot be used. All of the conflicting ideas rehearsed in the previous poems provide no helpful answer to the difficulties of the human condition.

Bibliography

Abel, Darrel. "I Look, You Look, He Looks: Three Critics of Melville's Poetry." *ESQ* 21.2 (1975): 116–23.

———. "'Laurel Twined with Thorn': The Theme of Melville's *Timoleon*." *Personalist* 41 (1960): 330–39.

Arvin, Newton. *Herman Melville*. New York: Viking, 1957.

———. "Melville's Shorter Poems." *Partisan Review* 16 (October 1949): 1034–46.

Barrett, Laurence. "The Differences in Melville's Poetry." *PMLA* 70 (September 1955): 606–23.

Baym, Nina. "The Erotic Motif in Melville's *Clarel*." *Texas Studies in Literature and Language* 16 (Summer 1974): 315–28.

———. "Melville's Quarrel with Fiction." *PMLA* 94 (1979): 909–23.

Bercaw, Mary K. *Melville's Sources*. Evanston: Northwestern UP, 1987.

Berthold, Dennis. "'Melville and Dutch Genre Painting." In Sten, ed., *Savage Eye*, 218–45.

Bezanson, Walter. "Melville's *Clarel*: The Complex Passion." *ELH* 21 (1954): 146–59.

———, ed. *Clarel: A Poem and a Pilgrimage in the Holy Land*. By Herman Melville. New York: Hendricks House, 1960.

Bridgman, Richard. "Melville's Roses." *Texas Studies in Literature and Language* 8 (Summer 1966): 235–44.

Brodwin, Stanley. "Herman Melville's *Clarel*: An Existentialist Gospel." *PMLA* 86 (May 1971): 375–87.

Bryant, John. "Melville's Rose Poems: As They Fell." *Arizona Quarterly* 52.4 (Winter 1996): 49–84.

———, ed. *A Companion to Melville Studies*. New York: Greenwood Press, 1986.

Bryant, John, and Robert Milder, ed. *Melville's Evermoving Dawn: Centennial Essays*. Kent, Ohio: Kent State UP, 1997.

Buell, Lawrence. "Melville the Poet." In Levine, ed., *The Cambridge Companion to Herman Melville*, 135–56.

Cannon, Agnes D. "Melville's Concept of the Poet and Poetry." *Arizona Quarterly* 31 (1975): 315–39.

———. "On Translating *Clarel*." *Essays in Arts and Sciences* 5.2 (July 1976): 160–80.

Chapin, Henry, ed. *John Marr and Other Poems.* Princeton: Princeton UP, 1922.

Chase, Richard. *Herman Melville: A Critical Study.* New York: Macmillan, 1949.

Coffler, Gail H. *Melville's Classical Allusions: A Comprehensive Index and Glossary.* Westport, Conn.: Greenwood Press, 1985.

Cohen, Hennig, ed. *The Battle-Pieces of Herman Melville.* New York: Thomas Yoseloff, 1964.

———. *Selected Poems of Herman Melville.* Carbondale: U of Southern Illinois P, 1968.

Cowen, Walker. *Melville's Marginalia.* 2 vols. New York: Garland, 1987.

Davis, Clark. *After the Whale: Melville in the Wake of Moby-Dick.* Tuscaloosa: U of Alabama P, 1995.

Dettlaff, Shirley. "Ionian Form and Esau's Waste." *American Literature* 54 (May 1982): 212–28.

Djelal, Juana Celia. "All in All: Melville's Poetics of Unity." *ESQ* 41 (1995): 219–35.

———. "Melville's Bridal Apostrophe: Rhetorical Conventions of the Connubium." *Melville Society Extracts* 110 (September 1997): 1–5.

Dillingham, William B. *Melville and His Circle: The Last Years.* Athens: U of Georgia P, 1996.

Donahue, Jane. "Melville's Classicism: Law and Order in His Poetry." *Papers in Literature and Language* 5 (1969): 63–72.

Dryden, Edgar A. "*John Marr and Other Sailors*: Poetry as Private Utterance." *Nineteenth Century Literature* 52 (December 1997): 326–49.

Finkelstein, Dorothee. *Melville's Orienda.* New Haven: Yale UP, 1961.

Fogle, Richard Harter. "*Billy Budd*: The Order of the Fall." *Nineteenth Century Fiction* 15 (1960–61): 189–205.

———. "Melville and the Civil War." *Tulane Studies in English* 9 (1959): 61–89.

———. "Melville's Poetry." *Tulane Studies in English* 12 (1962): 81–86.

———. "The Themes of Melville's Later Poetry." *Tulane Studies in English* 11 (1961): 65–86.

Freeman, John. *Herman Melville.* New York: Macmillan 1926.

Freibert, Lucy M. "The Influence of Elizabeth Barrett Browning on the Poetry of Herman Melville." *Studies in Browning and His Circle* 9 (1981): 69–78.

Garner, Stanton. *The Civil War World of Herman Melville.* Lawrence: U Press of Kansas, 1993.

Hillway, Tyrus. "The Poetry." In *Herman Melville.* Rev. ed. Boston: Twayne Publishers, 1979. 122–34.

Hook, Andrew. "Melville's Poetry." In Lee, ed., *Herman Melville: Reassessments*, 176–98.

Howard, Leon. *Herman Melville: A Biography.* Berkeley: U of California P, 1951.

Jarrard, Norman Eugene. "Poems by Herman Melville: A Critical Edition of the Published Verse." Ph.D. diss., University of Texas, 1960.

Kelley, Wyn. "Haunted Stone: Nature and City in *Clarel*." *Essays in Arts and Sciences* 15 (June 1986): 15–29.

Kelley, Wyn. *Melville's City: Literary and Urban Form in Nineteenth Century New York.* New York: Cambridge UP, 1996.

Kenny,Vincent. "Clarel." In Bryant, ed., *A Companion to Melville Studies*, 375–406.

———. *Herman Melville's Clarel: A Spiritual Autobiography*. Hamden, Conn.: Shoe String Press, 1973.

Knapp, Joseph G. *Tortured Synthesis: The Meaning of Melville's Clarel*. New York: Philosophical Library, 1971.

Kramer, Aaron. *Melville's Poetry: Toward the Enlarged Heart—A Thematic Study of Three Ignored Major Poems*. Cranbury, NJ: Associated UP, 1972.

Lee, A. Robert, ed. *Herman Melville: Reassessments*. London and New Jersey: Vision and Barnes & Noble, 1984.

Levine, Robert S., ed. *The Cambridge Companion to Herman Melville*. New York: Cambridge UP, 1998.

Mason, Ronald. *The Spirit Above the Dust*. Lonson: John Lohmann, 1951.

Melville, Herman. *Clarel, A Poem and a Pilgrimage*. Ed. Harrison Hayford, Alma A. MacDougal, Hershel Parker, and G. Thomas Tanselle. Evanston and Chicago: Northwestern UP and the Newberry Library, 1991.

———. *Correspondence*. Ed. Lynn Horth. Evanston and Chicago: Northwestern UP and the Newberry Library, 1993.

———. *Journals*. Ed. Howard C Horsford with Lynn Horth. Evanston and Chicago: Northwestern UP and the Newberry Library, 1989.

Milder, Robert. "Melville's Late Poetry and *Billy Budd*: From Nostalgia to Transcendence." In Milder, ed. *Critical Essays on Melville's Billy Budd, Sailor*, 212–23.

Milder, Robert, ed. *Critical Essays on Melville's Billy Budd, Sailor*. Boston: G. K. Hall & Co., 1989.

Miller, Edwin Haviland. *Melville: A Biography*. New York: George Braziller, 1975.

Mumford, Lewis. *Herman Melville*. New York: Literary Guild of America, 1929.

Parker, Hershel. "The Character of Vine in Melville's *Clarel*." *Essays in Arts and Sciences* 15 (June 1986): 91–113.

———. *Herman Melville, A Biography*, Vol. 1: *1819–1851*. Baltimore: Johns Hopkins UP, 1996.

———. "The Lost *Poems* (1860) and Melville's First Urge to Write an Epic Poem." In Bryant and Milder, eds., *Melville's Evermoving Dawn*, 260–75.

Philbrick, Nathaniel. "Hawthorne, Maria Mitchell, and Melville's 'After the Pleasure Party.'" *ESQ* 37 (1991): 291–308.

Pommer, Henry F. *Milton and Melville*. 1950. Reprint. New York: Cooper Square Publishers, 1970.

Renker, Elizabeth. *Strike Through the Mask: Herman Melville and the Scene of Writing*. Baltimore: Johns Hopkins UP, 1996.

Robertson-Lorant, Laurie. *Melville: A Biography*. Amherst: U of Massachusetts P, 1996.

Robillard, Douglas. *Melville and the Visual Arts: Ionian Form, Venetian Tint*. Kent, Ohio: Kent State UP, 1997.

———. "Melville's *Clarel* and the Parallel of Poetry and Painting." *North Dakota Quarterly* 51 (1983): 107–20.

———. "Melville's Late Poetry: Sources and Speculations." *Essays in Arts and Sciences* 27 (October 1998): 23–35.

———. "Theme and Structure in Melville's *John Marr and Other Sailors.*" *English Language Notes* 6 (March 1969): 187–92.

———. "Wrestling with the Angel: Melville's Use of the Visual Arts in *Timoleon.*" In Sten, ed., *Savage Eye*, 246–56.

Ryan, Robert C. "Melville Revises 'Art.'" In Bryant and Milder, eds., *Melville's Evermoving Dawn*, 307–20.

———. "'Weeds and Wildings Chiefly: With a Rose or Two' by Herman Melville, Reading Text and Genetic Text, Edited from the Manuscripts, with Introduction and Notes." Ph.D. diss., Northwestern University, 1967.

Sandberg, Robert A. "'House of the Tragic Poet': Melville's Draft of a Preface to His Unfinished Burgundy Club Book." *Melville Society Extracts* 79 (November 1989): 1, 4–7.

———. "'The Adjustment of Screens': Putative Narrators, Authors, and Editors in Melville's Unfinished *Burgundy Club* Book." *Texas Studies in Language and Literature* 31 (Fall 1989): 426–50.

Sedgwick, Ellery. *Herman Melville: The Tragedy of Mind*. Cambridge, Mass: Harvard UP, 1944.

Short, Bryan. "Form as Vision in Herman Melville's *Clarel.*" *American Literature* 50 (January 1979): 553–69.

———. "Memory's Mint: Melville's Parable of the Imagination in *John Marr and Other Sailors.*" *Essays in Arts and Sciences* 15 (June 1986): 31–42.

———. "'The Redness of the Rose': The *Mardi* Poems and Melville's Artistic Compromise." *Essays in Arts and Sciences* 15 (July 1976): 100–112.

Shurr, William H. "Melville's Poems: The Late Agenda." In John Bryant, ed., *A Companion to Melville Studies*, 351–74.

———. *The Mystery of Iniquity: Melville as Poet, 1857–1891*. Lexington: U of Kentucky P, 1972.

Stein, William B. "'The New Ancient of Days': The Poetics of Logocracy." *Essays in Arts and Sciences* 5 (July 1976): 181–93.

———. *The Poetry of Melville's Late Years: Time, History, Myth, and Religion*. Albany: State U of New York P, 1970.

Sten, Christopher, ed. *Savage Eye: Melville and the Visual Arts*. Kent, Ohio: Kent State UP, 1991.

Stern, Milton. *The Fine-Hammered Steel of Herman Melville*. Urbana: U of Illinois P, 1957.

———. "The Politics of Melville's Poetry." In Milder, ed., *Critical Essays on Melville's Billy Budd, Sailor*, 143–56.

Vincent, Howard P., ed. *The Collected Poems of Herman Melville*. Chicago: Hendricks House, 1947.

Wallace, Robert K. *Melville and Turner: Spheres of Love and Fright*. Athens: U of Georgia P, 1992.

———. "Melville's Prints: The Ambrose Group." *Harvard Library Bulletin* 6 (Spring 1995): 13–50.

———. "Melville's 'Venice,' Turner's Vignette, Ruskin's *Stones*, and Darwin's *Voyage.*" *Mediterranean Perspectives* 2 (1997): 21–35.

Warren, Robert Penn, ed. *Selected Poems of Herman Melville.* New York: Random House, 1970.

Wegener, Larry Edward, ed. *A Concordance to Herman Melville's* Clarel: A Poem and Pilgrimage in the Holy Land. 4 vols. Lewiston, N.Y.: Edwin Mellen Press, 1997.

Wright, Nathalia. "The Poems in Melville's *Mardi.*" *Essays in Arts and Sciences* 15 (July 1976): 83–99.

The Poems of Herman Melville

was designed & composed by Will Underwood

in 10.8/14 Bembo on a Power Macintosh G3

using PageMaker 6.5; printed by sheet-fed

offset lithography on 50-pound Turin

Book Natural Vellum (an acid-free, totally

chlorine-free paper), notch bound in signatures

and glued into paper covers printed in two colors

finished with polypropylene matte film lamination

by Thomson-Shore, Inc.; and published by

The Kent State University Press

KENT, OHIO 44242

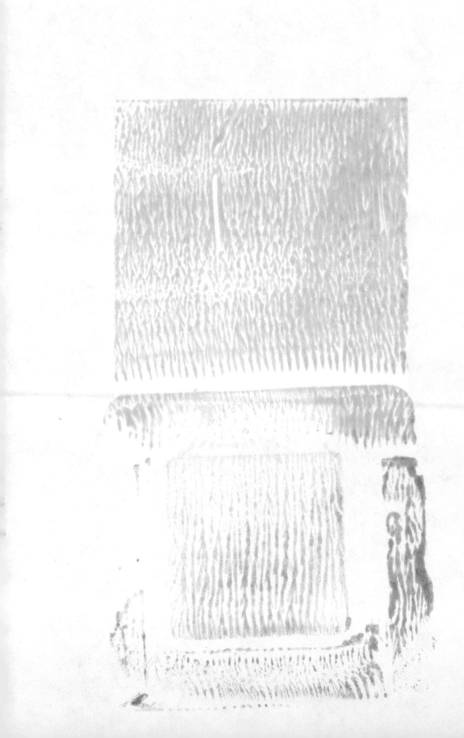

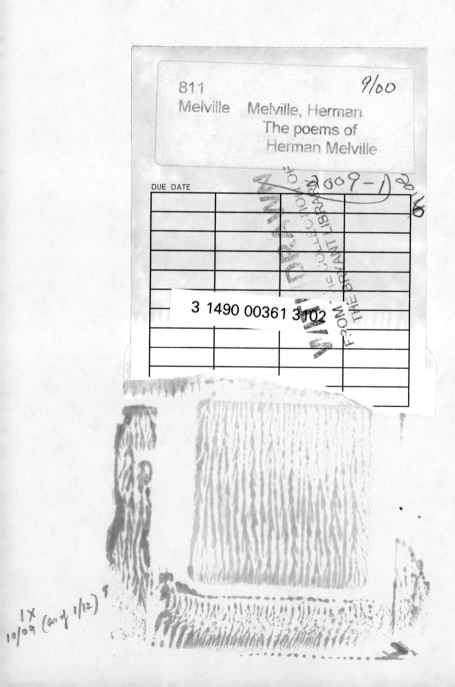